W9-BLE-301

# Practical
## Intelligence

**JB** JOSSEY-BASS

# Practical Intelligence

## The Art and Science of Common Sense

Karl Albrecht

BICENTENNIAL
1807
WILEY
2007
BICENTENNIAL

John Wiley & Sons, Inc.

Copyright © 2007 by Karl Albrecht
Published by Jossey-Bass
A Wiley Imprint
989 Market Street, San Francisco, CA 94103-1741
www.josseybass.com

No part of this publication may be reproduced, stored in a retrieval system, or transmitted in any form or by any means, electronic, mechanical, photocopying, recording, scanning, or otherwise, except as permitted under Section 107 or 108 of the 1976 United States Copyright Act, without either the prior written permission of the Publisher, or authorization through payment of the appropriate per-copy fee to the Copyright Clearance Center, Inc., 222 Rosewood Drive, Danvers, MA 01923, 978-750-8400, fax 978-646-8600, or on the web at www.copyright.com. Requests to the Publisher for permission should be addressed to the Permissions Department, John Wiley & Sons, Inc., 111 River Street, Hoboken, NJ 07030, 201-748-6011, fax 201-748-6008, or online at http://www.wiley.com/go/permissions.

Limit of Liability/Disclaimer of Warranty: While the publisher and author have used their best efforts in preparing this book, they make no representations or warranties with respect to the accuracy or completeness of the contents of this book and specifically disclaim any implied warranties of merchantability or fitness for a particular purpose. No warranty may be created or extended by sales representatives or written sales materials. The advice and strategies contained herein may not be suitable for your situation. You should consult with a professional where appropriate. Neither the publisher nor author shall be liable for any loss of profit or any other commercial damages, including but not limited to special, incidental, consequential, or other damages.

Readers should be aware that Internet websites offered as citations and/or sources for further information may have changed or disappeared between the time this was written and when it is read.

For additional copies/bulk purchases of this book in the U.S. please contact 800-274-4434.

Jossey-Bass books and products are available through most bookstores. To contact Jossey-Bass directly call our Customer Care Department within the U.S. at 800-956-7739, outside the U.S. at 317-572-3986, fax 317-572-4002, or visit www.josseybass.com.

Jossey-Bass also publishes its books in a variety of electronic formats. Some content that appears in print may not be available in electronic books.

**Library of Congress Cataloging-in-Publication Data**

Albrecht, Karl.
  Practical intelligence : the art and science of common sense / Karl Albrecht.
    p. cm.
  Includes bibliographical references and index.
  ISBN 978-0-7879-9565-2 (cloth)
  1. Common sense. 2. Success. 3. Conduct of life. I. Title.
  B105.C457A43 2007
  153.9—dc22
                                2007013594

Acquiring Editor: Lisa Shannon                         Editor: Rebecca Taff
Director of Development: Kathleen Dolan Davies          Production Editor: Dawn Kilgore
Manufacturing Supervisor: Becky Carreño                Wiley Bicentennial Logo: Richard J. Pacifico
Printed in the United States of America
Printing   10   9   8   7   6   5   4   3   2   1

# CONTENTS

## APPENDICES

# PREFACE

SOME TIME DURING THE PERIOD AROUND 200 BC, a famous general named Hannibal, who fought for the North African empire of Carthage, launched a ferocious attack on the Roman army in the African desert at a place called Zama.

Hannibal employed an innovative weapon in his attack: elephants. He had become a big fan of elephants as instruments of war. They were huge, frightening beasts, and enemy soldiers were usually intimidated by their mere presence. His father, Hamilcar, had experimented with elephants, largely without success, and Hannibal himself had led an army equipped with elephants across the Italian Alps to attack the farther reaches of the early Roman empire. The fact that he lost half of his army and most of the elephants on the way did nothing to dampen his enthusiasm for this military innovation.

Hannibal, his soldiers, and his elephants confronted the famous Roman general Scipio, who commanded a force of about an equal number of soldiers. Hannibal was utterly convinced that the elephants would provide him with the decisive advantage.

The battle began with a full frontal assault, with Hannibal's soldiers following more than a hundred elephants charging into the center of Scipio's infantry line. Scipio, however, was known as a clever general who could think up strategies and tactics to suit the unique situations he encountered. He had worked out a simple method for dealing with the elephants.

As the charge developed, Scipio's army re-formed, opening large alleys into which they redirected the charging elephants. Rather than attacking the elephants, they killed their drivers, rendering the elephants uncontrollable and useless in the battle. By shouting and banging their swords against their shields, Scipio's soldiers raised an enormous din, which frightened the elephants. The riderless elephants, now completely out of control and terrified, turned and stampeded, trampling hundreds of Hannibal's soldiers. Scipio had transformed Hannibal's elephants into weapons against him.

The battle turned into a complete rout, and Hannibal was so utterly defeated that he advised the rulers of Carthage to surrender, ending the Second Punic War.

Yet, curiously, even though the elephants had been a colossal failure in almost every campaign, Hannibal—even to his death bed—never admitted it. "If I had only had more elephants," he insisted, "I could have defeated them."

One definition of "intelligence" is the capacity to cope: to function effectively in an environment of some kind—to meet its challenges and capitalize on its possibilities in order to get what we want, need, and deserve. By that definition, we *Homo sapiens*—"thinking humans"—may need to get a lot smarter as a species, and soon.

*For the first time in the history of our species, our environment is evolving faster than our brains.* We might have fewer than fifty years left to get our act together, individually and collectively, to cope with the chaotic new environment we've created around ourselves.

But most of us know more about the electronic computers sitting on our desks than we know about the biocomputers we carry around in our heads. We know how to operate machine software better than we know how to operate our own mental software. Recent findings from three fruitful areas of study—brain research, hypnotherapy, and information systems—have given us an exciting new window into the workings of the competent human mind. Not only can we define and describe what effective thinking is, in simple street language, but we can also learn and teach its habits and methods.

With the publication of his landmark book *Frames of Mind: The Theory of Multiple Intelligences* in 1983, Harvard Professor Howard Gardner won many converts to his view that using a single "IQ" number to sentence a person to a specified level of potential in life is not only unrealistic, but in many ways destructive. He and others have long argued that we have a whole constellation of "intelligences."

The bulk of Gardner's early work involved a set of some seven independent intelligences: linguistic, logical-mathematical, musical, spatial, kinesthetic, intrapersonal (emotional intelligence), and interpersonal (social intelligence). He also posited the existence of an eighth dimension, "naturalist," which seems less clearly defined.

Other experts have diced up the various dimensions of intelligence into other categories, and presently there is no one universally accepted set of definitions. Later in this book I will present a somewhat more simplified taxonomy, with as few as six primary categories, using more commonplace street-language names. Regardless of one's favorite model, however, few experts deny the importance of Gardner's original contribution.

These "intelligences" are now becoming increasingly familiar in the conversation of the popular culture. There is talk of "spiritual intelligence," "moral intelligence," and "emotional intelligence." In the business world it's "executive intelligence" and "organizational intelligence." In pop literature, there is "sexual intelligence." I suppose we'll eventually hear about "financial intelligence," "real estate intelligence," and "gardening intelligence."

By referring to a particular "intelligence," those who are using the term are presumably trying to capture the notion of a unified constellation of skills that are important or interesting in a particular context.

This new vernacular—some would say profane—use of the formerly sacred term "intelligence" is causing intellectual heartburn for many in the academic community. Some of the more rigorous academic advocates of the single-number theory of IQ—the so-called universal "g-factor"—still question Gardner's model, and the controversy will almost certainly continue for decades to come. But for better or worse, the concept of intelligence is being irreparably secularized. This term that traditionally connoted a fixed, immutable trait has now morphed into one that signals a learnable competence. Gardner's "MI" concept has reached the tipping point of acceptance in certain sectors, particularly education and business, at least in the United States.

Surprisingly perhaps, it has taken a rather long time for other experts and practitioners to lend a hand and support the build-out of Gardner's MI model into its component parts. The first notable contribution in this area was Daniel Goleman's landmark book *Emotional Intelligence: Why It Can Matter More Than IQ* in 1995, which became a best seller and earned considerable respect in the business sector.

In 2005 my book, *Social Intelligence: The New Science of Success,* was released and has also met with a very strong response in the marketplace. Daniel Goleman followed suit with his own book on social intelligence late in 2006.

Considering the steadily gathering momentum behind the multiple-intelligence concept, and the popularity of both *Emotional Intelligence* and *Social Intelligence,* the next category of intelligence "up to bat" would seem to be *Practical Intelligence:* the art and science of common sense.

For as long as I can remember—certainly all of my adult life—I've been interested in and fascinated by the workings of the human mind. My first attempt to throw a rope around the subject was in 1980, with my book *Brain Power: How to Improve Your Thinking Skills,* which remains in print to this day. For a number of years I taught my "Brain Power" seminar to executives and managers in business organizations, as well as educators. I investigated the concept of cognitive styles, and developed the *Mindex* self-assessment profile to enable individuals to understand more clearly how they and others organize and arrange their thought processes.

Over a career of more than thirty years, I've found myself drawn again and again to this field of study. I've found applications in strategic thinking and planning, executive leadership, organizational intelligence, innovation, organizational culture, and team effectiveness, to name a few. And after all those years I remain convinced that the gray matter—the human software—is the last real unexploited capital asset we have in business today.

I recently organized the Brain Power Institute, which is a community of interest intended to bring together practitioners in business, education, mental health, research, and human development, to further define and develop the body of knowledge for practical intelligence, and to teach and promote the methods and concepts of competent thinking.

Many other thinkers, writers, and practitioners have contributed to the current state of knowledge in practical intelligence, and I try diligently to give credit where it is deserved in this book. My own small contribution, I hope, can be in offering a new conceptual structure for defining and describing practical intelligence, inspired partly by the philosophy of Gardner's MI concept. I'm a fairly competent "model-maker"; I relish the challenge of linking concepts together into constellations of thought that can serve as useful tools. That's what I've attempted in this book, and I hope I've succeeded to some small extent.

I've made no attempts in this book to "dumb down" the treatment of the subject, or to try to reduce it to a set of inspirational slogans. For better or worse, I'm asking my readers to engage these ideas thoughtfully, seriously, and with the intentions to learn. I hope that educators will use this book as a text or a supporting resource for teaching courses on practical intelligence.

Above all, I've tried to make the subject *interesting*—hoping to convey some sense of the awe and excitement that it holds, and has always held, for me.

# ABOUT THE AUTHOR

D R. KARL ALBRECHT is a management consultant, executive advisor, futurist, researcher, speaker, and prolific author. In his thirty-year career he has worked with many kinds of business, government, and nonprofit organizations in a wide range of industries world-wide. He has consulted with senior executives and lectured to conferences on all inhabited continents.

He is the author of more than twenty books on various aspects of individual and business performance, including *Social Intelligence: The New Science of Success*; *Brain Power: Learn to Improve Your Thinking Skills*; *The Northbound Train: Finding the Purpose, Setting the Direction, Shaping the Destiny of Your Organization*; *The Power of Minds at Work: Organizational Intelligence in Action*; and co-author of the best-selling *Service America!: Doing Business in the New Economy,* widely credited with launching the "customer revolution" in the U.S. and abroad, which has sold over a half-million copies in seven languages.

He devotes much of his effort to finding and developing promising new concepts for both organizational and individual effectiveness. His research and development activities have spanned a wide range of issues, from individual creativity all the way to corporate strategic vision. He is widely regarded as a key thought leader in the field of emerging strategic business issues.

He can be contacted at www.KarlAlbrecht.com.

# 1

# *A PROBLEM AND AN OPPORTUNITY*

"One should, each day, try to hear a little song, read a good poem, see a fine picture, and if it is possible, speak a few reasonable words."
—Johann Wolfgang von Goethe

ONE OF THOSE CHARMING STORIES that circulate in the public education community concerns an essay exam assigned by an American fifth-grade teacher. The essay question asked the students to name as many parts of the human body as they could think of, and tell what they do. One child wrote:

The human body consists of the Brainium, the Borax, and the Abominable Cavity. The Brainium contains the brain. The Borax

contains the lungs, the liver, and other living things. The Abominable
Cavity contains the bowels, of which there are five—a, e, i, o, and u.[1]

This is the kind of experience that causes some teachers to retire
early, and others to wonder whether the whole process of education
makes sense.

Yet, as the English novelist and futuristic thinker H.G. Wells
observed: "History becomes more and more a race between education
and catastrophe." As long ago as 1895, Wells saw the potential for human
beings to exterminate themselves, and our possibilities have only grown
more numerous in the intervening years. We "thinking humans" might
not be smart enough to avoid outsmarting ourselves.

The artificial world we've created around us now seems to have us by
the throat—or by various other elements of our collective anatomy—and
we're enduring the frustrating experience of not being able to control it.
Both individually and collectively, we seem hypnotized by the increasingly
strange social, political, and technological landscape that now seems to be
unfolding with an inexorable life of its own. We live in a world of instantaneous information, by turns bemused, amused, and frightened by the
highly charged images that bombard us constantly.

The information environment we've created around ourselves
now creates us. The swirling images, the sounds, the stories, the conversations—all become part of a shared electronic consciousness, a
kind of cultural hive-mind that binds us to our circumstances. We've
hypnotized ourselves, and this collective media-trance now shapes our
thinking processes at very deep levels.

We're now facing an important choice point in our individual and
collective lives. Most of us may take the "default" choice without ever
realizing we're *making a choice*. The choice will be whether we will be
creatures *of* our environment or creatures living *in* our environment.
The first option is the default choice: it requires no thought at all. The
second option requires that we wake up and start thinking.

# ACCIDENTAL INTELLIGENCE:
# THE TERMINAL ASSUMPTION

"The cream always rises to the top."

There seems to be one deeply submerged and seldom-questioned assumption at the very foundation of the public education process in almost all of the developed countries—an assumption that now *must* be questioned. It's the taken-for-granted, given-by-God, approved-by-scientists belief that, by the time a person arrives at young adulthood, that person is about as smart as he or she is ever going to be.

The source of this "terminal assumption," as I have named it, is the widespread confusion of "IQ" with the ability to think. They are not the same and, in fact, are only loosely related.

If you want to permanently impair your belief in the idea that IQ equates to mental ability, consider that one Ted Kaczynski, a.k.a. the famed "Unabomber" who murdered three people and injured scores of others with mail bombs, was a Harvard-educated professor of mathematics.

Many students of human mental competence—including myself—consider the introduction of IQ testing into public school systems to be one of the most destructive episodes ever witnessed in that benighted sector of our society. Aside from slotting children into an arbitrary caste system—a practice of highly questionable value—one is hard-pressed to name *any* useful application of IQ doctrine in raising or educating children. Other than amusement for university researchers, employment security for educational psychologists, and a sense of satisfaction for normatively minded school administrators, measuring IQ scores seems to have no known positive value.

If, as many IQ theorists contend, intelligence is a fixed, innate characteristic of human beings and cannot be improved significantly by education, training, or experience, then what would be the point of trying to measure it in children? How does saying to a child, "You're smarter than Johnny, but you're not as smart as Jenny" help Johnny, Jenny, or the child who receives the news?

If you keep the IQ scores secret from the children, presumably so as not to make them feel vain or insecure, then who should get the numbers? Wouldn't giving the scores to teachers make them more likely to treat certain children like superstars and value the others less? How does a parent benefit by knowing his or her child's IQ score? As revered as the IQ theory is in academic circles, it seems to have no demonstrable value in educating children, and is likely to be a net negative in its influence.

Nevertheless, the damage has already been done; the vast majority of educators and educational administrators seem to have bought the idea that children are distributed with respect to some innate mental competence, and that there is little hope of them moving higher than their numerical destiny. "Even if we don't know a child's actual IQ score," the conscious or unconscious reasoning goes, "we know that he or she has a certain potential that cannot be significantly exceeded."

Consider the effects of the Terminal Assumption on the thinking of teachers, administrators, and curriculum designers who subscribe to it: the child's mental software is programmed by some mysterious process as he or she grows toward young adulthood—a process not accessible to either the child or the child's caregivers. If the mental software is what it is and can't be influenced significantly, then the only function left to the educational establishment is to supply the data—the information.

To use a primitive analogy, it would be like having a personal computer on your desk but not being allowed to choose the software installed on it. If you were forced to use whatever software came with it, you could only do the things that software allowed you to do. You could supply the information, but only in the way the computer was set up to process it.

As another analogy, equating IQ with thinking ability is somewhat like deciding which race car will win based on comparing engine performance and ignoring the know-how of the driver. Even if human beings do have certain pre-wired features of their nervous systems, there is far more variability in the *use* of their endowments than in the endowments themselves.

This Terminal Assumption, if accepted by educators—and more and more of them are *rejecting* it these days—leads unavoidably to the mindset that education is all about delivering information, or "content," as curriculum designers used to call it. This leads to learning designs based on a "container model" of the child as learner: we figuratively unscrew the top of a kid's head, pour in some history, or music, or math, or literature, put the top back on, and we've educated the kid.

The consequence of the Terminal Assumption and the container model of the learner is that cognitive skills of various kinds tend to get lost within the educational experience, and not consciously identified to the learner as explicitly valuable and worthy of study in their own right. A group-study project, for example, might present an opportunity to learn skills like brainstorming, suspending judgment, accurate listening, paraphrasing, comparing and contrasting points of view, and formulating hypotheses. But if it is presented as an exercise in "content"—dates, kings, and wars, in the case of history, for example—then the opportunity to understand the skills as skills, independent of content and context, gets scrambled into the process of finding the "correct" answers.

> "You must adjust. . . . This is the legend imprinted in
> every schoolbook, the invisible message on every
> blackboard. Our schools have become vast factories
> for the manufacture of robots."
> —Robert M. Lindner

However, even in the face of formidable institutional support for the IQ doctrine, the idea of directly teaching cognitive skills to children has always hovered at the fringes of educational practice, and more than a few teachers and schools have made significant efforts to establish it as an accepted methodology. With some exceptions, this commitment to "mental skills training" has tended to center on schools in "better" neighborhoods, where funding, talented teachers, and highly educated parents with high expectations come together in a fortunate combination. So far, however, this insurrection against the fixed-intelligence doctrine hasn't reached anything like a critical mass, and still awaits a revolutionizing influence.

The Terminal Assumption found its way into the business world many years ago and still resides there comfortably, with some notable exceptions. As explained in the following section, business executives, managers, personnel experts, and company trainers have largely bought into the idea that the workers they hire are like the graduating students: they're about as smart as they're ever going to be.

About two decades ago, many American businesses flirted with training courses on critical thinking, creative thinking, problem solving, and team effectiveness, with mixed results. Some well-known companies committed significant resources to the objective of developing smarter people, and some still do. Conferences and seminars on thinking skills were popular, and many trade and industry conferences included an obligatory session on creativity or some related topic.

However, with the executive stampede toward "quality improvement," brought on as a reaction to the threat of Japanese competition in the mid-1980s, many American businesses shifted their thinking toward normative methods like "total quality management," or "TQM," which attempted to copy the hyper-methodical practices of Japanese firms like Toyota. "Soft skills" like clear thinking and innovation were often relegated to the "maybe later" category. Now, with many organizations evolving toward more knowledge-intensive operations, coping with a shortage of workers with high-level mental skills, and facing intense competition from foreigners, we're seeing a resurgence of interest in the gray matter.

Many executives who spent lavishly on information technology to modernize and upgrade their operations, often investing tens of millions of dollars on computer hardware and software, saw no particular value in spending a few tens of thousands of dollars on upgrading the "human software." Indeed, it wouldn't have even occurred to most of them.

The extension of the Terminal Assumption from education to business worked like a two-edged sword: the public education system saw little value in teaching the skills of competent thinking, and the business sector assumed that the employees they were receiving from the education system were as competent at thinking as they were ever going to be.

As we'll see in a later chapter, businesses now have the opportunity—and increasingly the inclination—to develop their own smart people. Having spent thirty years of my life as a consultant to businesses and an advisor to executives, I'm gratified to see the possibilities appreciated again. As business leaders increasingly reject and refute the Terminal Assumption, the "back pressure" exerted on the educational establishment will, hopefully, lead to its rejection there as well.

## THE WIDENING "SMART GAP"

During his tenure as CEO of the pioneering Internet job-matching service *monster.com,* Jeff Taylor compared the kinds of jobs that businesses were seeking to fill with the kinds of skill sets applicants were offering. What he saw caused him considerable dismay. The comparison of "skills offered" against "skills sought" showed a very significant mismatch. Across the board, businesses were seeking a higher caliber of mental skills than they were finding.

Taylor predicted that this ever-growing "smart-people gap" would increasingly confound executives' efforts to grow and develop their enterprises, to innovate, and to implement breakaway competitive strategies. In fact, Taylor warned, "Increasingly, the knowledge worker will be at the center of company desperation."

The smart gap has become a prominent topic of the strategic conversations business leaders engage in. Most of them seem to have little faith that the public education system will begin delivering "smarter" people to the workplace any time soon. This leaves them, as they consider it, in the position of having to compete more aggressively for talent.

"Talent management" is the new term of art for personnel directors, and increasingly for CEOs themselves. For many firms, talent management degenerates to a grim acceptance that they will have to bid ever-higher salaries to attract people who can think, plan, organize, analyze, research, decide, design, lead, manage, communicate, and— above all—solve problems. Able-bodied workers are fairly easy to find; able-*minded* workers are not.

Yet our schools, for the most part, still don't seem to "get it." Turning out high-school graduates who know how to use computers and surf the Internet is not the same as turning out *knowledge workers*— people who can think.

Indeed, we now have to redefine the term "knowledge workers." Management guru Peter F. Drucker made that term a permanent part of the vocabulary of business in the 1950s, when he predicted that by 1960 at least half of the U.S. workforce would be doing "think-work" instead of "thing-work." However, Drucker could not have anticipated the all-pervasive influence of computers and information technology.

The bank teller, for example, whom Drucker classified as a typical knowledge worker, now has to be down-classified to the status of a *data worker*. Most large businesses now have an invisible "data factory" operating in parallel with the normal operation; it's the collection of people and resources that process information to support and shape the familiar operations we typically think of as "the business."

In this sense, the young worker at the fast-food restaurant who pushes a coded button on a keyboard or taps an icon on a screen contributes almost nothing in the way of knowledge work. It's data work, and low-skilled data work at that. With the kinds of technology readily available now, the job of a bank teller, for example, is really no more knowledge-intensive than that of, say, a welder in a factory. Information technology has not necessarily made people smarter;

instead, it has made many jobs easier to perform by people with limited mental skills.

As business leaders are forced to redefine Drucker's concept of knowledge work and knowledge workers, it becomes more and more apparent that true knowledge workers are relatively scarce. At the same time that businesses are becoming ever more knowledge-intensive in their operations, schools do not seem to be turning out a higher proportion of skilled thinkers.

With occasional exceptions, the kinds of educational experiences that challenge and develop knowledge skills tend to be concentrated mostly in the schools that serve wealthy or upper-middle-class families. Most of the schools in economically disadvantaged areas can barely cope with their basic mission, to say nothing of delivering a true third-wave educational experience.

Beginning in the decade of the 1990s, and increasingly since 2000, business leaders in the United States have become increasingly vocal about the general failure of the school system to equip young people with the skills they will need to succeed over the coming decades. As we'll see in a later discussion, many of them have turned from complaining about it to correcting for it as best they can.

Businesses, to some extent, are becoming the educators of last resort, and they're beginning to look carefully at ways to grow their own smart people instead of merely trying to steal them from one another. For more and more business leaders, the familiar term "ROI" has morphed from "return on investment" into "return on intelligence." Workers can no longer be just individual "production units"; businesses must now look upon them as "ITUs"—individual *thinking* units.

## THE DUMBING OF AMERICA AND THE CULTURE OF AMUSEMENT

Karl Marx, the father of communism, reportedly remarked, "Religion is the opiate of the people." Were he alive and trying to sell his political theory these days, he would very likely say, "*Television* is the opiate of the people."

One of the most popular television shows ever broadcast in the United States, "American Idol," probably best exemplifies what's happened to the level of mental activity in the mainstream popular culture. During one round of competition in mid-2006, more votes were cast for the winning "Idol" contestant than for any presidential candidate in U.S. history.

> "Nobody ever went broke by underestimating the
> taste of the American public."
>
> —H.L. Mencken

The late professor Neil Postman, of New York University, devoted considerable study to the effects of the electronic media on the culture, and on the development of mental capacities of children. In his provocative book, *Amusing Ourselves to Death: Public Discourse in the Age of Show Business,* he asserted that the rise in popularity of television coincided with a decline in rational thinking and discussion in the consciousness of American society. Postman traced three phases in the development of what he called "the culture's conversation with itself."[2]

Phase one, extending back to our very origins, was an oral phase. People shared knowledge, ideas, and their history through discussion and story-telling. Phase two, the rise of literate communication through the printed word, peaked in its impact during the nineteenth century, according to Postman. Phase three, with the arrival of what he called the "televisual" media, began the inexorable transition to a pervasive "culture of amusement."

Postman contended that, while print media have long served as a robust platform for the reasoned exchange of ideas, the televisual media—most notably commercial TV—have proven themselves poorly suited for explaining complex concepts and for managing conversations about them. Philosopher Marshall McLuhan had already given us the familiar but puzzling slogan "The medium is the message,"[3] and Postman seconded his views with the idea that every medium limits, controls, and distorts the information we try to push through it. "The medium is the *metaphor*," he claimed. Just as a metaphor is a figure of speech that re-codes a complex and abstract idea into a familiar concrete example, television re-codes complex information into its own unique and simplified way of presenting it.

For example, it would be very difficult to have an effective discussion of philosophy using only smoke signals; the "bandwidth" of that particular medium is simply too limited. Similarly, the experience of watching television involves the passive acceptance of a steady flow of disconnected entertainment units—audiovisual packets that are condensed, simplified, and sweetened to fit the short attention-span limitations of the medium.

With the minimal exceptions of government-supported broadcasting such as America's PBS and England's BBC, the economic structure of the TV industry requires that the content be selected for its commercial potential—the number of eyeballs looking at the screen when the commercial comes on. And in recent years, the intense competition for viewers has forced media producers to fight for attention by pandering ever more aggressively to a jaded public, with material that is increasingly sexualized, violent, lurid, and voyeuristic.

> "America is the only nation in history that has gone
> directly from barbarism to decadence without the
> usual interval of civilization."
> —Georges Clemenceau

In what remains of "the news," according to Postman, we're treated to a steady parade of "talking hairdos" tantalizing us with the latest secrets about the personal lives of celebrities, robberies, shootings, car chases by police, and the mudslinging of political adversaries. We see news segments, file clips, and sound-bites of public figures so brief that one can only assume that the people who create them are convinced that we have the attention span of a gnat. The product, of course, *is* the talking hairdo, not the information.

Even the websites that serve as extensions of the broadcast media operations, such as CNN Online and others, have the look of online candy stores, with carefully tuned topic headlines promising lurid video footage, celebrity news tidbits, pop-science jelly beans, and easily digestible factoids.

Television, according to professor Postman and others, is a medium forever doomed to the status of the court jester—capable only of distracting and amusing us.

In fact, Postman asked: Could television actually be making us a dumber society? By analogy, if the muscles in our bodies atrophy when we don't use them, and if abilities such as sports, singing, dancing, playing musical instruments, drawing, and painting fade with disuse, doesn't it seem that our mental faculties such as critical thinking, comparative thinking, curiosity, imagination, judgment, and logic also atrophy with disuse?

If we can't look to the televisual media to help us keep our minds sharp and support the development of the minds of our children, then what other viable media do we have for developing and exercising the faculties of clear thinking and intelligent discourse? What of the literary channel—the world of ideas as expressed in print?

The news there is not good. Americans have been reading fewer books with each passing year, and U.S. publishers have been putting out fewer of them. In fact, 2006 marked the turning point at which, for the first time, the United States lost its leadership in publishing more titles than any other country. The UK—with one-fifth the people and one-sixth the economic size of the United States—took over as the new leader in book publishing.[4]

Most newspapers in the United States have seen declining readership, and a spate of special-topic popular magazines has not slowed the decline in the numbers of people who read. *Sports Illustrated,* a traditional men's magazine, saw its circulation stalled for a number of years, until it introduced its annual "swimsuit" issue, which put it into the light pornography business. For a male-oriented magazine, it discovered sex rather late in life, but eventually had to accept the realities of the saturated marketplace.

Big-brand marketers are using less print-based advertising and have taken to subsidizing the production of movies and TV shows in order to "place" their products into the public attention stream, where prospective customers can't tune them out or turn them off. The huge migration of advertising funds to the Internet also testifies to the steady transition of America to an electronically based culture from a print-based culture.

Screen-viewing, defined broadly as paying attention to information presented visually on display screens of various types—TVs, video players, computer monitors, movies, cell phones, PDAs, and electronic games—has displaced much of the experience of reading print on paper. The American Academy of Pediatrics has formally expressed its concern about protracted screen-viewing by children, and has recommended that parents not permit children younger than two to view *any* screen-based devices, including television.[5]

NYU's Professor Postman pointed out that television, as the least interactive of the televisual modes of information, diverts the most mental energy away from the experience of active cognition—for hours at a time. "Chewing gum for the mind," he called it. It's probably no accident that obesity in the Western cultures, particularly in America, has been steadily rising since television took over as the dominant activity in leisure time.

Brain research has demonstrated clearly that the experience of watching television for more than two to three minutes induces a trance-like state nearly indistinguishable from hypnosis. Advertising messages, in this sense, are post-hypnotic suggestions and embedded directives: "The next time *you have a headache* . . . ," or "Flu season is here and . . . [it's time to get the flu and then buy our medicine]."

Noted historian David McCullough, widely praised for making history come alive in his best-selling books, worries about what he and others have called "cultural amnesia," which is the loss of a sense of shared history and culture by a population ever more entranced by the provocative images dancing before their eyes. More and more people, says McCullough, devote their discretionary time and attention to the synthetic reality of the entertainment media rather than the active cognition that comes with reading and discussing interesting ideas. According to McCullough,

> "Reportedly the average American watches twenty-eight hours of television every week, or approximately four hours a day. The average person, I'm told, reads at a rate of 250 words per minute.
>
> "So, based on these statistics, were the average American to spend those four hours a day with a book, instead of watching television, the average American could, in a week, read:
>
> - The complete poems of T.S. Eliot;
> - Two plays by Thornton Wilder, including "Our Town";
> - The complete poems of Maya Angelou;
> - Faulkner's *The Sound and the Fury*;
> - F. Scott Fitzgerald's *The Great Gatsby*; and
> - The Book of Psalms.
>
> "That's all in one week.
>
> "If the average American were to forsake television for a second week, he or she could read all of *Moby Dick*, including the part about whales, and make a good start, if not finish, *The Brothers Karamazov*."[6]

Another significant development of the American popular media, best exemplified by talk shows on radio and television, has been the increasingly strident, polarized, antagonistic pattern of discourse. With the shifting of "the news" business toward an entertainment model of design and production now virtually complete, and the increasingly saturated media environment in the United States, those who sell us our media fix are forced by sheer competition to pander to our most primitive fears and appetites.

Media celebrities and spokespeople who formerly may have modeled thinking processes such as open-minded discourse, tolerance for differences, and respect for honest political opposition, now model the lowest levels of rudeness, intolerance, extremism, information-twisting, character assassination, and polarization. Our children have little chance of seeing role models for intelligent discourse anywhere in the popular media.

In fact, none other than *Time* magazine demonstrated its best two-valued thinking with a cover that featured New York Senator Hillary Clinton, who at the time was in the news as a possible presidential candidate for 2008. The cover layout showed a close-up view of her face along with two check-boxes, one labeled "Love Her" and the other labeled "Hate Her." Inside, readers were invited to vote: "How do you feel about Hillary Clinton? Check one of the boxes on this week's cover, and mail to TIME Magazine Letters, [address]."[7]

Allen Ginsberg, beat poet of the 1960s, remarked:

"We're in science fiction now, man. Whoever controls the images— the media—controls the culture."

On a more optimistic note, however, we must acknowledge that neither Postman nor Ginsberg, nor other scholars who seemingly despaired of the decline of the intellectual culture in America, could clearly foresee the coming impact of the Internet and the World Wide Web. It seems clear, at the time of this writing, that the culture of ideas is now rapidly and energetically migrating toward the Internet—a previously unrecognized *fourth medium* that deserves to be included in Postman's progression of the cultural conversation.

The web page, which may turn out to be one of the most important inventions of modern time, is—potentially, at least—*both* a televisual medium *and* a text-based reading medium. Perhaps the most remarkable feature of the web is that people of all intellectual stripes can find the information that suits the level of consciousness they choose for themselves. Alternatively, the downside of this migration of intellectual activity may exaggerate the impact of the culture of amusement, possibly reinforcing a new and more worrying polarization of the society.

## No Time to Read?

Excerpt from the commencement address by author and historian David McCullough, to the University of Connecticut, May 15, 1999.

"We're being sold the idea that information is learning and we're being sold a bill of goods.

"Information isn't learning. Information isn't wisdom. It isn't common sense necessarily. It isn't kindness. Or trustworthiness. Or good judgment. Or imagination. Or a sense of humor. Or courage. It doesn't tell us right from wrong.

"Knowing the area of the State of Connecticut in square miles, or the date on which the United Nations Charter was signed, or the jumping capacity of a flea may be useful or valuable, but it isn't learning of itself.

"If information were learning, you could become educated by memorizing the World Almanac. Were you to memorize the World Almanac, you wouldn't be educated. You'd be weird.

"My message is in praise of the greatest of all avenues to learning, to wisdom, adventure, pleasure, insight, to understanding human nature, understanding ourselves and our world and our place in it.

"I rise on this beautiful morning, here in this center of learning, to sing again the old faith in books. In reading books. Reading for life, all your life.

"Nothing ever invented provides such sustenance, such infinite reward for time spent as a good book.

"Thomas Jefferson told John Adams he could not live without books. Adams, who through a long life read more even and more deeply than Jefferson, and who spent what extra money he ever had on books, wrote to Jefferson at age seventy-nine of a particular set of books he longed for on the lives of the saints, all forty-seven volumes.

"Once upon a time in the dead of winter in Dakota Territory, with the temperature well below zero, young Theodore Roosevelt took off in a makeshift boat, accompanied by two of his ranch hands, down-stream on the Little Missouri River in chase of a couple of thieves who had stolen his prized rowboat. After days on the river, he caught up and got the draw on them with his trusty Winchester, at which point they surrendered. Then, after finding a man with a team and a wagon, Roosevelt set off again to haul the thieves cross-country to justice. He left the ranch hands behind to tend to the boat, and walked alone behind the wagon, his rifle at the ready. They were headed across the snow-covered wastes of the Bad Lands to the rail head at Dickinson, and Roosevelt walked the whole way, forty miles. It was an astonishing feat, what might be called a defining moment in that eventful life. But what makes it especially memorable is that during that time, he managed to read all of *Anna Karenina*.

"I often think of that when I hear people say they haven't time to read."

## KNOWS AND KNOW-NOTS: THE NEW SOCIAL DIVIDE

During the most intensive phase of the U.S. military operations in Iraq, the National Geographic Society commissioned a study by the Roper Public Affairs firm to find out what American high school students knew about the Middle East. The Geographic's leaders, as well as many educators, were stunned by the results.[8]

According to the study, 63 percent of the students couldn't find Iraq on an unlabeled map that showed only the countries of the Middle East. Seventy-five percent of them couldn't locate Israel on the same map. Less than half could point out India on a map of only the Asian continent.

Many students did no better with a map of their own country. Less than one year after the legendary hurricane Katrina nearly destroyed New Orleans, 30 percent of the high school students surveyed couldn't locate the state of Louisiana, or even figure out where the hurricane had struck. Forty-eight percent of them couldn't find the state of Mississippi, which borders Louisiana.

The poll also showed that 72 percent of young Americans— between the ages of eighteen and twenty-four—did not consider it important to know anything about other countries. Fewer than 10 percent considered it important to know another language besides English, and a majority of them mistakenly estimated that English is the world's most-used language.

The Roper/Geographic poll matches up with another interesting fact: *fewer than 25 percent of Americans have passports.*

Fewer Americans visit museums than in the past. Fewer of them attend live theater performances. Fewer of them visit libraries, patronize bookstores, or visit historical sites.

Professor Jon Miller of Michigan State University found that fully one-third of the Americans he surveyed completely rejected the scientific concept of evolution: *they simply didn't believe it.* The only country in Miller's comparative surveys with a lower acceptance of evolution was Turkey.[9]

In this new, so-called "Third-Wave" world of information glut, 24/7 news, and continuous entertainment, Americans seem, paradoxically, to be getting collectively dumber—or at the very least not getting smarter.

Every developed society eventually differentiates itself into various levels of wealth, status, and power. Differences in human capacity and human ambition sooner or later show up in the material standard of living. So it is with the process of education. Every developed society also develops an educated elite, and their material fortunes generally tend to correlate with their mental capacities. For many years, an article of faith in the American culture has held that a large middle class was the economic destiny of the country, and that a growing educated class was one of the primary causes of this democratization of wealth. This may not hold true indefinitely.

In recent years, the economic gap between the wealthy class and the middle class has been widening. If it continues to widen at its recent pace, the so-called American middle class may begin to fuse with the lower class, to form what may again look like a two-class society. Some futurists believe that the dumbing down of the popular media-based culture, together with the lack of progress in public education, may lead to an educational two-class society—the "knows" and the "know-nots."

By about 2000, more than half of the graduate students majoring in science and technology in U.S. universities were foreign-born. That disparity continues to grow. It's also interesting to note that while the number of women enrolled in colleges and universities in the United States has been growing steadily, the number of men enrolled has been declining. In fact, by about 2005, female students outnumbered males at the bachelor's, master's, and doctoral levels. Some sociologists believe that this steady shift in mental preparedness may lead to a significant change in the balance of influence and political power, and ultimately perhaps to a "feminization" of leadership in business and politics.

## WHO CARES? WHO NEEDS TO CARE?

"But the schools are out to teach patriotism; the news [media] are out to stir up excitement; and politicians are out to get re-elected. None of the three, therefore, can do anything whatever toward saving the human race from reciprocal suicide."

—Bertrand Russell (mathematician, philosopher)

"So what?" "Why should I care about any of this? Why is this my problem?" "What do you want me to do about it?" "What *can* I do about it?" Those are, of course, all legitimate questions—variations on the same basic question, actually. If the person who answers the question answers only for him- or herself, and only within the confines of his or her own immediate self-interest, then perhaps the answer is "I *don't* care. I have my own life to live. Don't bother me with other people's problems."

But if one answers from a somewhat larger perspective, say that of a parent, a teacher, a counselor, a social services professional, a business owner or executive, a political leader, a community activist, or maybe just someone who's concerned about where the country and culture may be heading, then perhaps there is reason to care. A person need not be a hyper-intellectual egghead to be at least vaguely concerned about the widely discussed dumbing-down of the American culture.

Practical intelligence, as we will define and explore it, could serve as a unifying concept, an organizing principle around which to structure the discussion of what some activists are calling the American "restoration agenda." The restoration agenda is a set of priorities for bringing back a number of key values, traditions, and institutions that many feel have been lost in the transition to a here-and-now culture of electronic experience. This restoration agenda is not unique to the American culture; many thoughtful people in virtually all of the developed countries are concerned about the same kinds of issues as their American counterparts are.

More and more social commentators have been blaming the pervasive media-based culture of amusement—not always fairly, perhaps—for a variety of sins. These include the coarsening of public entertainment with the ever-increasing use of sexualization, violence, and voyeuristic content; the destruction of childhood innocence; the commercial exploitation of children by cynical marketing methods; and the polarization of political discourse with mean-spirited, narrow-minded, and antagonistic personal attacks exchanged by warring ideological camps.

All of these symptoms and others, one might argue, are indicators of a culture that has "gone dumb."

Some will say that the battle has already been lost, that "it can't be done." Surely it's too much to expect that several hundred million people will all suddenly discover the rewards of thinking clearly, reading exciting ideas, and exchanging their views intelligently with one another. But revolutions don't start with the masses; they start with the few—those who can articulate the case for a new way of doing things and who can show others the road to get there. The masses learn by imitation and social modeling.

In 1975, the government of Venezuela created a new cabinet position: Minister for the Development of Human Intelligence. Dr. Luis Machado, a noted scholar and activist, was appointed to head the department. His mission was to influence as many public institutions as possible throughout the country to devote attention and resources to supporting the development of intelligence in its citizens, beginning at—and even before—birth. Machado launched an ambitious campaign to educate parents, healthcare professionals, educators, and caregivers of every imaginable variety about how intelligence develops in children and how to support and accelerate its progress.

To the best of my knowledge, this remarkable venture has not been replicated at the national level in any other country. The Venezuelan venture had a fatal flaw: the government gave Machado a small office, one assistant, and no budget. He labored mightily for several years to advance his mission, but eventually the government changed hands and the program was killed. Possibly the government leaders had second thoughts about the implications of millions of citizens learning how to use their gray matter more skillfully. There's a bigger demand for sheep than for shepherds.

Malcolm Gladwell, in his best-selling book *The Tipping Point: How Little Things Can Make a Big Difference*, described the domino-like process by which ideas and ideologies sell themselves across cultures.

One of the contagion dynamics he identified was "mavenhood," the role of people who are uniquely well positioned to promote an idea to others. Mavens, according to Gladwell, are people who have the attention of large numbers of people and who can influence them by way of the roles they play. A maven who takes a personal interest in some particular idea or movement can have a huge impact in bringing the idea to the attention of others, and making it part of the public consciousness.[10]

Who are the potential mavens who can promote the teaching, application, and appreciation of PI in our culture?

**Parents** can educate themselves about PI, upgrade their own PI skills, and teach their children every day how to use their minds more effectively. Starting with the very youngest children, parents can help them develop superior language skills, learn to love reading, make decisions for themselves, think in terms of options and possibilities, develop tolerance for ambiguity and complexity, articulate problems and work their way through to solutions, think up original ideas, and share their ideas with others. Parents can work with teachers to encourage schools to implement the teaching of PI concepts and skills.

**Teachers** can educate themselves about PI, upgrade their own PI skills, and change the focus of the educational experience from teaching kids what to think to teaching them *how* to think. Teachers can change the vocabulary of their practice to focus more on competence and less on content. They can bring the concepts and methods of PI to the surface, rather than leave them haphazardly scrambled into the teaching-learning experience. They can work through their professional associations to encourage schools to implement the teaching of PI concepts and skills.

**Educators** who train teachers in colleges and universities can educate themselves about PI, upgrade their own PI skills, and change the focus of the teacher-education process from teaching kids what to think to teaching them *how* to think. Educators can encourage teachers to play a more active part in encouraging schools to implement the teaching of PI concepts and skills.

**Mental health professionals** can educate themselves about PI, upgrade their own PI skills, and learn to view human adjustment through the multi-faceted prism of practical mental competence. A large aspect of the therapeutic experience is unlearning and relearning, and the concept of "therapy as learning" has much to recommend it.

**Executives and managers** in business organizations can educate themselves about PI, upgrade their own PI skills, and allocate training resources toward upgrading the thinking skills of their employees—all of them, not just the elite or the star performers who are anointed for success. They can make *organizational intelligence,* both individual and collective, a high priority within the cultures of their enterprises. They can use their positions of visibility and influence to encourage schools to implement the teaching of PI concepts and skills.

**Consultants to business** can educate themselves about PI, upgrade their own PI skills, and promote the training and development of mental skills among employees as one avenue for increasing the capacity of the enterprise to compete. Consultants can introduce the methods of effective thinking and problem solving as part of their contribution in advising executives and helping teams work more effectively.

**Legislators and political leaders** can educate themselves about PI, upgrade their own PI skills, and provide the leadership needed to raise the level of discourse needed to encourage schools to implement the teaching of PI concepts and skills.

**Celebrities and media leaders** can educate themselves about PI, upgrade their own PI skills, and provide the leadership needed to raise the level of discourse in the popular media, disavowing the practices that pander to fear, ignorance, and bigotry. They can use their positions of visibility and influence to encourage schools to implement the teaching of PI concepts and skills.

If my prescription seems rather repetitive, with the same commitment required of the influencers in various sectors of our society, then maybe that's the message. If we're going to rescue the culture of ideas from its captivity at the hands of the culture of amusement, we'll have to make the conversation about the "restoration agenda" ever more widespread, intense, and interesting. One modest hope for this book is to strengthen the case and provide a street-language vocabulary that can inform that strategic conversation.

## Notes

1. *Reader's Digest.* April 1978, p.132.
2. Postman, Neil. *Amusing Ourselves to Death: Public Discourse in the Age of Show Business.* New York: Penguin, 1985.
3. McLuhan, Marshall. *Understanding Media: the Extensions of Man.* Cambridge, MA: MIT Press, 1994 (reissued). Originally published in 1964. See also McLuhan, Marshall, *The Medium Is the Message.*
4. "U.S. Book Production Plummets 18K in 2005." News release. RR Bowker, May 9, 2006.
5. An AAP policy paper on the association's website recommends: "Pediatricians should urge parents to avoid television viewing for children under the age of two years. Although certain television programs may be promoted to this age group, research on early brain development shows that babies and toddlers have a critical need for direct interactions with parents and other significant care givers (e.g., child care providers) for healthy brain growth and the development of appropriate social, emotional, and cognitive skills. Therefore, exposing such young children to television programs should be discouraged." See http://aappolicy.aappublications.org/cgi/content/full/pediatrics;104/2/341
6. Excerpt from the commencement address by author and historian David McCullough to the University of Connecticut, May 15, 1999.
7. *Time* magazine, August 28, 2006, cover.
8. *National Geographic*-Roper Public Affairs, 2006 Geographic Literacy Study. November 2006. See *National Geographic* website at www.national geographic.com.
9. "Americans Less Likely to Accept Evolution than Europeans." News release, Michigan State University website, www.msu.edu.
10. Gladwell, Malcolm. *The Tipping Point: How Little Things Can Make a Big Difference.* New York: Little, Brown, 2000.

# 2

## MULTIPLE INTELLIGENCES
### *The Possible Human*

"A human being should be able to change a diaper,
plan an invasion, butcher a hog, conn a ship,
design a building, write a sonnet, balance accounts, build
a wall, set a bone, comfort the dying, take orders, give orders,
cooperate, act alone, solve equations, analyze a new problem,
program a computer, cook a tasty meal, fight efficiently,
die gallantly. Specialization is for insects."
—Robert Heinlein (science fiction author)

THE GAP BETWEEN SCIENCE AND THE POPULAR PERCEPTION may be wider in the area of human mental process than for almost any other topic—with the possible exceptions of global warming and losing weight. Scientists and researchers toil away in their laboratories and clinics, trying to accumulate an agreed-on body of knowledge about the human biocomputer and its capacities. Meanwhile, educators, parents, business managers, publishers, writers, and advisors of every stripe are left to evolve a street-level understanding of how we think and how we might think better. It would seem that the exchange of knowledge between "gown and town" could be much richer and more useful than it has been.

For example, one of the charming "scientific facts" that seems to have become firmly embedded in the popular consciousness is that we humans use only a small part of the brain's thinking capacity. This seems eminently reasonable—especially after having read or watched a typical day's "news." However, somewhere in the foggy zone between science and experience we've developed a peculiar cliché: "Well, studies show that we only use 7 percent of our brain's capacity."

The percentage number varies, but is almost invariably low. And it's usually an odd number: 5 percent, 7 percent, but sometimes 10 percent. The next time you hear someone—including yourself—make such a "scientific" pronouncement, you might pause and ask the speaker: "By the way, how *do* scientists measure the brain's capacity? Do they measure it in thoughts per second? Megabytes? Megahertz? RPM? Furlongs per fortnight?" There is no credible method for measuring mental capacity; we don't even know how to define it. Nevertheless, this "fact" has remained popular for a long time.

Unfortunately, the journey we've embarked on in this book must necessarily traverse that foggy zone between science and experience. My academic friends are probably already appalled at my cavalier acknowledgement of Gardner's multiple intelligence theory, which many feel has little basis in research. Some will take me to task for not being sufficiently "rigorous" in my assertions and in the evidence I adduce for their support. Some will cry "foul" in protest of what they see as prostituting the whole concept of intelligence as the academic community has traditionally defined it—for allowing the barbarians to overrun the palace. And some of them get *really mad* about it.

At the same time, many of my colleagues in the business sector, where I earn my livelihood, seem convinced that even if there are multiple intelligences, so what? It doesn't matter. The competitive process sorts it all out: the cream will always rise to the top. All you have to do is hire the smartest people you can find or afford and pay them well. Maybe they'll act a bit smarter if you treat them nicely, but beyond that, why concern yourself with trying to make them any smarter? The smart ones will make it to the head of the pack anyway. This is the same logic that governs the educational system.

The difficulty presented by the gap between science and experience in this case lies in the confusion of terms like smart, intelligent, intelligence, skill, talent, and thinking ability. Clearly, they do not all mean the same thing in the academic world, and the secular world seems rather confused about what they do mean.

In the discussion that follows, I have no aspiration to narrow the gap between science and experience, but I do recognize an obligation to explain what I myself mean when using those terms and others related to them, and to explain what I believe is possible. The best I can hope for is to request an armistice with both gown and town, while I attempt to trace what I believe can be a practical framework for thinking about thinking: practical intelligence.

## IQ DOESN'T TELL THE WHOLE STORY

We needn't belabor the "IQ debate" much further, considering that the multiple intelligence concept is already rather widely accepted, for better or worse. For our purposes, it's only necessary to put the dimension of *abstract intelligence*—the IQ kind—into perspective with the other intelligences.

Having a high IQ is proof of the ability to get a high score on an IQ test, and possibly a few other things, although it's uncertain exactly what those are. IQ test scores do tend to predict success in life, but *only to a small extent and within a relatively small range of scores.*

A person with a very low IQ test score, say 85 or less, is very likely to have difficulty coping with the kinds of tasks presented by life in a modern society. A person with a mid-range IQ score, say 95 through 120, will very likely cope with life more successfully than people with very low scores. However, scores above 125 or so are only loosely correlated with life success. And even within the "normal" range of 95 to 125, the effects of the differences tend to get washed out by a host of other factors.

In other words, it would not be reasonable to expect that a difference of five or ten IQ points would make a direct and measurable difference between two people in terms of income, net worth, or even subjective measures of success. The effect of the IQ differences is too weak, and there are many other factors that contribute to success in life. In highly controlled educational settings, performance differences on written tests may be more noticeable, but in "real life" the other factors come into play in unpredictable ways.

Many leading thinkers in the field of developmental psychology have advocated eliminating intelligence testing completely from public schools, but with limited success. Even eminent intelligence psychologist Arthur Jensen has said, "Achievement itself is the school's main concern. I see no need to measure anything other than achievement itself."

IQ testing suffers from another, perhaps more important limitation—one not necessarily of interest to researchers but one certainly of concern to parents, for example, who are trying to raise kids who can use their gray matter successfully in life. That limitation, or flaw if you prefer, is built right into the method of IQ testing that is almost universally used.

Standardized IQ tests typically present questions or problems in a written format—with pen and paper—and with multiple-choice answers. This practice probably came about because of the need to test large numbers of people at low cost, so it became necessary to eliminate any kind of experiential or contextual challenge and get the whole testing process into the multiple-choice format.

The unfortunate limitation of the pen-and-paper test design is that the test can only present questions or problems that have one "right" answer. Such a design makes it easy to test what psychologists call *convergent thinking* skills—narrowing down many possibilities to find the one correct choice. It makes it virtually impossible to test the complementary mental skill of *divergent thinking,* which is critical for creativity, innovation, imagination, and invention.

For example, if you give a coin to a child and ask, "How many things can you think of to do with this coin?" the youngster will probably come up with quite a few possibilities: use it as a guide to draw a circle; use it to turn a screw or pry something open; use it to measure something; flip it to make a decision; give it to someone as a gift; and, of course, use it to buy something. With this divergent thinking process, the number of possible options is unbounded, and can't be reduced to a fixed set of "right" answers.

Show a picture to a child and ask him or her to tell you a story about the picture. You'll get lots of different stories from different kids, all of which are "correct," in that they're all natural products of the child's "intelligence." Yet conventional IQ testing leaves out the entire range of divergent, generative, projective, and inventive thinking processes.

Many educators believe that the unconsciously held idea that intelligence is confined to a process of convergent thinking has led to educational approaches based on "right" answers. Many of them—and I agree with them—believe that the skills of "far-out" thinking get systematically eradicated as children go through the educational experience to adulthood.

# THERE ARE AT LEAST
# SIX KINDS OF "SMART"

Enter Harvard Professor Howard Gardner. With Gardner's theory of *multiple intelligences,* theory may have caught up with common sense.

Beginning in about 1980, Gardner had become interested in some fundamental questions arising from psychological testing: Why do some people with very high IQ scores fail miserably in their personal lives? Do tests of mental competence miss certain obvious aspects of human ability, such as artistic, musical, athletic, literary, and social competence?

Gardner came to the inevitable conclusion: the outdated concept of "intelligence" as a singular measure of competence has to go. He posited that human beings have a whole range of primary competencies—intelligences—and they exist in various proportions in various persons. His provocative book *Frames of Mind: The Theory of Multiple Intelligences,* published in 1983, dealt a body-blow to the established notion that IQ defines or controls the ability to think, and set in motion a new way of looking at human competence.[1]

Placing practical intelligence ("PI") within Gardner's "MI" framework requires a bit of conceptual acrobatics, inasmuch as Gardner himself—at least at the time of this writing—continues to evolve his categories and definitions. The bulk of his early work involved a set of some seven independent intelligences. He has also posited the existence of an eighth dimension, less clearly defined. Some other researchers have diced up the macro-intelligences into other categories.

Consequently, for our exploration, we'll need to settle on some working definition of these multiple intelligences, in order to place PI clearly into that perspective. While Gardner uses rather scientific sounding labels for his categories—verbal-logical, mathematical-symbolic, spatial, kinesthetic, interpersonal, intrapersonal and musical—we probably do little harm by re-coding them into street language and simplifying them conceptually. With appropriate respect for Professor

Gardner and his theory, I've found it helpful to rearrange these "multiple smarts" into six primary categories:

1. *Abstract Intelligence:* symbolic reasoning, mathematics, and formal logic.
2. *Social Intelligence:* understanding social contexts and dealing with people.
3. **Practical Intelligence: common sense (the topic of this book).**
4. *Emotional Intelligence:* awareness and management of one's inner experience.
5. *Aesthetic Intelligence:* the sense of form, design, music, art, and literature.
6. *Kinesthetic Intelligence:* whole-body skills like sports, dance, or flying a jet fighter.

Others might argue for a somewhat different set of subdivisions, but these six categories work fairly well, and they have the modest extra advantage of spelling out a memorable acronym: ASPEAK.

Presumably the "Renaissance human," the success model most of us admire, would have a strong and well-integrated combination of all key intelligences.

Gardner's notion of multiple intelligences seems to fit with our common experience. Consider the disparity between *abstract intelligence*—the IQ kind—and *social intelligence*. I've met many members of Mensa, the international society of people with high IQs—the only requirement for membership. I've often marveled at the number of them who, despite their impressive cognitive credentials, seemed incapable of connecting with other people and, in some cases, incapable of maintaining a reasonable degree of emotional resilience.

IQ-intelligence doesn't necessarily translate to the ability to raise children, plan a wedding, run a business, manage people, or compose a song. Nor, to be fair, does the ability to fly a jet fighter—kinesthetic intelligence—necessarily translate to the ability to solve differential equations.

Presumably, we can approach each of these six key dimensions as a learning adventure in and of itself. The evidence from developmental research suggests that the basis for each of the six intelligences takes shape early in life. We know less—actually, very little—about the extent to which adults can make significant gains in all of these dimensions. Certainly the hope for that possibility appeals to many of us.

## BUILDING OUT: APPLYING THEORIES TO EVERYDAY LIFE

Each of the primary intelligences deserves attention in its own right. Interested experts will eventually "build out" each of the dimensions with diligent study and clear conceptualization. This book will attempt a fairly systematic build-out of only one of them, the PI dimension. To guide our exploration, it may be worthwhile to learn from the progress of the build-out of two of the other important dimensions, emotional intelligence and social intelligence.

My friends in the academic community are quick to remind me that the study of the broad field of "intelligence" has been going on for a very long time, and that very few of the key concepts and theories can be fairly attributed to only one individual expert. Even the concept of multiple intelligences has been foreshadowed in earlier research, and certainly the component intelligences such as emotional and social have been specifically identified in the past. Researchers have at least speculated about most of them at some time and to some extent.

Books such as Professor Daniel Goleman's *Emotional Intelligence* and my *Social Intelligence* have made these topics accessible to a broader populace outside of the academic community, but don't necessarily advance the theoretical frontiers of their study. The contribution of the "popularizers," while not always regarded with admiration by academic researchers, can also be to lend clarity by bringing together a number of scattered concepts into a useful body of knowledge. This is largely what I mean when I refer to the "build-out" phase in the life cycle of a concept like any one of the intelligences.

# BUILD-OUT 1: EMOTIONAL INTELLIGENCE

Arriving in 1995, Daniel Goleman's *Emotional Intelligence: Why It May be More Important than IQ*,[2] could be considered the first step in bringing the MI concept out of the academic realm and into the lives of ordinary civilians. One could argue that most of the "self-help" literature has dealt with EI in some form or another, but *Emotional Intelligence* deserves credit for crystallizing the idea of an "intelligence" as a useful focus of attention in the popular culture.

Goleman's book became a best seller and very quickly gained a following in the business sector. Executives, personnel managers, trainers, consultants, coaches, and a whole population of human performance practitioners jumped on the wagon and began to sell their services to businesses. Conferences, seminars, books, training materials, and websites sprang up to carry the EI build-out forward.

Goleman's first attempts to frame a practical model of EI identified five dimensions of competence:

1. Self-awareness.
2. Self-regulation.
3. Motivation.
4. Empathy.
5. Relationships.

One of Goleman's five dimensions, however—the relationship dimension—seemed to stretch the model and the concept beyond its practical boundaries. The four primary competencies do clearly identify elements of the internal emotional landscape, which influence one's behavior in fundamental ways. And certainly they influence in a very fundamental way a person's capacity to interact well with others. But trying to force-fit social competence into an already broad model of emotional competence seemed to risk doing too little with too much.

Indeed, as previously explained, Professor Gardner clearly separates them in his formulation: he posits an *intrapersonal* intelligence (emotional intelligence), for all practical purposes, and an *interpersonal* intelligence—competency in human situations. The value of this clearer delineation of concepts seems to lie in the opportunity to coordinate and inter-relate them, rather than trying to squash them all into a single conceptual container.

Goleman and others eventually evolved a conceptual structure for EI that attempted to balance EI and SI, although still trying to keep them fused together under one "brand" name. This dual-concept framework subdivided each of the two dimensions into two sub-scales—awareness and control. The emotional dimension broke down into self-awareness and self-control (or self-management), while the social dimension broke down into social awareness and management of one's interactions with others.

As of this writing, the majority of EI practitioners seem to embrace this four-quadrant view, insisting for the most part that the EI umbrella adequately incorporates the social component and that there is no need for a separately identified dimension of social intelligence. However, Goleman himself has apparently rethought his own approach to EI, and practitioners in the field may have to make some adjustments if they want to stay aligned with the "Vatican view."

## BUILD-OUT 2: SOCIAL INTELLIGENCE

Social Intelligence, as with the other MI dimensions, has been knocking about the academic community for many years. Early researchers debated whether they should consider it simply a sub-skill, or a talent, under the broad umbrella of IQ-type intelligence, or whether it deserved a separate identity. (Questions like this, by the way, are exceedingly important to researchers, some of whom get considerably worked up about these theoretical distinctions.)

Several books dealing with SI, either directly or tangentially, have appeared in the academic press and the popular press over several decades, but none seems to have captured the attention of a very large readership.

My book, *Social Intelligence: The New Science of Success,*[3] arrived on the planet in late 2005, as an attempt to clarify the body of knowledge, help people assess their own SI status, and prescribe some learning methods for increasing one's SI. My hope was that *Social Intelligence* would serve as a bridge between the academic world and the worlds of business and private life. My intent was to present neither an academic work nor a breezy "self-help" book; I hoped to establish a credible conceptual foundation, and at the same time present a "how-to" approach that might be personally useful to readers.

My particular interest in SI, according to my yellowed research notes, traces to about 1985, although I only recently began to apply that label explicitly. I was interested in developing new ways to help business people increase their personal effectiveness, and it seemed to me that the pop-science label of "people skills" tended to devalue the "wisdom" component I felt could be clarified and developed.

By about 2000 I had finally evolved a descriptive model or framework (perhaps I'm a slow learner in some ways), which I believed could capture the "intelligence" aspect of human interaction, while incorporating the common-sensical features of social skills we've always understood at a practical level.

I evolved a model of SI with five components, embodied in the acronym "S.P.A.C.E.," which means:

**S** = Situational Awareness; "reading" situations, people, interactions, and contexts.

**P** = Presence; also known as "bearing"; how one presents one's self in situations.

**A** = Authenticity; behaving honestly, with integrity, and from a clear sense of self.

**C** = Clarity; skill at asking, telling, persuading, and getting one's ideas into the minds of others.

**E** = Empathy; the skill of connecting with people, on a personal and meaningful level; getting them to move with and toward you rather than away and against you.

I also developed a self-assessment questionnaire, the *Social Intelligence Profile,* for use by educators, trainers, coaches, and business leaders to understand their individual competencies and developmental needs.[4]

Curiously, about a year after the publication of my book, *Social Intelligence: The New Science of Success,* Daniel Goleman released his own book *Social Intelligence: The New Science of Human Relationships.*[5] (The use of an identical title and a near-identical subtitle for a book following so closely on the heels of another is a rare practice in publishing, and somewhat mysterious in its reasoning.)

Goleman had been thinking about social intelligence as possibly a separate dimension, on a par with emotional intelligence instead of included within it. This cleavage of the Goleman model into two distinct parts caused somewhat of a theoretical brain cramp, inasmuch as the EI build-out was more than ten years underway, and devotees of the Goleman theory had been working hard to keep EI and SI welded together in the same structure.

As of this writing, it's too early to anticipate the impact of Goleman's change of position on his EI theory or to predict the development of EI and SI as a result of the conceptual realignment. My view is that the realignment will help clarify and simplify the study of both EI and SI, and possibly rather soon.

# THE NEXT BUILD-OUT:
# PRACTICAL INTELLIGENCE

Now, with some history and an understanding of the development of EI and SI as separate but related bodies of knowledge, we have some guidelines for the next intelligence that's a candidate for a build-out, namely practical intelligence.

If we're going to build a framework for describing, teaching, and learning practical intelligence, then it needs to be . . . well . . . practical, above all. It has to show us useful, helpful, learnable methods and habits of thought. It needs a defining vocabulary that can help us capture and articulate its key principles. It needs some visual-graphic models that can constellate various key concepts and ideas into useful packages of meaning. And it needs a "story line," a sense of continuity that leads us from one level of understanding to another.

Such a model or framework is what I hope to present in this book, and only time and the reactions of readers of all kinds will tell the extent to which I may have succeeded.

## Notes

1.   Gardner, Howard. *Frames of Mind.* New York: Basic Books, 1983. See also Gardner, Howard. *Intelligence Reframed.* New York: Basic Books, 1999.
2.   Goleman, Daniel. *Emotional Intelligence: Why It Can Matter More Than IQ.* New York: Bantam, 1995.
3.   Albrecht, Karl. *Social Intelligence: The New Science of Success.* San Francisco: Jossey-Bass, 2005.
4.   Karl Albrecht International. *Social Intelligence Profile.* San Diego: 2006. www.KarlAlbrecht.com.
5.   Goleman, Daniel. *Social Intelligence: The New Science of Human Relationships.* New York: Bantam, 2006.

# 3

## *WHAT IS PRACTICAL INTELLIGENCE?*

"... if we once start thinking, no one can guarantee
where we shall come out—except that many ends,
objects, and institutions are doomed. Every thinker
puts some portion of an apparently stable world
in peril, and no one can wholly predict what
will emerge in its place."
—John Dewey (American educator)

ACCORDING TO A WIDELY CIRCULATED STORY that quickly became an Internet parable—or possibly a legend—a bricklayer had injured himself while working on a repair project at the top of a low-rise building. On his claim form for medical insurance, he tried to minimize the incident by answering the question, "What caused the accident?" with the brief response, "Faulty judgment." When pressed by the company's claims department for a full and detailed description of the accident, he related a tale that could indeed tempt the casual reader to question his common sense.

According to his account of the incident, he had been repairing a brick chimney on the roof of an older four-story building. When he finished, he still had a large number of unused bricks and needed to get them back down to the ground. Not wanting to make many trips up and down the service stairwell, he decided to rig a rope and pulley system to lower the bricks to the ground.

Spotting a pulley mounted on an existing beam that extended over the edge of the roof, he chose a wooden barrel as a container for the bricks. He passed a rope through the pulley, attached one end to the barrel, and threw the other end down to the ground. Then he went down and attached the bottom end of the rope firmly to a cleat mounted on the wall.

Next he went back up, hung the empty barrel over the side of the wall, and proceeded to fill it with bricks. When it was full, he went down and proceeded to lower it to the ground. He wrapped the end of the rope securely around his hand and then released the rope from the cleat. Too late, he realized that the barrel of bricks weighed a lot more than he did.

He suddenly shot upward, hanging onto the rope, as the barrel rapidly descended. He met the barrel on its downward trajectory, getting severely bruised in the process. As he arrived at the pulley, the barrel hit the ground. Unfortunately, the weight of the bricks tore the bottom out of the barrel, which—now empty—weighed much less than he did. Now the barrel shot upward as he descended rapidly, still attached to the rope. He met the barrel a second time, sustaining additional bruises.

He hit the ground as the barrel hit the pulley. By then, he had become disentangled from the end of the rope and, as he lay on the pile of bricks looking upward, he saw the barrel on its third trip, now heading straight for him. Before he could get up and move out of the way, the barrel landed on him, inflicting a final humiliating insult.

No, it's not inhuman to laugh at this incident; we're laughing at the human condition, not the condition of any one human. If you have guilt feelings about laughing at the slapstick nature of the incident, just imagine that it might not be true. But . . . we all know that it *could* be true, don't we?

There's something primal and archetypal about incidents like these. They're the stuff of comedy, cartoons, and jokes. Failure of common sense is a common theme in theater, movies, and even songs. And if we're honest with ourselves, we have to admit that we've all had similar lapses of "common sense."

My neighbor's teen-age son, while drilling a hole in the fender of his bicycle to mount a headlight, vigorously drilled down through the metal fender and straight into the front tire. It's a necessary part of the experience of being a teen-ager—it comes with the territory.

> "There is nothing so frightening
> as ignorance in action."
>
> —Goethe

I'm a fan of definitions; I often find that I can clarify my understanding of an issue, a topic, or a concept if I can frame it succinctly into a concise definition. And sometimes trying a variety of definitions helps us understand a concept from multiple angles. For this discussion, I use the following definition:

> *Practical Intelligence: the mental ability to cope*
> *with the challenges and opportunities of life.*

What counts as practical intelligence, common sense, or wisdom depends on the *context* in which we hope to find it. It's situational. A person might be wise in the ways of business, but not at all wise in his or her dealings with fellow human beings. Someone might be considered wise in the practice of some scientific specialty, but not wise in managing his or her personal finances.

Practical intelligence, perhaps more than the other intelligences in the MI framework, needs a view through a wide-angle lens. It incorporates a wide range of mental processes, skills, and habits. We understand that it isn't "IQ," and in fact that it's *more than IQ*, but: What is it?

Moving on from this simple definition, we begin a fairly broad investigation of human mental competence, in its many dimensions.

## THINKING IS A BODILY FUNCTION

How many of your best ideas have come to you in the shower? While brushing your teeth? While walking or jogging? How often have you experienced strange, surreal, and creative images flowing through your mind as you were falling asleep or coming out of sleep? Have you had an important idea or a realization come to you in a dream, or while daydreaming? Has the solution to a problem flashed into your mind while you were doing something completely unrelated to the problem?

> "Never trust any thought you have
> while sitting down."
> —Friedrich Nietzsche

The very first principle of practical intelligence to be understood is that *you think with your whole body,* not with some individual circuit somewhere in the cortex of your brain. In fact, your brain is not really a whole computer—it's one key part of an *extended computer,* your *biocomputer,* which includes your whole nervous system, various information-processing subsystems located in your organs and muscles, and even your chemical messenger systems such as your hormone systems and your immune system.

*Case in point:* controlled clinical studies have shown that, immediately after test subjects meditated for as little as fifteen minutes, concentrations of an immune-system chemical known as *Immunoglobulin A* (IgA) in their saliva registered significantly higher than before meditation. These changes were not observed when the subjects merely rested or slept. The particular nature of any mental activity potentially has a corresponding physiological impact on the body.

*Case in point:* controlled clinical studies have also shown that listening to counter-classical types of music such as hard rock, grunge, rap, and other strident acoustical patterns induced a significant *drop* in salivary IgA levels. Working in very high-noise environments tends to have the same debilitating effects on immune function. In Chapter 5 we'll explore further the effects of environmental stressors on mental health and wellness and discover some strategies for managing our sensory environment and filtering out a major part of the toxic input.

Clearly, mental activity of any kind is expressed throughout the body, down to the level of individual cells. In some sense, we can even say that the cells themselves have intelligence—they "think" at a microscopic level. Certainly the individual organs do. A mountain of scientific and anecdotal evidence supports the conclusion that mental activity can make a person sick or well, a point we hardly need debate here. The emerging scientific field of *psychoneuroimmunology* reports astonishing instances of remission of cancer and recovery from a host of diseases using meditation, intensive imaging, and even prayer, where conventional medical treatment strategies have failed.

A thought—any thought—is a whole-body event. It might arise from within an organ, say with a change in blood glucose level, which you sense as a changed feeling, or mood. That change in mood will have a subtle—or significant—effect on the conscious aspect of your mental process, which is only a part of the whole of what you're "thinking" about. What you decide, what you say, and how you perceive what's going on around you are all moderated by these bio-information events that are constantly flashing throughout your body. Your brain is usually involved, but may not necessarily be controlling the process. What we think of as "moods," for example, are actually bio-informational states that pervade the body.

In order to clarify our vocabulary from the outset, let's agree on a simple working definition of the word *thinking*:

> *Thinking: a never-ending multi-level process of*
> *information flow, which involves or affects every cell*
> *in the human body.*

By extension, we can define a *thought* as:

> *Thought: a whole-body information event that*
> *re-patterns the bio-informational structure of*
> *the body.*

You think—in the broadest sense of the term—even while you're sleeping. Even in the deepest level of sleep, classified as Stage 4 sleep, you can still respond to signals from your environment. How does a sleeping mother's biocomputer tune out traffic noises, barking dogs, and a snoring mate, and yet wake her instantly when her infant cries? What enables you to wake up five minutes before your alarm goes off?

Sleep researchers report incidents of *lucid dreaming,* a dream state in which the dreamer somehow "knows" that he or she is dreaming. This seems to be a paradoxical state of consciousness that incorporates aspects of waking thought and vivid dream images.

Every one of those countless thought-events that continually flash through our bodies makes us a different person—physiologically, psychologically, and informationally. We may be conscious and aware of some of these bio-informational events, which we specifically refer to as "thoughts," only vaguely aware of others, and incapable of experiencing others at a conscious level. Nevertheless, we're continuously "thinking."

# MEET YOUR BIOCOMPUTER

"The purpose of your body is to carry
your brain around."

—Thomas Edison

Imagine building a computer that can store a hundred years' or more worth of information; analyze and seamlessly combine multi-media data—images, sounds, numbers, words, and even sensations and smells; recognize and recall complex patterns; generate its own data from scratch; and even write its own software.

Make it able to control complex mechanical, electrical, and chemical processes equivalent to those of a small factory, and make sure it can connect instantly to any of billions of others like it.

Make it portable, keep it smaller than a fair-sized grapefruit, keep its weight under about three pounds, make it operate with no battery and no cooling fan, on less power than a twenty-five watt bulb, and you have something like the human brain.

*Your* brain. It's the most advanced biological structure found anywhere in nature.

Have you ever considered what a phenomenal gift you have in this biological computer? Let's take a closer look at this remarkable system and understand more fully the potential it offers for living more intelligently and joyfully.

Referring to Figure 3.1, we see the general physical structure of the brain and spinal cord, which form the central processor and the primary communication axis for the whole extended biocomputer.

Although not visible in the simplified diagram, your brain floats inside a shockproof vault—your *cranium.* Three layers of tough tissue, the *meninges,* protect it and cushion it from bouncing against your skull. It's the best-protected organ in your body, and it enjoys the highest priority when blood, oxygen, and nutrients are distributed. It produces and floats in its own *cerebro-spinal fluid,* which circulates nutrients and flows downward to the body, carrying waste products with it.

## Figure 3.1. Architecture of the Brain

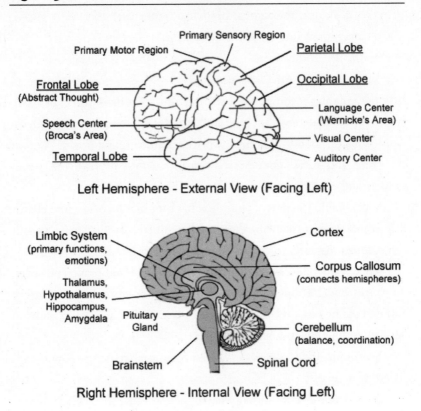

Left Hemisphere - External View (Facing Left)

Right Hemisphere - Internal View (Facing Left)

Also not shown in the diagram is the whole system of arteries and veins, which supply the brain with blood. The absence of a properly oxygenated blood supply to the brain for longer than about four minutes usually causes irreversible brain damage or death.

Your brain consumes about 20 percent of your body's glucose supply and a similar amount of its oxygen. It burns energy at a rate about equal to a twenty-five-watt bulb. (We'll forego the obvious jokes about people whose bulbs are dimmer than others.)

## Hemispheres, Lobes, and Functions

At first glance, one notices that the outer portion of the brain is partitioned fore-and-aft into left and right halves, or *cerebral hemispheres.* Your two hemispheres are physically separate, but they're joined by a thick band of nerve fibers called the *corpus callosum* ("callous body" in Latin), as illustrated by the interior view in the figure. The corpus callosum carries signals back and forth between the hemispheres, enabling them to share information constantly.

The outer part of your brain's convoluted surface—the *cortex*—is demarcated by deep fissures, each referred to by scientists as a *sulcus* (collectively, *sulci*), separating various mounds or ridges, each referred to as a *gyrus* (collectively, *gyri*). This sulcus-and-gyrus formation tends to maximize the surface area of the *gray matter* of the cortex, where the billions of *neurons* do the heavy work in our thinking processes.

It's also well known that the left hemisphere of the brain controls the right side of the body, and *vice versa.* Similarly, the sensory signals coming to the brain from the two sides of your body cross over to the opposite hemispheres, where they're processed.

Rather peculiarly, your visual neurons, which emerge from the retinas of your eyes, are segmented into left and right "fields." That is, the nerves from the left half of your left retina and the left half of your right retina both go to your right hemisphere's visual processing center, located in the occipital lobe at the rear of your brain. Similarly, the nerves from the right half of each retina go to the visual center in the occipital lobe of your left hemisphere.

The *optic nerves,* which emerge from the back of each eyeball, fuse together into a junction called the *optic chiasm,* and immediately separate again, with each outgoing nerve branch switching over to the opposite hemisphere.

This "crossover" effect, in which motor control and sensory processing are swapped between the two sides of the body and the two cerebral hemispheres, remains a mystery to scientists. The functional value of this design feature is open to speculation.

Much of what we know about the functions of the brain comes from the study of brain-injured people. Scientists and physicians have long associated various cognitive, behavioral, and motor impairments with specific traumas to the brain and nervous system. Conversely, they can often diagnose specific brain injuries by testing for impairment of these specific functions. Incidentally, your brain cannot directly perceive the effects of trauma to itself. It has no sensory nerves of its own.

Amid the convolution of visible blobs and crevices on the surface of each hemisphere, one can discern four general subdivisions or *lobes*: the *frontal lobe,* which sits just behind your forehead; the *temporal lobe,* located on the side; the *parietal lobe,* which spans across the top of your brain; and the *occipital lobe,* located in the back of your skull. Each lobe is responsible for certain specific aspects of the thinking process. The left and right hemispheres each have the same four lobes, although the assignment of the functions differs somewhat between the two. Between any two people, these functional divisions of activity are very similar, although certain areas can vary somewhat from person to person.

Two functional areas that seem to vary somewhat from person to person are the speech and language centers. For about 70 to 95 percent of us, these functions probably reside in the left hemisphere, as illustrated in the figure. Slightly above and behind your left ear, *Wernicke's area,* named after German scientist Carl Wernicke (in science, you get to name a part of the body after yourself if you're the first to discover it) handles the complex process of encoding ideas into language and interpreting the meaning of incoming verbal information. Just forward of your left ear, *Broca's area* (named after French scientist Paul Broca) controls your vocal apparatus. These two centers must work together closely for you to understand and use language.

"Handedness"—the preference for using either the left or right hand—is also not so simple as one might first think. Early researchers believed that handedness and speech were mostly *contra-lateral*—right-handers had their speech centers in their left hemispheres, so therefore left-handers must carry speech in their right hemispheres.

More recent research indicates that left-handers are not simply the opposites—cranially speaking—of right-handers. Apparently, some of them are right-brained for language and some are not. Ambidextrous people complicate the question even further. It's difficult for scientists to settle this question, because it would require opening up the skulls of a large number of people and probing their brains—not a very humane approach to research.

Your brain receives information from the various parts of your body and sends back instructions of various kinds by means of twelve pairs of cranial nerves, or nerve bundles (not shown in the figure), which emerge from the base of your skull and plug into your spinal cord. Each cranial nerve coordinates a particular collection of functions. Some of them only transmit information *to* the brain—the *sensory nerves*; some only transmit commands *from* the brain—the *motor nerves;* and some do both.

The neurons—you have over two hundred different kinds of them in your cortex, stacked in six layers—are specialized cells that seem to be designed to communicate with one another and with other cells in the body. A typical neuron has a blob-like central body with thousands of thread-like receiving connections, or *dendrites.* Branching out from the cell body is a long tail, or *axon,* with a fatty *myelin* sheath, from which radiate many other outgoing connectors called *axon terminals.* These axons and their terminals make up the thick, fatty structure known as the *white matter* of the brain. Brain tissue, overall, is highly concentrated in fat, and people in certain cultures consider various animal brains a culinary delicacy.

Each neuron receives information through its dendrites and passes it on through its axon terminals. These axons can vary in overall length from a small fraction of an inch to several feet. Unlike other body cells, neurons cannot replace themselves, with a few interesting exceptions.

Neurons are continually flashing pulses to one another, at speeds of about two hundred miles per hour. The astronomical number of these potential neuron-to-neuron connections makes it possible for the brain to store vast amounts of information. The well-known *brainwaves,* measured by the *electroencephalograph,* portray a kind of electrical "music" created by the simultaneous, rhythmic firing of millions of neurons.

> "... an enchanted loom where millions of flashing
> shuttles weave a dissolving pattern, always a mean-
> ingful pattern though never on abiding one."
> —Sir Charles Sherrington

Actually, neurons only account for about 10 percent of your brain's cell count. There's another type of cell, the much more abundant *glial cell* (from the Latin word meaning "glue"), which doesn't carry nerve impulses, but supports the neurons in many ways. Scientists have previously thought of glial cells as a kind of passive "pudding" that surrounds and supports the neurons. New findings, however, suggest that the glial cells communicate chemically with one another, and may act in concert to help transmit information throughout the brain. They also transport nutrients, digest the bodies of dead neurons, guide the development of neurons in infancy, and manufacture the fatty *myelin,* which surrounds the axons of the neurons.

The part of the brain we've been seeing from the outside—the *cerebrum*—is just one of three main divisions that reflect the evolutionary history of human development. This so-called *cortex* of the brain (from the Latin word meaning "tree bark") is the most recent of the three primary structures, and it's what makes us essentially human. To see the other, more primitive levels of our biocomputer we need to peek inside the brain, as is shown in the second diagram of Figure 3.1.

The three primary brain structures are sometimes labeled the *basal region,* the *mid-brain,* and the *cerebral cortex.* (*Note:* scientists differ somewhat in the use of these labels and subdivisions, but these three seem to represent the most widely accepted architecture.)

## The Basal Region: Your Reptilian Brain

At the *basal region* of your brain, your spinal cord enlarges to form the *medulla oblongata,* and above it a bulbous structure called the *pons,* two structures that regulate and control the most primitive aspects of life: breathing, heartbeat, arousal, and primary motor control. This portion of the system is sometimes called the *brainstem,* considered by scientists to be the most ancient part of the brain, evolutionarily speaking. We share this primary type of structure with reptiles, birds, and probably with the dinosaurs.

Your spinal cord itself is a miniature computer of sorts, where some primitive processes are controlled by in-built *spinal reflexes.* These include the familiar patellar knee jerk, which the physician tests with a little hammer, and automatic recoil responses to sharp pain, heat, or cold. When you put your weight on your feet as you get out of bed or rise from a chair, your spinal reflexes automatically activate the muscles that raise the arches of your feet so that they will support you properly. This *stretch reflex* is a in-built spinal feature that serves most of the muscles in your body. Sexual orgasm also qualifies as a spinal reflex, although it is mediated in complex ways by cortical activity and a dozen or more hormones and neurotransmitters.

At this basal level, various other specialized structures control your *autonomic,* or involuntary, functions, such as hunger, thirst, sleep and wakefulness, sexual drives, various organ processes, blood pressure, and the general level of activity of your entire nervous system. The *pupillary reflex*—the automatic dilation and constriction of the pupils of your eyes in response to light—is a fairly reliable indicator of these autonomic functions, which emergency medical workers test to assess for brain injury.

Curiously, the processes of falling asleep and waking up are not controlled by the main regions of the brain, but rather by a small patch of cells in the brainstem known as the *reticular activating system* (RAS). By means not yet well understood, the RAS apparently "turns on" your cortex as you wake up and figuratively turns it off to put you to sleep.

Although we can resist falling asleep, it's well proven that a human being cannot voluntarily stay awake indefinitely. General anesthetics typically work their effects on the RAS. While the RAS doesn't "cause" consciousness, it seems to be necessary for conscious mental activity to occur. It may also be implicated in *attention deficit disorder,* and possibly *hyperactivity disorder.*

The brainstem contains specialized cells that secrete *neurotransmitters,* the chemical messengers that enable the neurons to communicate with one another. These include *serotonin, dopamine, acetylcholine,* and a number of others. The relative concentrations of these messenger molecules in the brain tends to reflect the current state of brain activity. Some researchers claim that romantic infatuation, for example, is signaled by an increased concentration of dopamine (hence the name).

This same basal region has another special structure that easily qualifies as a computer—or at least a sub-computer—in its own right. This is the *cerebellum,* a plum-sized blob of special nerve tissue that handles your habitual motor functions, such as balance and coordination, walking, routine hand and arm movements, speech, eye movements, and other well-learned motor processes such as a golf swing or tennis serve, typing into your computer, or dancing.

The cerebellum (Latin for "little brain") is also divided into left and right hemispheres. Its neurons, known as *granule cells,* are very tiny, and while it occupies only about 10 percent of your brain's volume, your cerebellum has nearly 50 percent of all the neurons in your brain. It receives about two hundred million input fibers, compared to, say, the optic nerve, which contains about one million fibers.

It's the job of the cerebellum to reduce the information-processing load on the cerebral cortex, freeing it for more abstract mental activity. Although the *motor control region* of the cortex can send commands to various muscles throughout the body, it typically delegates responsibility to the cerebellum for "over-learned" activities that become "second nature."

As you learn any new motor activity, such as writing, singing a song, or reciting multiplication tables, your cerebellum tunes in to the neural activity in your cortex and begins to mimic the patterns in its own neurons. After a number of repetitions, the cerebellum has recorded a script of sorts, which it can call on to control the activity itself. Once the function has been fully learned, the cerebellum takes over control and it actually becomes difficult for the cortex to over-ride it.

As an experiment, try to take over conscious control of the process of walking across the room or up a flight of stairs. Note how the cerebellar auto-pilot seems to operate almost independently of your effort, making it very difficult to control it by conscious intention. These learned scripts actually account for a large proportion of your brain's activity.

## The Mid-Brain: Your Auto-Pilot

From the basal region, nerve channels branch out to the *mid-brain* region, which has a set of secondary control systems. Scientists also refer to this collection of structures as the *limbic system.* The mid-brain area produces various hormones, or "messenger molecules." These include such hormones as the *pituitary* gland's *growth hormone* and activating chemicals that cause your *adrenal glands* to secrete the excitatory hormone familiarly known as *adrenalin.* Other structures stimulate your *thyroid gland* to secrete *thyroxin,* which controls the overall pace of your body's cellular combustion processes, better known as your *metabolism.*

The *pituitary,* or *hypophysis,* is a busy little gland. About the size of a pea, it sits in its own private chamber, a small cavity hollowed into the bony *brainpan,* just above the roof of your mouth. Even this tiny brain structure is further divided fore-and-aft into two lobes, an anterior lobe and a posterior lobe. Operating largely under the supervision of the *hypothalamus,* the pituitary helps to regulate blood pressure; water retention; thyroid gland function; certain aspects of sexual function; aspects of pregnancy, childbirth, and lactation; overall body growth and size; and the conversion of food into energy.

Other components in this limbic or mid-brain system include your *thalamus,* which serves as the central collection point for almost all sensory data going up to your cortex. The single exception to this thalamic centralization of data is the *olfactory* data, or the sense of smell, which goes directly to its own processing center in the cortex. The sense of smell is so ancient, evolutionarily speaking, that the olfactory nerves pass upward from the sinuses, through the *cribiform plate*—the floor of the brainpan—and into the olfactory bulb, a sensory sub-computer that sends its data directly to a special processing area of the cortex.

The *hypothalamus* mediates arousal and emotion (and supervises the pituitary). The *hippocampus* plays a part in transforming short-term memory into long-term memory. A nearby structure, the *amygdala,* serves as an early-warning sensor, detecting patterns in the incoming stream of sensory data that might imply threats to your survival or well-being.

Many neuroscientists believe that this constellation of structures in the limbic system, probably coordinated by the hypothalamus, plays a part in psychosomatic illness and psychosomatic healing. By some yet-undiscovered process, it seems that the hypothalamus and its partners transform our various levels of conscious and non-conscious ideation into direct physiological consequences, as we'll explore in more detail in a later chapter. As we'll learn further, the developing field of *psychoneuroimmunology* seeks to understand the causative connections between conscious mental activity and immune function, as mediated through these primitive, non-conscious processes.

## The Cortex: Your Mental Pilot

> "Brain, n. An apparatus with which we
> think that we think."
>
> —Ambrose Bierce

The third, and evolutionarily highest, level of your brain's hierarchy is the *cerebral cortex.* This region manages the more complex, abstract, relational, and consciously experienced mental processes. It interacts constantly and intimately with the other two levels, as previously described.

As we've already noted, thinking is not merely a whole-brain function—it's a *whole-body* function. Almost all of the body's processes, and particularly those processes we refer to as thinking, intertwine closely with the other processes.

To illustrate the closely integrated nature of these various brain and body elements, consider the experience of explaining a complicated idea in a conversation. You must begin by forming the concept in your mind; then you find the words to express it; then you switch on your speech apparatus; you modulate the pitch, rate, and volume of your voice to convey the nonverbal meaning; you may make facial expressions or hand gestures to punctuate your message; you study the other person's reactions for cues that tell you how well you're getting through; and you sense the emotional tone—the "feeling"—of the situation. Your own emotional and non-conscious responses register your reactions to the situation, and to whatever the other person may be saying.

Another familiar experience of the close integration of these brain regions is the so-called "fight-or-flight" reaction, which mobilizes your body in response to a stressful event. The conscious mental activity triggers automatic routines in the limbic or mid-brain region, which in turn mobilize various primitive responses in the basal region. Your whole-body response to a sudden provocation, or to a chronic experience of stress, forms a well-orchestrated syndrome, in which many parts of your biocomputer participate.

There is probably much more about the cortex that is yet to be learned than that which we know. We still understand very little about how the brain dreams or why it dreams. We still have no robust theory of how the brain stores its memories. And of course, the entire notion of consciousness remains largely a mystery to neuroscientists.

"I think I am, therefore I am. I think."

—George Carlin (American comedian)

## Two Brains in One: The Hemispheres

As a result of a series of remarkable surgical experiments in the mid-1960s, neuroscientists discovered an astonishing fact about the brain's hemispheres: *they operate as two separate, independent computers,* with two uniquely different ways of processing data.

Surgeons Joseph E. Bogen and Philip J. Vogel, working at CalTech, began performing a controversial, last-resort surgical technique on patients suffering from severe epilepsy. They theorized that, by severing most of the corpus callosum, the thick band of nerve fibers that connect the two hemispheres, they could prevent epileptic seizures from spreading across the entire brain, or at least limit their severity.

Most surgeons had previously believed that such an extreme insult to the brain's structure would totally incapacitate the patient, or at the least seriously impair his or her general mental functions. But experiments by neuroscientists Roger Sperry and Ronald Myers with cats and monkeys had indicated no observable impairment. As a result, Bogen and Vogel applied the procedure in a number of cases, with positive results for the epilepsy and no noticeable impairment in mental function.

In addition to providing a last-resort treatment for intractable epilepsy, which was eventually rendered unnecessary by more effective drug treatments, the surgical transection of the *corpus collosi* produced a small population of very unusual human beings. *They all had divided brains.* Sperry, Myers, and their colleague Michael Gazzaniga performed a wide range of cognitive experiments with these special split-brain people, over a number of years. Here's what they discovered.

In normal humans (not including the split-brain population), each hemisphere knows what the other hemisphere knows, as a result of the constant swapping of information across the corpus callosum. But each hemisphere "knows" in a different way.

The left hemisphere, or "left brain" as pop-psychology fans like to call it, responds much more readily to certain aspects of the data stream than to others. Conversely, the "right brain" responds to its own preferred aspects of the data. Working together they get the job of thinking done, but each makes a different kind of contribution.

The left hemisphere—let's call it "LH"—is more attentive to *elements* of data—words, phrases, sentences, numbers, repetitive parts of patterns, procedures, sequences, time intervals, and logical "if-then" progressions of ideas. It specializes in noticing, reacting to, and thinking with the "bits and pieces" of information that flow through it. Logic, mathematics, and structure are the home territory of LH thinking.

The right hemisphere—the "RH"—is more attentive and more skillful in processing *patterns* in the data. These include recognizing spatial forms and structures, colors, sound patterns such as musical melodies, and the patterns of intonation of speech. Your RH creates your subjective *body image*—your sense of your own physical structure, bodily boundaries, and the location and movement of your limbs in space, also known as *proprioception*. The RH also seems to be much more attentive to the social and emotional meanings of what it's perceiving. And, of course, we typically associate the term *intuition* with the RH style of processing.

To simplify and sloganize the differences for convenience: the LH specializes in "parts" and the RH specializes in "patterns."

In most normal people, the two hemispheres cooperate so closely that these profound differences are typically concealed. This probably explains why scientists only discovered the phenomenon of hemispheric lateralization in the 1960s when the split-brain surgeries lifted the veil on the brain's exquisite integration and cerebral synergy.

Consider the very ordinary experience of singing a song. Most likely, your RH would conjure up the melody and supply the cues for pitch, intonation, and phrasing, while your LH would retrieve the lyrics (the words). All of this information would flow to your vocal apparatus through the LH speech center, the parietal lobe's motor center, and probably the cerebellum as well. It's no wonder that most of us have to practice diligently to learn to sing competently. There's a lot going on in your head when you sing.

Since the discovery of brain lateralization, many scientists and many science popularizers have taken an interest in the implications of the discovery for personal growth and individual effectiveness. Unfortunately, myth and imagination have displaced science in some areas, and various popular myths have sprouted out of wishful thinking.

For example, physiological studies indicate certain variations in brain structure and lateralization between males and females and different patterns of learning and competence during childhood. However, the interpretation of this domain of research is so burdened with socio-political controversy that it's impossible to do it justice within the scope of this book. Consequently, I've cravenly elected to limit this discussion and to refer interested readers to the abundant research literature to be found on the Internet.

## What Is Our Real Potential?

One aspect of the human biocomputer that seems to fascinate us all is the existence of a small number of people with abnormally competent brains, many of whom are simultaneously beset by underdeveloped brain functions. Throughout medical history, scientists have studied these unusual people, often with great curiosity but with little practical result.

Often referred to as *idiot savants* (from the French for "wise idiot"), or sometimes just as *savants,* they demonstrate a combination of remarkable information processing capabilities with impaired primary faculties. One such person, Kim Peek, is a savant with a "photographic" or *eidetic* memory, combined with severe developmental disabilities.

Born with an enlarged head, an *encephalocele* (a protrusion of brain tissue through a fissure in the skull), an impaired cerebellum, and *no corpus callosum,* he nevertheless displayed remarkable skills in memory and information processing before the age of five. Although he reportedly tests well below average on standardized IQ tests and has difficulty interpreting abstract concepts such as proverbs and metaphors, he far surpasses most "normal" humans on data-processing tasks.

Affectionately known by his friends as "Kimputer," he has reportedly read over seven thousand books—typically finishing a book in about an hour—and can quote extensively from them. He rattles off baseball scores, geographic information, highway maps, Zip codes, calendars, particulars of popular movies, books, historical events, current news events, and the details of classical music.

Peek was the inspiration for the movie *Rain Man,* starring Dustin Hoffman. He holds down a clerical job that enables him to use his mental calculating abilities, and he also travels and speaks about disabilities as he demonstrates his own unusual abilities.

As far as I have been able to determine, neuroscientists and psychologists have learned little or nothing from studying these remarkable savants that might be used to help the rest of us "normal" people to use our biocomputers more effectively. The ironic paradox of a person possessed of phenomenal mental skills that we'd all like to have, combined with severe impairments that none of us want, offers a poignant counterpoint to our concept of ordinary "intelligence." But we can continue to hope, and to strive to understand.

In Chapter 10 we'll explore a number of practical applications of this knowledge of our biocomputer's operation, particularly hemispheric lateralization, including the concept of thinking styles, which shape the way we perceive, react, listen, learn, decide, and communicate.

## BRAINCYCLES, BRAINWAVES, BRAINSTATES, AND THE DAILY TRANCE

We know so much about the human biocomputer, and yet we know so little. And we make use of very little of what we do know. Although we don't need to know as much as neuroscientists, maybe we should know at least as much about our brains as we know about our cars and our computers. And this simple knowledge can translate directly into greater personal effectiveness, career success, and greater contributions to our organizations. Let's start with a better understanding of the patterns of mental process. In the following discussion, when we refer to the brain, let's keep in mind that we're usually referring to the entire biocomputer, of which the brain is the central processor.

## Braincycles

Scientists have long known about "braincycles," but few people in the general public seem to understand them or make good use of that knowledge, except perhaps intuitively or inadvertently. Braincycles are variations in the brain's focus of attention, ranging through a period that averages roughly ninety minutes. In one part of the cycle, your brain pays close attention to the outside world, that is, the incoming "data" from the senses. During this phase, you're consciously involved in interacting with your environment, such as when reading or listening attentively to what someone is saying.

During the other phase of the braincycle, your brain withdraws its attention from the sensory data stream and turns inward, processing its own stored images, sensations, reveries, thoughts, and musings. In everyday language, we say that your mind is "wandering." This brain-state is usually easily observed in another person by watching his or her eye movement, facial expression, and diminished motor activity.

One can immediately think of practical applications for just this one simple but important aspect of brain function. For example, you may observe that your boss seems to be distant and detached from the conversation, indicating that his or her brain is temporarily "off line" (to use an Internet analogy). You might decide to wait until another time to bring up a complex or critically important issue that requires his or her full concentration—your raise, for example—a time when the brain is back "on line."

As another example, consider that there are certain times when you seem to be in the mood for work that requires close attention and concentration, and at other times you find it more difficult to focus on details. To the extent that you can choose, you can tackle certain tasks when your brain cycle is in the right phase for the job.

We can directly apply findings like these to human performance management. How many data-entry errors, short-changed customers, industrial accidents, car crashes, surgical blunders, and maybe even plane crashes might be associated with braincycles? Can we provide job aids and skill training to reduce these effects?[1]

This *attention cycle*—the shifting of attention between on-line and off-line phases, is just one of many cyclic patterns exhibited by the biocomputer. When we consider the number and variety of other cycles, we can see that the system is like a collection of oscillators, or perhaps like a collection of musical instruments, each playing its own melody.

Scientists refer to daily cyclic patterns as *circadian* rhythms—from the Latin root, which means "about a day." Perhaps the most obvious circadian pattern is the cycle of sleep and wakefulness. Researchers also identify *ultradian* cycles, or patterns that repeat several times within a day, and *infradian* cycles, which span across multiple days.

Among the *ultradian* patterns we have the obvious but taken-for-granted cycles of heartbeat and respiration. Somewhere in the biocomputer, or perhaps at various points, we have oscillators that keep our vital processes going. Our body temperature tends to rise and fall throughout the twenty-four-hour period. The chemical composition of our blood and various other bodily fluids tends to cycle throughout the day. Appetite and digestion follow their own cycles. Sexual arousal and release follows its own cycle. The attention cycle, described above, is also a primary ultradian pattern.

A particularly curious ultradian pattern is the so-called *nasal cycle,* which seems to vary over a period of about ninety minutes. At various times over the cycle, one nostril or the other will be more dilated, with a freer flow of air—provided your nasal passages aren't congested—and the other will be less open. Sometimes during the cycle they'll both be about the same. To test this, press one nostril closed with your fingertip and notice the volume of air as you inhale through the other nostril. Then switch to the other side and compare the flow rates. Some researchers have speculated that this nasal cycle is linked to a cycle of cerebral activity in which either the left cerebral hemisphere or the right one is more active, although there seems to be some controversy about this connection.

One of the most noticeable *infradian* patterns is the female menstrual cycle of about 25 days. Over a much longer span, the gestation period for human females is about 280 days. In between, there seem to be human cycles of adaptation based on changes in seasons, the weather, and the amount of daylight.

We have many other cycles built into our biocomputers. Consider various rhythmic physical activities such as walking, which are controlled by the cerebellum. Keeping time to music, singing, dancing, and marching all involve built-in oscillators. Even commonplace motor activities such as knocking on a door, brushing your teeth, and washing your hands involve rhythmic patterns. The compelling rhythm of sexual intercourse responds to oscillators programmed deeply into the biocomputer.

Consider also the cadence of ordinary speech. The native users of any particular language all tend to follow a distinctive rhythm, or alternating pattern of emphasis. Read the following passage from a poem by A.E. Housman and sense the rhythmic pattern of the language, marked off by the rhyming syllables:

> And how am I to face the odds
> of man's bedevilment, and God's?
> I, a stranger and afraid
> in a world I never made.

## Brainwaves

Nowhere do we see the rhythmic, cyclic pattern of the biocomputer's activity so compellingly illustrated as in the electric signals coming from the brain. In about 1920, German physiologist Hans Berger demonstrated that electrodes attached to the scalp could detect the minute voltage differences between different areas of the brain and could monitor the voltage oscillations caused by the simultaneous firing of millions of neurons. He referred to his device as the *electroencephalograph*. Researchers and physicians now use these "brainwaves" to study the brain's operation and to diagnose and treat a wide range of neurological disorders.

Neuroscientists have divided up the range of brainwave frequencies into a series of bands, much like musical notes on a scale. By adjusting their equipment to select only certain ranges of frequencies, they can see the relative proportion of energy that goes into each range. If one band of frequencies is getting much more energy than the others, researchers say that this particular band—or brainwave—is predominant at the moment, and they are able to associate the individual's reported mental state with the brainwave that's most prominent. Although there is no precise agreement on the exact frequency ranges. the most commonly identified brainwave frequency bands (in cycles per second, or Hertz, abbreviated "Hz.") are:

- *Beta Waves.* The range of frequencies from about 12 to 16 Hz. upward is usually associated with active, conscious thinking, concentration, problem solving, and forming ideas in preparation for talking. The beta zone is the "alert" state of mental activity, possibly the "standard" state we use most often. If you become anxious, highly vigilant, or expectant, your beta activity will usually increase.

- *Alpha Waves.* The range of frequencies from about 8 Hz. to about 12 to 16 Hz. is usually associated with a relaxed, alert state of consciousness. When you close your eyes, your alpha activity usually increases. The mental process in the alpha state is usually less purposeful, somewhat detached, possibly somewhat of a reverie, but not necessarily "tuned out." Alpha activity diminishes with the onset of sleep, opening the eyes, and physical movement, or the intention to move.

- *Theta Waves.* The range of frequencies from about 4 Hz. to about 8 Hz. is usually associated with drowsiness, reverie, and various states such as trances, hypnosis, deep daydreams, lucid dreaming and light sleep, and the preconscious state just upon waking and just before falling asleep. Theta activity tends to be higher in young children, diminishing into young adulthood. Curiously, the theta pattern can sometimes be increased significantly by hyperventilation.

- *Delta Waves.* The range of frequencies from 0.5 Hz. up to about 4 Hz. is usually associated with deep sleep, deep trance states achieved by experienced meditators, and sometimes by drugs, medication, or neurological dysfunctions. Very young children tend to exhibit higher proportions of delta activity than older children or adults.

In addition to these four primary zones of brainwave activity, scientists study other patterns for evidence of abnormal brain activity. Brainwave energies also shift due to the effects of drugs, dementia, general anesthesia, and brain lesions.[2]

As we'll see in a later discussion, variations in these brainwaves—particularly their frequency of oscillation—are associated with particular kinds of mental activity, ranging from conscious purposeful thinking to emotional arousal, to meditation, to reverie, to drowsiness, and to sleep. And the more important reason for knowing about these brainwaves and brainstates, or mindzones, is to realize that we can choose the state we want to be in at a particular moment. We can use this knowledge of brainstates to reduce stress, improve our concentration, increase our creative ideation, and solve problems more effectively.

For example, here's a simple method for going into the alpha state, which can help you relax, de-stress, and become more centered in yourself:

Sit still, stop moving, close your eyes, suspend all intention, and begin listening. Imagine that you're listening for a particular sound—say the tinkle of a tiny bell—and that, paradoxically, you know it will not happen. Imagine what the bell *would* sound like if it did tinkle, but at the same time imagine that it has not, does not, and will not. In a sense, you're meditating on the idea of the bell. As you perform this simple mental procedure, your biocomputer will shift toward the alpha state, the alpha frequencies of your cerebral cortex will increase, and your state of consciousness will change. A few minutes spent in this state every day can help you become more calm, more centered, and less reactive to any stress or conflict going on around you.

## Brainstates

We all recognize, at least occasionally, that our "state of mind"—the momentary configuration of mood, ideation, attention, intention, and expectation—can take various forms. Our mental activity can range all the way from deep sleep through light sleep; drowsiness; reverie; detached attention; concentrated attention; reactive attention; proactive attention; engagement; excitement; agitation and stress; fear and apprehension; and even hysteria. Each of these brainstates—more accurately thought of as a state of the whole biocomputer—has its own unique arrangement of programs in the biocomputer.

Researcher Charles T. Tart, one of the pioneers in the study of consciousness, identifies a wide variety of brainstates, each with subtle differences. His book *States of Consciousness* became a foundation work for the study of consciousness, and what some practitioners refer to as "altered states of consciousness." For example, Tart contrasts the state associated with going into sleep, which he labels the *hypnogogic* state, from the state associated with emerging from sleep, which he calls the *hypnopompic* state. "Micro-dreams," those momentary images—like video clips or excerpts of dreams—that arise during the state of "half-sleep," can be very vivid but often make no apparent sense as one returns from them.[3]

I often find that new ideas, fragments of ideas, strange verbal expressions, and half-formed concepts come to me during dreams or while going into or out of sleep. This is one reason why I keep a stack of index cards and a pen on the night table next to my bed.

Brainstates such as apprehension, fear, strong intention, anger, intense concentration, amazement, amusement, disappointment, suspicion, guilt, shame, elation, and many others have scientific interest to researchers. To us ordinary civilians, they're significant because they're all part of our mental software.

Harvard professor, psychologist, and researcher Herbert Benson, an authority on the subject of meditation and its biocognitive effects, traveled to remote Tibetan monasteries in the Himalayan mountains to study the monks who lived there. The monks, who practiced a method known as g Tum-mo meditation, could raise the temperature of their fingers and toes by as much as 17 Fahrenheit degrees above their average body temperature.

Similar measurements on advanced meditators in Sikkim, India, found that the monks there could reduce their metabolism by as much as 64 percent. To understand the significance of that finding, consider that metabolism, or oxygen consumption, typically drops by about 10 to 15 percent during sleep, and slightly more than that during simpler states of meditation. These practitioners could reduce their metabolic functioning to levels below what researchers had previously considered necessary for survival.

Benson and his researchers caught the attention of the popular culture by making a video of nearly nude monks in states of deep meditation, drying cold, wet sheets with body heat, in temperature-controlled rooms at 40 degrees Fahrenheit.

According to an account in the *Harvard Gazette*:

"In a monastery in northern India, thinly clad Tibetan monks sat quietly in a room where the temperature was a chilly 40 degrees Fahrenheit. Using a yoga technique known as g Tum-mo, they entered a state of deep meditation. Other monks soaked 3-by-6-foot sheets in cold water (49 degrees) and placed them over the meditators' shoulders. For untrained people, such frigid wrappings would produce uncontrolled shivering.

"If body temperatures continue to drop under these conditions, death can result. But it was not long before steam began rising from the sheets. As a result of body heat produced by the monks during meditation, the sheets dried in about an hour.

"Attendants removed the sheets, then covered the meditators with a second chilled, wet wrapping. Each monk was required to dry three sheets over a period of several hours."[4]

Benson and his colleagues also videotaped monks sleeping through a winter night without shelter, at an altitude of 15,000 feet in the Himalayas. The event took place in February on the night of the winter full moon, with temperatures dropping to 0 degrees Fahrenheit. The video documentary showed no indication of symptoms of hyperthermia, or even normal shivering.

Accounts of super-normal human capabilities associated with special states of consciousness are so well-documented and verified that we can reasonably take them as proven. The question we now seek to ask is: Can these advanced methods ever be accessible to "normal" human beings who don't spend their lives studying and meditating? Is it possible that all of us have the possibility of increasing our mental functions to much higher levels than we've previously dreamed of? Maybe we won't be able to find a magic pill that does it, but there is the hope that, by learning more about the human biocomputer and its software, we may be able to transform ourselves and our lives in ways heretofore unimagined.

## The Daily Trance

Have you ever found yourself standing in some room in your house and you couldn't remember why you went there? It's as if you've come back to consciousness after having passed through some mental never-never-land. You struggle to re-orient yourself. You've lost *continuity*—the normal sense of the connectedness and progression of experiences from one to another. Although substance abusers and people with cognitive impairment experience this state of mind fairly often, mentally healthy people also do. It's a normal feature of the way your biocomputer operates.

The simplest description of your experience is that *you went into a trance.*

Unfortunately, the word "trance" tends to conjure up ideas and images of strange and supernatural experiences. Folk myths about hypnosis, often perpetuated by the popular media and the antics of stage hypnotists, tend to color the meaning of the term.

The simple fact is that *we all slip into and out of trance states many times in a typical day.* So, if trances are merely one particular kind of normal mind-state, we can learn to understand and demystify them.

We all have a general sense of what a trance, or a trance-like state, is. Yet psychologists and neuroscientists cannot seem to agree on a working definition. There seem to be a variety of trance states, ranging from the specialized state of hypnosis to the kinds of religious and ritualistic trances experienced by various native cultures, to various meditative experiences that are different from "normal" waking consciousness.

Aside from the normal "daily trance," as we might label it, trance states can be caused by a number of experiences. Hypnosis, of course, is the deliberate induction of a trance state by means of hyper-focused concentration. Meditation and prayer can also induce trance-like states. People in some cultures chant, sing, and dance to put themselves into trance states.

But accidental, momentary trances are also quite common. A magic trick, or almost any similar astonishing experience, will cause most minds to go into a fixated state, at least for a matter of seconds. Sudden fear, extreme anxiety, and other pathological states can also cause trance.

A more mundane example of the daily trance is the experience of watching television. After about five minutes, a person watching TV typically slips into a light trance state.

One key characteristic of virtually all trance states, including the normal daily trance, is a condition psychologists refer to as *dissociation.* In our normal waking mental processes, our mind—or minds—are continually weaving our perceptions and our thoughts into coherent patterns. These *associative* patterns are what we store away in our memories, and they're what we recall when we access any element of an experience. In a condition of dissociation, however, the associating process temporarily stops. The brain no longer weaves the elements of perception together.

The effect of dissociation could explain to some extent the *repressed memory syndrome,* in which victims of trauma cannot access certain parts of the experience that caused the trauma. The conventional psychological explanation is "ego defense," the notion that one of our minds is protecting us from the unbearable experience of recalling the unpleasant material. But another explanation, based on dissociation, is that the information became dis-integrated, or unpatterned, and the memory elements have lost their associative connections. Typically, a trained therapist can help a person retrieve these lost memories by a process of guided recall, in which they are brought to consciousness and then properly reassociated, after which they can indeed be remembered.

The daily trances we slip into and out of many times in a typical day seem to be a normal and necessary part of the biocomputer's operation. Neuroscientists aren't sure why they happen, or exactly what their function is.

It's conceivable, although by no means proven, that we could learn to manage our mental energies and emerge from the typical microtrance by a conscious procedure. Presuming that the biocomputer typically gets as much trance time as it needs over the course of a day or so, can we recapture our attention and redirect it toward the mental activities we prefer and the things we want to accomplish?

Here's a method you can use to bring your mind back to a conscious state and focus your attention more clearly. It involves three steps or attentional "scans":

- *The Body Scan.* When you become aware that your mind has been wandering—which implies that it has stopped wandering for a moment—bring your attention to your body. Close your eyes if you like, and tune in to as many signals as you can detect that are coming from your body. Feel the sensation of your clothes on your skin. Does anything itch or tickle? Can you feel any activity in your stomach or digestive tract? What's your overall energy level? Can you feel the pressure of the chair, couch, bed, floor, or whatever you're sitting or lying on? Rub your fingertips against your thumbs and feel the sensation. Move your head around and feel the sensation of movement. Get messages from as many parts of your body as you can.

- *The "Bubble" Scan.* Next, extend your attention to your immediate physical environment—the imaginary bubble that extends about three to five feet outward from your body. What's there? Is anyone close enough to you to make physical contact? What are the movements, colors, textures, and patterns you can sense? What do you hear? What are you doing with your hands? What are you holding, if anything? What are the various things around you: a pen and some index cards; your computer keyboard, mouse, or display; papers and other items on your desk; if you're in a car, the arrangement of the compartment you're sitting in; if you're on a plane, the people, seats, and other items around you. Tune in as intently as possible as you scan your close-in environment.

- ***The "Field" Scan.*** Next, extend your attention outward to the larger environment around you. Who and what do you see? What are people doing? What sounds do you hear, and where are they coming from? If you're outdoors, how far can you see and what do you see? Can you feel and smell a breeze? What does the sky look like? Can you feel the sun? What colors and patterns do you become aware of? If you're indoors, study the arrangement of the room or the space you're in. How is it designed? How do people move around in it? What materials, textures, and patterns do you see? Tune in to the "meaning" of what's going on in the extended space around you.

With this simple three-step scan, all you've done, basically, is to activate your sensory system. You've coaxed your biocomputer out of its dissociated, trance-like reverie state and given it a job to do. If you make a habit of this three-scan method, using it occasionally during a day, you may find that you feel more focused, more present, more mentally clear, and more connected to what you're doing.

You can use it in any number of situations. While you're waiting for someone; sitting in your car waiting for a traffic light to change; while shopping or taking care of routine errands; you can do a quick "triple-scan" and bring your mind back to consciousness.

Of course, it's probably not advisable to try to avoid the daily micro-trances altogether, even if we could. Most likely, your biocomputer will find the trance time it requires, and you can make use of the rest as you see fit.

## MINDMODULES: YOU HAVE MANY "MINDS"

Another key principle of practical intelligence is that *you have more than one "mind."* In fact, you have lots of minds. The customary division of two minds—the "conscious" and "unconscious" minds—can't possibly do justice to the rich constellation of *simultaneous mental processes* that make us what we are. There are many levels of consciousness and many levels of "unconsciousness," as we shall see when we explore the key dimensions of mental process in later chapters.

In his provocative book *Multimind: A New Way of Looking at Human Behavior,* psychologist and researcher Robert Ornstein presented a compelling case for thinking of the human biocomputer as a *true multiprocessor.*[5] Most of the electronic computers we're becoming ever more familiar with give us the impression of doing lots of things at the same time—you can be reading a web page, waiting for a document to print, and receiving email—but in fact most computers can't actually multi-process. They only do one thing at a time. What they actually do is called "time slicing": they hop around rapidly from one task to another, doing a bit here and a bit there, and they usually do it so quickly that we think it's all happening at once.

In your biocomputer, however, lots of things really are happening at the same time. According to Ornstein, your biocomputer uses a priority sorting system to figure out what to think about next. It's constantly sampling the sensory inputs coming in on the channels of sight, hearing, smell, taste, and body sensations, checking for any "emergency" messages. If you stumble and start to fall over while you're walking and talking, your biocomputer will instantly redirect its attention and its "processor cycles"—to borrow a term from the techie community—to deal with this threat to your physical safety. Sudden noises, sharp pains, and rapid movements of things in your visual field will capture the processor first, until it figures out that there's nothing to be concerned about. Only after it has evaluated those primal signals does it allocate resources to so-called "higher level" thinking processes.

Common expressions of our everyday language reflect our intuitive understanding of these multiple levels of thinking: "I'm of two minds about this." "Something tells me. . .," "My gut tells me. . .," "My heart tells me. . . ." Scientifically speaking, the gut and the heart actually do have "minds."

The human digestive system is organized around its own built-in sub-computer, which controls most of its complex processes locally, without the need for the brain's directions. The heart has its own built-in computer, and every heart cell has the potential to act as a pacemaker cell, triggering a heartbeat on its own.

Your cerebellum, previously described, is a remarkable sub-computer in its own right. It manages all motor activity that is "overlearned," that is, so well learned that it no longer needs conscious attention. Walking, talking, speaking, and reciting familiar information are handled by the cerebellum, leaving the cerebrum free to manage other, more complex activities.

The cerebellum learns to handle coordinated motor activities by mimicking the electrical patterns that occur in the cerebral cortex as you learn to serve a tennis ball, play a guitar chord, or sing a song. Once you've learned the procedure thoroughly, the cerebral cortex "delegates" the task to the cerebellum, which usually handles it afterward.

Problems can arise when you become anxious about your performance, as with a critical point in a tennis match or presenting detailed data from memory. Under anxiety, the cerebral cortex tries to take over the activity, not trusting the cerebellum to carry it out expertly. Bad serves, bad baseball pitches, strikeouts, bad golf shots, forgotten words to songs, missed comedy lines, and many other "flubs" occur at this instant of conflict between the cerebrum and the cerebellum.

Accomplished athletes learn to trust their well-trained bodies—or cerebella—and to prevent their conscious minds from trying to take over at critical moments. Sports psychologist Timothy Gallwey explained this aspect of brain function well in his landmark book *The Inner Game of Tennis,* in which he prescribes mental techniques for preventing the higher brain processes from interfering with the well-learned and instinctive skills.[6]

We can even think of the body's *immune system* as a "mind," or a sub-computer. It takes in information about the status of the body, makes evaluations about what is and is not part of "the self," and mobilizes an army of defender cells to attack intruders. When the software of the "immune mind" malfunctions, one can get an *auto-immune* disease such as rheumatoid arthritis, lupus, or Addison's disease, in which the immune system erroneously attacks the body itself.

We can define a *mind* very simply, as:

*Mind: a collection of mental functions.*

With these simple definitions—thinking, thoughts, and minds—it makes sense to think in terms of lots of minds and lots of thoughts inter-acting in an orchestrated way to allow us to function at the biological level, various unconscious levels, and various conscious levels. These various minds, or modules, as Ornstein identifies them, all cooperate— or fail to—to make us what we are.

A third key principle to keep in mind is that these multiple minds are *always at work all the time,* doing their jobs simultaneously. While we're thinking "consciously"—usually verbally or logically—our non-conscious thinking processes are feeding information from all levels, offering it to the gatekeeper modules that admit new information into our awareness.

Where do hunches come from? Where do great new ideas come from when they flash onto our mental view-screens? The creative thinking concept of *incubation,* for example, depends on this "behind the scenes" mental activity; we consciously think about a problem or a situation for a certain amount of time, and then we move on to think about other things. But other mindmodules may go to work on the problem below the level of our awareness. Then, suddenly, seemingly without invitation, an idea flashes into our consciousness that gives us the solution we were seeking.

Careful study of the varieties of mental process suggests more and more strongly that what we call the "conscious mind"—or just "the mind" to most people—is more like a projection screen than a functioning computer. So much of our real thinking goes on at *precognitive* and *non-conscious* levels, that it often seems that the viewing screen of consciousness simply displays the results of what the other minds are doing at any particular moment.

If we think of a mind or a mindmodule as a collection of mental functions and recognize that we have many mindmodules processing information for us simultaneously on multiple levels, it's intriguing to wonder about how these modules manage to get along. Who's in charge?

According to psychologist and researcher Michael Gazzaniga, *none of them are.* Gazzaniga and other researchers argue—to the dismay and consternation of many of their colleagues—that the human biocomputer may not actually have an "executive module." There may not be a single master program in control of our thinking processes. In his research with split-brain patients, described above, Gazzaniga presented tasks that placed the two separated hemispheres in competition with one another.

For example, by flashing an image to the left half of each visual field of the subject's eyes (using a divided viewing device), he could make it known to the right hemisphere without allowing the left hemisphere to know what it was. In normal, undivided people, the information would immediately cross over to the left hemisphere, through the corpus callosum, and the left hemisphere would activate its speech center to name the object.

With the split-brain subjects, however, the right hemisphere would recognize the object, but the information could not pass over to the left hemisphere. Consequently, the subject's left hemisphere, having control of speech and believing that it was the "real" brain, would claim not to know what the object was.

But if the image was presented to the right half of the visual field, traveling through the cross-over optic circuit to the left hemisphere, the subject could easily name it, because the same hemisphere that controlled speech received the information.[7]

From his research with split-brain subjects over about a decade, Gazzaniga arrived at, and began to promote within the scientific community, a very provocative proposition. He argued that our brain-mind systems are composed of multitudes of processing modules, and there is no "master module," no "executive mind."

Further, he contended, our left brains are home to a specialized module he called the "interpreter" module, which might also be called the "explainer." The function of the interpreter module, according to Gazzaniga, is simply to explain why we just behaved the way we did. His theory touched off an explosion of argument and theorizing among brain researchers, and well it might.

Gazzaniga's proposition has four parts, all of them distressing to the conventional "free-will" model of human mental process:

1. That we have no executive module—"No one is really in charge," as he says;
2. That our behavior arises out of impulses not known to consciousness;
3. That our "explainer" module simply makes up reasons for our behavior, after the fact, so to speak; and
4. That what we call our "values" are simply the explanations we give for our behavior, and not the causes of it.

Gazzaniga's proposition has been the subject of debate and theorizing in the psychological community for almost two decades, and the discourse becomes ever more complex and intricate. We certainly can't resolve it here, but it does seem that the multi-mind, modular concept of the biocomputer's organization has merit.

In later chapters we'll frequently refer to this modular aspect of the human mental process and capitalize heavily on the idea of mindmodules as normal components of our information processing biosystem.

# MINDMODELS: YOUR PORTABLE REALITY

A story circulated many years ago in the psychiatric community about a man who came to visit a psychiatrist, claiming that he was dead. He'd been telling his friends and acquaintances that he was dead, and he made a habit of referring to himself in the past tense. The psychiatrist was unable, using ordinary counseling procedures, to shake him loose from his attachment to the morbid idea that he was dead.

The psychiatrist decided to provide the patient with a very powerful emotional experience that would disconfirm his faulty concept of himself as a dead person. He asked the man to stand in front of a mirror, roll up his sleeves, clench his fists tightly, and say with emphasis, "Dead men don't bleed." He asked him to practice this procedure a dozen times every day, and then to return at the same time next week.

The man faithfully carried out the instructions, practiced diligently, and returned the next week. The psychiatrist asked him to stand in front of the mirror, roll up his sleeves, and repeat the procedure. The reason for having him clench his fists was to cause the veins in his forearms to distend. As the man repeated the statement "Dead men don't bleed," the psychiatrist produced a small scalpel and nicked the vein at the inside of his arm.

Blood spurted out of the vein. The patient looked at the blood trickling down his forearm, and with an astonished expression, exclaimed, "By God! Dead men *do* bleed!"

We human beings carry around in our heads our own portable versions of reality—a *model,* or actually a huge inventory of models, that represent the parts of the world we've experienced so far. The fact that each of us has our own mind full of memories seems so self-evident as to deserve no further thought. Yet it's one of the most fundamental and significant facts of all about our existence as a species.

Without our memories—our *mental models* of the parts of reality we've experienced—we couldn't function in even the most primitive way. Our cave-era ancestors could never have survived to sire the generations that led to us if they weren't able to remember which animals were their prey and which were their predators, and countless other facts about their environment and their functioning in it.

If you didn't have a memory model of your house, for instance, how could you find your way back home whenever you left? How could you recognize your car, your place of work, the coffee shop where you meet you friends, your spouse, your children, or your relatives? People with profound loss of long-term memory often can't call to mind even the standard mental models that we take absolutely for granted.

We're constantly accumulating these mental models as we keep living. Some people continue to accumulate them—it's called *learning*—throughout life, while others tend to slow down and lose their curiosity and eagerness to learn. Our ability to think and to cope with our experiences depends on the size and richness of the inventory of mental models we've accumulated and can put to use as we need them.

We know, of course, that every one of our mental models is a very limited replica of reality—a proxy for what we understand some sample of reality to be. All mental models are limited, flawed, distorted, and contaminated. Most of them work well enough for us to make use of them in our lives. But when they no longer represent reality in a sufficiently meaningful way, they affect our mental performance.

Much of what we recognize as human maladjustment, ranging from mild eccentricity to downright craziness, is caused by "mangled models"—*distorted versions of reality* from which we think and react. People with adjustment difficulties have typically constructed a particular collection of mindmodels that drastically misrepresent reality, and that cause them to perceive, reason, conclude, decide, and behave in dysfunctional ways.

We can think of human beings as functioning mentally at various points along a spectrum, or continuum of mental competence, which is basically practical intelligence, as illustrated in Figure 3.2.

For the sake of discussion, we could further divide human beings—including ourselves—into three broad camps, in terms of their levels of practical intelligence (not to be confused with "IQ"–type intelligence.

**The Insane.** At one end of the figurative bell curve of human mentality, we have the certifiably "crazy" people. Some people don't like to use the term "crazy," but it's a popular word, we know generally what it means, and it works. Crazy people—the insane, if you prefer—are *muddled thinkers*: their muddled models prevent them from functioning successfully in the typical environments most human beings have to cope with. When they become crazy enough, the rest of us get to lock them up for our own good.

**The Sane.** At the upper end of the figurative bell curve we find the very sane people, those who have somehow learned to cope at a very high level of effectiveness and who've learned not to get co-opted into the craziness in the society that surrounds them. They're *meta-thinkers*: they think about thinking and they're more highly conscious of their own mindmodels, and that enables them to think more effectively than others.

## Figure 3.2. Bell Curve of Mental Competence

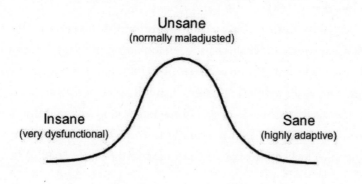

*The "Unsane."* In the broad middle of the bell curve we find most of society—the "normally maladjusted" majority. They function well enough to get along in the world; they grow up, find mates, hold jobs, raise families, save for their retirement, and are generally convinced that they "think for themselves." They're *reflex thinkers*: they think mostly with "standard" models, pre-established archaic patterns they learned early in life.

The models we carry around in our heads dominate our thinking incessantly. At any instant, we form our thoughts from two sources, usually simultaneously: what we're taking in through our senses, and what we're calling up from memory—our models. We automatically combine these two channels of information as we decide what to do. We call on our mindmodels so regularly, so routinely, and so habitually that they sometimes provide the largest share of the raw material that we think about.

Visual illusions provide a compelling way to illustrate the dominating effects of our learned models on our perceptions, reactions, and conclusions. Consider the arrangement of elements in Figure 3.3. Do you "see" a star?

Of course, there's no star there. What you "see" is a memory model your brain superimposes over this ambiguous figure. The five black circles with the wedges removed offer what psychologists call a *subjective contour*: the suggestion of a figure that your brain seizes on to make a real figure—at least "real" enough for it to conclude that it knows what it's looking at.

Consider this: *We don't actually see reality.* What we see are the retinas of our eyes. Our brains have been looking at our retinas for so long that they believe the retinas are reality. Consider, however, that color-blind people see a different reality than full-color perceivers see.

On the few occasions when I order a steak in a restaurant that doesn't specialize in steaks, I find it amusing to observe how food servers are sometimes locked into the standard models they've learned. When the

## Figure 3.3.   "Star" Illusion

server asks, "How would you like your steak cooked?" I usually reply, "I'd like it to be just slightly pink at the center." *Almost invariably,* the server will offer one of the standard steak-cooking categories: "Medium?" he or she will ask, expectantly. Presumably I'm supposed to ratify the conversion of my model of a steak to the restaurant's model.

My usual response is, "You can call it whatever you like, but I call it slightly pink at the center." At this point, the furrowed brow and the confused look lead to another try: "How about Medium Rare?" I reply "You can call it whatever you like, but I call it slightly pink at the center."

I can imagine the mental wheels spinning as he or she tries to force-fit my model into the standard steak-cooking model. I may also politely remind the server, "May I presume that if it's not slightly pink at the center, the cook will be willing to redo it?" Almost invariably, the server will write down one of the standard categories.

Then, of course, the cook transforms the server's model, which was transformed from my model, into the cook's model. The steak typically comes out overcooked anyway, usually falling somewhere into the well-done zone.

These are simple and commonplace examples, chosen for their illustrative value. But at various other levels of behavior and social interaction, our mental models operate in just the same way as our recognizer circuits that see the star or the "medium" steak. We tend to see, in people and situations, what we've programmed our brains to see.

Forcing people and situations into our mental models is the basic mechanism of prejudice, bigotry, and intolerance. When one person or a group of people demonizes another, accusing them and attributing various disreputable motives to them, there is a strong tendency to perceive selectively. The antagonist tends to perceive and remember evidence that reinforces the stereotype and tends to overlook or minimize evidence that contradicts it.

An interesting news story a few years ago described a courtroom incident, in which an attorney was lambasting two physicians in a malpractice suit. Just before he finished his characterization of them as incompetent, self-serving, money-grubbing hacks, he was suddenly stricken with a severe heart attack—an acute *myocardial infarction*. The attack surely would have killed him if the doctors hadn't leaped to his rescue, administering first aid, and calling for medical assistance.

When the attorney left the hospital, he dropped the lawsuit.

## FOUR HABITS THAT UNLOCK YOUR MENTAL CAPACITY

If you've read this far, I'd like to thank you for your patience and acknowledge that you may be keen to know more about the "how-to" of practical intelligence. At least, that's what I would be feeling at this point. We have the needed inventory of basic concepts for understanding

PI, and now we need to get specific. How does it work? How do we learn it? How do we put the methods to use every day?

We will begin by "cleaning out the attic"—tuning up four key aspects of the way we process information that profoundly influence almost all of our other mental processes. These four mental habits—features of our mental "software"—enable us to put our natural, in-built range of mental skills to effective use. Let's review them briefly, and then explore each one in greater depth in the following chapters.

1. *Mental Flexibility*—the absence of mental rigidity. When you free yourself from narrow-mindedness, intolerance, dogmatic thinking and judgments, "opinionitis," fear-based avoidance of new ideas and experiences, and learn to live with ambiguity and complexity, you become more mentally flexible. Mental flexibility is at the very foundation of your ability to perceive clearly, think clearly, solve problems, persuade others, learn, and grow as a person.

2. *Affirmative Thinking*—the habit of perceiving, thinking, speaking, and behaving in ways that support a healthy emotional state in yourself as well as in others. This includes consciously and continually deciding what you will accept into your mind, what you will and will not devote your attention to, and which people and messages you will allow to influence your thinking and your emotional reactions. We'll go beyond the usual "positive thinking" slogans and the "glass is half-full" clichés, to explore how affirmative thinking *really* works.

3. *Semantic Sanity*—the habit of using language consciously and carefully so as to promote your own mental flexibility and affirmative thinking, think more clearly and less dogmatically, and persuade others much more effectively than by using the customary methods of arguing and verbal combat. Revising the way we talk forces us to revise the way we think; therefore, adopting language habits that are "semantically sane" contributes

to mental health and emotional well-being as well as more intelligent thinking, problem solving, and communicating.

4. *Valuing Ideas*—the habit of saying a "tentative yes" to *all* new ideas at the first instant of perception—however strange, unfamiliar, or different from our own—rather than reflexively shooting them down. Valuing ideas means letting the ideas of others live long enough to present their possibilities, capturing your own fleeting ideas with a pen and note cards, thinking up lots of new ideas—"option thinking"—and encouraging others to do the same. And we'll go beyond the usual slogans about "thinking outside the box," to learn about mental boxes and "metaboxical" thinking.

Once we've started working on these four upgrades to our mental software, and realizing that we need to upgrade them continually, we can then understand much more clearly how to make good use of the four "mega-skills" for thinking that all of us have.

## FOUR DIMENSIONS OF PI: YOUR MEGA-SKILLS

Much of our exploration into the concepts, practices, and skills of practical intelligence will involve four key dimensions of thinking— "sub-smarts," we might call them. Each of these four dimensions contributes in its own unique way to our total capability to cope with our environments. We can think of them as polarities—contrasting mental processes that go together—with *both* alternatives to be used to the fullest, rather than to be thought of as an either-or choice.

The four mega-skills, or competence polarities, are:

1. The range of *divergent and convergent thinking,* the "D-C" axis, which we shall refer to as "bivergent thinking," in terms of the ability to choose freely between both modes. Divergent thinking, as previously touched on, is the pattern of branching

out from an initial idea to explore various related ideas—much like tracing the many branches of a tree; it's how we think up great new ideas. Convergent thinking, by contrast, is the pattern of "de-branching"—narrowing down from many ideas and options to a critical few; it's how we make effective decisions.

2. The range of *abstract and concrete thinking,* the "A-C" axis, which we shall refer to as "helicopter thinking," in terms of the ability to move from one to the other. Concrete thinking is thinking about what we can sense—see, hear, feel, smell, or taste. The more concrete an idea is, the closer it is to something we experience directly. Abstract thinking is thinking about concepts rather than things—understanding things in general rather than one thing in particular. When we think and speak of some partic- ular human who has a face and a name, for example, we're closer to the concrete end of the scale. When we speak of "mankind," we're closer to the abstract end of the scale. Conceptual fluency involves being able to maneuver along the entire range of possi- bilities from concrete to abstract, much like flying a figurative helicopter from its landing spot on the ground up to an altitude from which we can see much more of the terrain.

3. The range of *logical and intuitive thinking,* the "L-I" axis, which we will refer to as "intulogical thinking," in terms of the ability to use either pattern freely and even to integrate the two into a single process when appropriate. Logical thinking is step- wise thinking; it's procedural, systematic, and progresses from one idea to another; it imposes order on information. Intuitive thinking is "all-at-once" thinking; it seems to originate pre- consciously, dealing with the raw material of thought, before the conscious mind dices it up and tries to apply logic to it. The capacity to respect both patterns of thinking and to use them in a compatible combination is one of the hallmarks of highly effec- tive problem solvers.

4. The range of *rational and emotive thinking,* the "R-E" axis, which we will refer to as "viscerational" thinking (a contraction of "visceral" and "rational" thinking), in terms of the ability to cherish and respect emotional experience while making it compatible with so-called rational or "unemotional" thinking. Although many people tend to think of "being rational" and "being emotional" as two opposing patterns of thinking, a more careful consideration invites us to treat them as compatible, and to some extent even simultaneous. Values, for example, can be considered an emotional aspect of thinking; we want our solutions and decisions to reflect our values and ethics. Compassion is also a worthy emotion that can guide our rational decisions and our problem-solving strategies. We can also learn to temper the influence of our emotions on our reactions and our choices.

As Figure 3.4 shows, we can think of these four key polarities as offering us a rich combination of mental processes, suited to the various situations and problems we encounter. At any one moment, we may find one of the four mega-skills especially useful, and in fact we may choose to dwell on one polarity or the other within a particular mega-skill. As we become fluent and versatile in using these various patterns at will, we become ever more effective in understanding the situations we face, communicating with others, solving problems, and managing our lives.

## GETTING STARTED: UPGRADING YOUR MENTAL "SOFTWARE"

It's time to switch on our biocomputers and do a "software upgrade." In the next four chapters we'll explore the four key habits of thinking and reacting—*Mental Flexibility, Affirmative Thinking, Sane Language,* and *Valuing Ideas*—that set the foundation for putting all of our mental capacities to practical use.

## Figure 3.4.   PI Dimensions

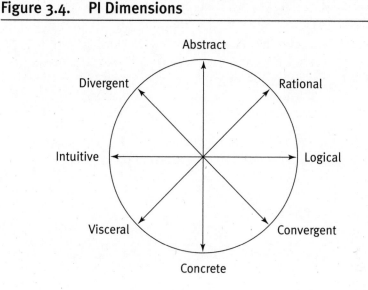

Then we'll explore each of the four key mega-skills—*Bivergent Thinking, Helicopter Thinking, Intulogical Thinking,* and *Viscerational Thinking*—and see how they provide us with the leverage to activate the natural levels of our intelligence and common sense.

## Notes

1. Adapted from an article on the author's website, "Brain Training: New Research, New Models, New Methods." http://karlalbrecht.com/articles/braintraining.shtml.

2. For more about brainwaves, see http://en.wikipedia.org/wiki/Electroencephalography.

3. Tart, Charles T. *States of Consciousness.* New York: E.P. Dutton & Company, 1975.

4. William J. Cromie. "Meditation changes temperatures: Mind controls body in extreme experiments." *Harvard Gazette,* archived. www.hno.harvard.edu/gazette/2002/04.18/09-tummo.html.

5. Ornstein, Robert. *Multimind: A New Way of Looking at Human Behavior.* New York: Anchor, 1989.

6.  Gallwey, W. Timothy. *The Inner Game of Tennis* (rev. ed.). New York: Random House, 1997.
7.  See "The Social Brain: It's a Case of the Left Brain Not Knowing What the Right Is Doing. And Therein Lies Our Capacity for Belief" by Michael S. Gazzaniga. *Psychology Today,* November 1985.

# 4

## *MENTAL SOFTWARE UPGRADE 1*
### *Developing Mental Flexibility*

"I am afraid to listen, for by listening I might understand,
and be changed by that understanding."
—Carl Rogers (American psychologist)

MENTAL FLEXIBILITY IS THE WILLINGNESS to let yourself be changed by your experiences—by new ideas, new points of view, opinions and beliefs that are different from your own, situations and experiences that can take you out of your familiar patterns and invite you to grow.

## ARE YOU A FINISHED PRODUCT?

As we set out on this exploration into the PI dimension of the multiple intelligences, we start by posing a very basic question, a challenge to each of us as an individual:

*Am I a finished product—or a work in progress?*

There are three main choices for an answer to this question: "Yes, I am a finished product"; "No, I'm not a finished product. I'm a work in progress"; and "Hmm . . . I've never thought much about it."

Actually, your behavior answers the question every day.

According to the late physicist and biomechanical researcher Moshe Feldenkrais, who became one of the pioneers of mind-body healing, *most human beings in their early lives develop only as far as necessary to cope adequately with their environments.* A smaller number, probably less than 20 percent of people, continue learning and growing more than necessary—all through their adult years. These are people who think of themselves as "works in progress," with a sense of growing and becoming that brings joy to their lives.[1]

As Feldenkrais explained it, all human beings are forced to acquire an astonishing range of capacities within the first few years of life, just to survive as living creatures. As we move into our adolescent years, we continue to learn and grow, but somewhat less rapidly than in the first few years. Then we become teen-agers and we start to form our individual identities—who we are, what we want and need, and what we believe is possible for us in life.

By the time we leave our main educational experience, which is some version of high school for most people in the developed societies, we begin to "harden" into the people we're going to be. We evolve a definition of ourselves in terms of our worth, our capabilities, and our strategies for getting our needs met. We tend to define ourselves as much in terms of what we're not, just as much as by what we are; what we won't do as much as by what we will do; what we're not capable of as much as by what we're capable of.

For most people, the hardening process runs its course by early adulthood, but not everyone succumbs to it completely. The capacity to *keep becoming*—to think of one's self as a work in progress and to behave accordingly—is something we can learn or re-learn.

The late John Gardner was a Renaissance man in both the academic world and in government. In 1965, he was appointed the Secretary for Health, Education, and Welfare and worked as an adviser on civil rights and social reforms to President Johnson. He founded the organization Common Cause and helped develop public television through his creation of the Corporation for Public Broadcasting. As a Stanford University professor, where he worked and taught until he left the planet in 2002 at the age of eighty-nine, he won the highest achievement award given by the university.

In his brief but insightful book *Self-Renewal: The Individual and the Innovative Society,* Gardner wrote of the need for people to take chances in their lives, to break old habits, to see things in new ways instead of always relying on what's certain and comfortable:

"As we mature we progressively narrow the scope and variety of our lives. Of all the interests we might pursue, we settle on a few. Of all the people with whom we might associate, we select a small number. We become caught in a web of fixed relationships. We develop set ways of doing things.

"As the years go by we view our familiar surroundings with less and less freshness of perception. We no longer look with a wakeful, perceiving eye at the faces of people we see every day, nor at any other features of our everyday world.

"It is not unusual to find that the major changes in life—a marriage, a move to a new city, a change of jobs, or a national emergency—break the patterns of our lives and reveal to us quite suddenly how much we had been imprisoned by the comfortable web we had woven around ourselves.

"One of the reasons why mature people are apt to learn less than young people is that they are willing to risk less. Learning is a risky business, and they do not like failure. In infancy, when the child is learning at a truly phenomenal rate—a rate he or she will never again achieve—he or she is also experiencing a shattering number of failures. Watch [any child]. See the innumerable things he or she tries and fails. And see how little the failures discourage him or her.

"With each year that passes [the child] will be less blithe about failure. By adolescence the willingness of young people to risk failure has diminished greatly. And all too often parents push them further along that road by instilling fear, by punishing failure, or by making success seem too precious.

"By middle age most of us carry around in our heads a tremendous catalogue of things we have no intention of trying again because we tried them once and failed—or tried them once and did less well than our self-esteem demanded.

"*By middle life, most of us are accomplished fugitives from ourselves.*"[2] [emphasis added]

Call it mental arthritis; "mentalpause"; or "hardening of the categories." It's a typical—*but not inevitable*—narrowing of the range and depth of our thinking processes, and a progressive reduction in our mental flexibility, just as lack of exercise and movement leads to a stiffness and reduced mobility in our joints.

> "Denunciation of the young is a necessary part of
> the hygiene of older people, and greatly assists in
> the circulation of their blood."
>
> —Logan Pearsall

As Gardner implies, one of the first casualties of the mental hardening process is *curiosity*: the passing years tend to make many people more sure of their opinions and less open to learning about other views. As we've previously noted, a relatively small fraction of Americans, for example, accounts for a large portion of the books sold and read, as well as a large fraction of the visits to museums, libraries, plays, and historical sites. Fewer than 25 percent of Americans travel abroad.

*Risk-taking,* as Gardner points out, is related to a factor psychologists call *tolerance for ambiguity,* which is the capacity to function when things are not necessarily clear and simple. Related to tolerance for ambiguity is *tolerance for complexity.* People who continue to learn and grow through their lives tend to look upon ambiguity and complexity as stimulating challenges to their skills of adaptation rather than threats to their ego-stability.

But people who are well along into the hardening process tend to react to ambiguity and complexity with discomfort. This discomfort, often rooted in fear, tends to show in their behavior as intolerance, bigotry, argumentativeness, and "opinionitis." It may also involve a gradual loss of one's sense of humor, a mental process closely connected with creativity, innovation, inventiveness, and the ability to see the world through multiple lenses. They expect less of themselves and less of their thinking processes. For many people at this stage of life, "good enough" is good enough.

This inspiring view of the self as a work in progress, rather than a finished product, will serve as a key guiding principle for our journey into the realms of PI, and a frequent reminder of the importance of humility.

*Perhaps we can start thinking of ourselves not as*
*"human beings," but as "human becomings."*

# DYNAMIC THINKING AND
# ARCHAIC THINKING

Perhaps the clearest expression of the difference between people who've developed a high level of practical thinking and those who haven't lies in the distinction between *archaic thinking* and *dynamic thinking*. This is a distinction we'll study and apply many times throughout this exploration.

*Archaic thinking* is automatic thinking. It's reflexive rather than reflective; it operates from decisions and conclusions made in the past; it's controlled by pre-established rules, policies, and boundaries; it's habitually judgmental; it's expressed in slogans, clichés, and dogma; it fears and resists the new, novel, and ambiguous; it seeks to preserve what's familiar and comfortable; it's often contaminated by unacknowledged emotions; and it filters, selects, distorts, and rationalizes information to reinforce existing beliefs.

*Dynamic thinking* is original thinking. It's reflective rather than reflexive; it responds to the current reality, here-and-now information, and possibilities; it respects evidence and is open to the "story" that emerges from thoughtful exploration; it parses information, particularly in verbal form, for nuance and complexity that can shape its meaning; it's capable of judging and unjudging; it values ideas as a form of wealth; it values originality of language and novel expressions of ideas; it seeks and values the new, novel, subtle, and ambiguous; it's evolutionary and open to updating itself; it's aware of and acknowledges the emotional sources that influence it; and it respects all forms of knowing.

As we'll see in the following chapters, many of the self-limiting mental habits that many people have acquired in their lives are forms of archaic thinking. The journey to practical intelligence is as much as a journey of *unlearning* as well as learning. We need to recognize and unlearn the archaic features of our mental process, and move toward a more dynamic expression of our natural intelligence.

# YOU MIGHT BE A MENTAL REDNECK . . .

Before we study the key mental habits and mega-skills of PI, let's take a common-sense check on our common sense.

American comedian Jeff Foxworthy draws on his heritage as a child of the South by inviting his listeners to consider whether "You might be a redneck." He poses various hypothetical behaviors to give his audience a "neck check."

- "If you have a complete set of salad bowls and they all say 'Cool-Whip' on the side," he advises, "you might be a redneck."
- "If you're wearing a strapless dress and a bra that isn't, you could be a redneck."
- "If you've been married three times and still have the same in-laws, you might be a redneck."

A redneck, in typical American usage, is an uncouth person of limited education—typically from the rural South—with an arrested social development, a narrow experience of culture and aesthetic experience, traditionalist attitudes and reactions, and self-indulgent preferences for experience. Rednecks stereotypically own guns, drive trucks or old rattle-trap cars, and like to fish and hunt.

Southerners in the United States also call them "bubbas." Australians call them "yobbos." In Hawaii, they're known as "mokes." They respond well to simple appeals such as patriotism or religious fundamentalism and take offense easily at perceived slights against the social or political groups they identify with. At their best, they are supposedly friendly, unassuming, and uncomplicated—"a glorious absence of sophistication," as Foxworthy affectionately describes them. At the extreme, a redneck is narrow-minded, bigoted, intolerant, boorish, and resentful of others who act "snooty."

Some people are "mental rednecks." They may not dress like stereotypical social rednecks, or even talk the way they talk, but nevertheless they *think* like rednecks. Mental redneck thinking is quite prevalent, including among supposedly "well-bred" people, who may have college educations, well-paying jobs, and comfortable living styles. It's a learned pattern of incompetence.

Mental redneck thinking is narrow, rigid, intolerant, resistant to change, unaccepting of other perspectives, and motivated by the need for simple answers and a comfortable sense of "law and order." Mental rednecks usually don't think of themselves as rednecks, of course. They typically like to think of themselves as having a firm grip on the problems and challenges of life, but paradoxically it's their fear of the loss of a sense of control, structure, and order—not having simple answers and simple solutions—that leads them to act out in ambiguity-avoiding patterns.

> "Elvis is dead. Deal with it."
> —T-shirt spotted in California

Mental redneck thinking is often selective: a person might think like a redneck on one topic, such as politics, and yet think more open-mindedly or creatively about others. People who are open to ideas in one area may snap into a reflexive, intolerant pattern of thinking when their hobby-horse topic comes up in conversation.

How do you know if you're a mental redneck—or "redbrain"? Taking a cue from comedian Foxworthy, here's a neck-check for the mind:

- If you get most of your information about the society you live in from watching television, you might be a mental redneck.
- If you take pride in having strong opinions and stoutly defending them, and you have no patience with wimps who don't, you could be a mental redneck.
- If you often say, "I don't care what anybody says, that's my opinion," you just might be a mental redneck.

- If you subscribe to three or more conspiracy theories about who's behind the bad things that are happening in the world today, you might be a mental redneck.
- If your car has more than one flag decal, religious bumper sticker, or political slogan, you could be a mental redneck.
- If you haven't been into a bookstore (or bought a book online) during the last year, you just might be a mental redneck.
- If the extent of your magazine reading is *People* magazine, *Cosmopolitan, Sports Illustrated,* or *Playboy,* you might be a mental redneck.
- If you know the names of all of the characters in the most popular TV shows but can't name the head of state of any foreign country, you could be a mental redneck.
- If you know more about the personal lives of movie stars, sports figures, or celebrity criminals than you know about the qualifications of the people you vote for, you just might be a mental redneck.
- If you vote for all the candidates on the ballot who belong to one political party, you just might be a mental redneck.
- If you emphatically claim, "I don't vote for any party, I vote for the individual" and then you vote for all the candidates on the ballot who belong to one political party, you might be a mental redneck.
- If you get all of your ammunition for political debates with your friends and acquaintances from a talk show host, you could be a mental redneck.
- If you've reduced your views and judgments about social and political issues to a set of standard slogans, which you routinely trot out in conversations, you just might be a mental redneck.
- If you're convinced that anyone who doesn't embrace your particular religious beliefs is doomed to burn in hell, you might be a mental redneck.

- If you're convinced that anyone who doesn't embrace your particular political opinions is mentally incompetent, morally corrupt, or otherwise defective, you could be a mental redneck.

There are many more clues, but presumably this short list adequately makes the point. Supposing that a person has a few redneck thinking habits—most of us do—how does one reform one's way of thinking and become more practically intelligent? How, if one wants to, can one cure one's self? That's one of the questions we'll explore on our journey into practical intelligence.

## THE CREATIVE PARADOX

I can still vividly recall an experience from many years ago when I was in about the third grade. I attended a small-town school in rural western Maryland. The teacher had given us a craft project: she had collected a number of pint-sized cardboard ice cream containers from the ice cream shop in the town. She gave one to each of us and instructed us to make a pencil holder as a gift for our parents.

It was a pretty simple-minded project, even for third-graders. All we had to do was decorate the thing in some way, with crayons or by gluing some colored construction paper around the outside of it. I think we had about a half-hour to get it done. (I learned later in life that the principal challenge in being an elementary school teacher is finding ways to keep the little buggers busy.)

Being the little entrepreneur that I was, and seldom inclined to take instructions too literally, I reconsidered the project from the "big picture" view. Both of my parents had very little education, and I couldn't remember seeing many pens or pencils around the house. My father always had a few carpenter's pencils he used in his occupation, but I didn't think we had any fountain pens or other fancy writing implements. We had few, if any, books as I recall.

It seemed to me that, if the purpose of the project was to make something our parents would like and enjoy (which I soon found out it was not), a pencil holder wasn't really the best choice. I studied the cylindrical container, which was about three inches in diameter and about five inches high. I turned it around to different angles and finally decided I could make a little house out of it. So I turned it upside down, drew a door and some windows on the outside of the cylinder, sketched in a pattern of bricks and some curtains, and built a makeshift roof with construction paper. I was just to the point of cutting open the little door with my pocket knife to make it open and close, when . . . *she caught me!*

Towering over my desk, she demanded in a loud voice, *"What in the world are you doing?!"* I looked up from my creation and tried to explain my rationale for going outside the bounds of the assignment. Exasperated, she snatched up my work-in-progress, gave me another container, and snarled, "You're *supposed* to make a pencil holder. Now do it!"

So I made a pencil holder.

Creativity and conformity don't usually go well together. *Yet we human beings crave both.* At one level, the human biocomputer cherishes routine, structure, order, and predictability. It's a pattern-maker, a pattern-recognizer, a pattern-follower, and a rule-follower. It often goes into stress when familiar, reliable patterns break down or no longer work. We like structure and order in our lives, we like it in our social environment, and we like it in our thinking processes.

Yet within each of us, at varying levels of depth and accessibility, is an appetite for something different; something new; something refreshingly unfamiliar; something that's uniquely us; for the exhilaration of creating something the world—or at least we—have never seen before. We need to express our individuality.

With the help of the people and environments we navigate as we grow up, each of us settles on some proportion of conformity and creativity. Some of us learn to bury our creative appetites deeply and settle for the comfortable predictability of a routinized life. Some of us invest so much energy into expressing our individuality that we may have trouble coping with the "law and order" of the environments we traverse. Most of us, perhaps, are somewhere in the middle.

With the help of early schooling experiences, many people conclude that they have no creative appetite or talents, and they adopt a pattern of thinking and behaving that reinforces this conviction. Others may be more lucky. In my own case, I have a sense that the "learning" I took from the classroom experience I described was not that "I'm not creative" or "Don't try to do things differently." I think what I got—fortunately—was "Just do what the teacher says."

This creative paradox has long been a topic of fascination with me: how does the biocomputer come to some equilibrium between creativity and conformity? Mental habits, structures, and patterns are, after all, quite powerful in their effects.

Socially, we seem to be highly programmed as well. I often think of the comic similarities between our automatic social behaviors and those of the "lower animals." Biologist Edward O. Wilson, widely considered one of the world's foremost authorities on ants, reportedly discovered that after ants die their bodies secrete a hormone messenger substance—one of a class of chemicals known as *pheromones*—which other ants detect and interpret as a signal of death. When they detect the pheromone on an ant's body, several of them will pick up the dead ant, carry it outside the nest, and throw it onto a kind of refuse pile.

Wilson managed to synthesize the death pheromone and—in one of those perverse comedic episodes of science—captured a live ant and painted some of the chemical on its body. Then he released it back into the ant population. Immediately, several of his colleagues picked him up, carried him outside, and threw him on the heap. The disgruntled ant got up and went back into the nest. Several other ants, oblivious to his protests and struggles, picked him up and, again, dragged him outside and threw him onto the heap.

The misunderstood ant continued to protest and to assert his right to join the group, and always he found himself unceremoniously carted outside and discarded. I don't know whether Wilson felt guilty about inflicting such a fate on an unsuspecting ant, or whether he considered it necessary to the advancement of science.

Are we humans really all that much more intelligent and aware than the ants?

In my occupation as a management consultant and executive advisor, I get to observe socially conditioned behavior in operation almost every day—at the level of the individual, the work team, the managers, and the whole organization. Most of their creative energies never get released, because the conformist pressures keep it bottled up.

I think we need to learn to respect and cherish our craziness. When we let go of the illusion that we're always sensible and logical creatures who always think and do the right things, life actually becomes more fun. And, in a strange way, that's part of the psychology of creativity.

> "You're only given a small spark of madness.
> You mustn't lose it."
> —Robin Williams (comedian)

## THE "BEGINNER'S MIND": INNOCENCE AND HUMILITY

An expression frequently attributed to various Zen masters is:

> "The biggest obstacle to learning something is the
> belief that you already know it."

Zen practitioners speak of the "beginner's mind," which is a state of awareness that is open to learning, understanding, and perceiving ideas and situations in new ways. As Zen Master Suzuki Roshi explains it:

> "In the beginner's mind there are many possibilities;
> In the expert's mind there are few."

A remarkable number of important inventions have been created by people who were not "experts" in the areas of their contributions. Many of them were beginners, often operating outside the boundaries of accepted practice. Many were ridiculed by the established experts and the keepers of the establishment.

*Case in point:* the "Xerox" process, which affects the lives of most educated people almost every day, was single-handedly pioneered by an amateur inventor, a man named Chester Carlson. Working at his kitchen table, Carlson managed to duplicate an image onto a piece of glass, using a clumsy makeshift apparatus. He saw the enormous potential of this technique, but knew he would need a lot of money to develop it to the point of commercial viability. Carlson was turned down by virtually all of the big names of business—more than twenty firms that would have been the logical candidates to bring it to market, including IBM and General Electric, as well as the U.S. Army Signal Corps. Carlson began his work in 1938, and it was 1959 when he finally saw his brainchild become the Xerox 914 copier, a product that founded the Xerox Corporation, made business history, and made him a very wealthy man.

*Case in point:* two college dropouts, both fascinated with electronic gadgets, pioneered the personal computer. In a now-legendary story, Steve Jobs and Steve Wozniak, working in the garage of Job's parents, created the prototype of the first commercial "PC," which at that time was only a scrambled mess of parts and wires. Jobs shopped the idea all around northern California—which was not yet known as "Silicon Valley," but eventually would be, largely as a result of their pioneering efforts. He was turned down by every major electronics firm in the area, including IBM, Hewlett-Packard, and game-maker Atari. They finally found a financial sponsor in Mike Markkula, an executive who had recently left Fairchild Semiconductor Corporation, and within a short time they created the first "Apple" computer.

It's axiomatic in the business world that the firms that dominate any particular area of business are almost never the ones to "reinvent" the business when times change drastically. The executives of IBM, the undisputed leader in the mainframe computer industry, never considered the PC an important product. Kodak, which absolutely dominated the photography business for decades, came late to the digital revolution, while other firms pioneered digital cameras and other popular gadgets. Giant telephone companies such as AT&T and others could have developed the Internet, but didn't.

Many years ago the American railroad companies were some of the most profitable firms in the country; they could have morphed into airline companies when the jet engine made air travel commercially practical, but none of them did. Typewriter manufacturers were going out of business as the computer printer became a phenomenal best-selling product; Hewlett-Packard, formerly a maker of electronic lab equipment, made it a reality. None of the dominant Wall Street brokerage firms—the traditional "wire houses"—pioneered online investing. It's a long list.

Many of us are experts in various aspects of what we do.

> *The most important thing every expert needs to*
> *learn is how to think like a beginner.*

Humility is a paradoxical state of thinking: it takes a healthy ego to be humble. People we think of as having "big egos" actually have small egos, and they keep trying to enlarge them by showing off. Of course, not all people who are quiet and withdrawn are humble; some of them just have deflated egos. Humility is the center zone between being inflated and deflated. It's an expression of the essence of mental flexibility.

## THE "PLEXITY" SCALE

In his fantasy novel *The Broken God,* David Zindell introduces us to the concept of "plexity," as explained by the elders of the Fravashi, a wise and highly evolved culture:

"... the ideal and practice of the art of *plexure.* This art—it is sometimes called *plexity*—aims at moving the student through the four stages of liberation. In the first stage, that of the *simplex,* one is caught within the bounds of a single worldview. This is the reality of a child or an Alaloi hunter [a Neanderthaloid race], who may not even be aware that other ways of perceiving reality exist.

"It is the great and deadly vanity of human beings to convince themselves that their worldview, no matter how unlikely or bizarre, is somehow more sane, natural, pragmatic, holy, or truthful than any other. Out of choice—or cowardice—most people never break out of this simplex stage of viewing the world as through a single lens, and this is their damnation.

"All of Old Father's students, of course, by the very act of adopting the Fravashi system, had elevated themselves to the *complex* stage of belief. To be complex is to hold at least two different realities, perhaps at two different times of one's life. The complex woman or man will cast away beliefs like old clothes, as they become worn or inappropriate.

"The third stage of plexure is the *multiplex.* If complexity is the ability to suspend and adopt different beliefs as they are useful or appropriate, one after another, then multiplexity is the holding of more than one reality at the same time. These realities may be as different—or even contradictory—as the old science and the magical thinking of a child.

"'Truth is multiple,' as the Old Fathers say. One can never become multiplex if afraid of paradox or enslaved by the god of consistency. Multiplex vision is paradoxical vision, new logics, the sudden completion of startling patterns. The mastery of multiplexity makes it possible to see the world in many dimensions; it is like peering into a jewel of a thousand different faces."[3]

Taking a cue from the "Old Fathers" of the Fravashi—and David Zindell's fertile mind—we can adapt these levels of *plexity* for our own study. We can build a bigger window on the world for ourselves. Modifying the labels slightly, I think of them as describing four kinds of thinkers:

- *Simplex thinkers*—people who, typically out of fear and ignorance, crave simple answers, simple world views, simple explanations, simple opinions, and simple solutions. They may be superstitious, "magical" thinkers, ultra-religious, and hostile toward others who don't look like them and who don't walk and talk and think like they do. They tend to be drawn toward powerful leader figures who promise them solutions to their lives' problems without taxing their gray matter. In primitive societies, simplex thinkers unquestioningly follow ancient beliefs and myths, rely on tradition and ritual to anesthetize their existential fears, and ostracize or even kill others who differ with their beliefs and values. In so-called advanced societies, they seek to impose their world views or religious beliefs upon all others, being utterly convinced that they are "right." Their hostility typically arises from a latent, suppressed fear that there might be multiple explanations for reality and that their personal worlds might crumble if they started considering complex options. They are easily manipulated by demagogues, appeals to patriotism, religious intolerance, and fear. They want to know what's right and what's wrong, who's right and who's wrong, who has the right answers, and whom they're supposed to hate.
- *Duplex thinkers*—people who have acquired a measure of social sophistication, but who have arrested their mental development at the level of *two-valued thinking*. Duplex thinkers tend to dichotomize situations, issues, and ideologies in terms of simple opposing distinctions: right or wrong, good or bad, normal or abnormal, moral or immoral, success or failure, liberal or conservative, friend or enemy, us and them, with us or against us. Formal education is not always a cure for this disorder, probably because it originates in a similar kind of fear that drives

simplex thinkers. Duplex thinkers are fond of saying, knowingly, things like, "Well, there are two sides to every story," not understanding that there may be many "sides" to any particular story. Many news writers seem incurably addicted to the duplex pattern of presenting stories, which drives them to frame almost every political issue in terms of conflict between two opposing sides. American politics has operated on a duplex model of thinking for so many decades, largely because there are only two viable political parties, that few Americans seem to be able to think beyond their two opposing ideologies.

- *Multiplex thinkers*—people who have developed a high tolerance—and even a preference—for ambiguity and complexity. They tend to see problems as having "more than one right answer." They think, react, and express their ideas respectfully and with concern for the conversational civil rights of others. Multiplex thinkers understand intuitively and consciously that what is true and right depends entirely on who is buying. They can acknowledge other points of view as valid for those who hold them, even points of view that contradict their own. They value their own learning and growth more highly than their need to be "right." They respect reason, evidence, honesty, and fair play, so they try to avoid the temptation to use their intellect to influence others in dishonest ways. Multiplex thinkers consider themselves works in progress, and consequently consider their own opinions works in progress—miniature construction projects that take shape and evolve as their learning and understanding evolve. They separate their opinions from their egos, and view opinions as merely impersonal constellations of ideas that organize what they know at a particular moment. Multiplex thinkers know how to persuade others by leading their ideas in non-aggressive ways, and they attach little value to confrontation as a general means of changing others' minds. Biologist Thomas Huxley said, "It is not who is right, but what is right that is of importance."

- *Omniplex thinkers*—people who have not only become tolerant of ambiguity and complexity, but who seem to enjoy it. They appreciate the mental stimulation of realizing that human beings only know an infinitesimal fraction of what can be known; they find the idea strangely exhilarating rather than frightening, and yet they seek to understand what they can understand. They react to paradox with wonder and amusement rather than frustration. They often see far beyond the boundaries that others apply to situations, issues, and problems. While multiplex thinkers may be skillful at "connecting the dots," omniplex thinkers tend to notice dots that others fail to see, because they see through a wider lens. They are open, at least in principle, to the most seemingly outlandish ideas, ethereal concepts, and preposterous options. They understand that ideas, like living things, are only partly formed when they come into being; that they die quickly if not protected; and that over time, they will prove themselves or fail to prove themselves by their merits. Omniplex thinkers have a reverence for knowledge, ideas, and intellectual honesty. One of the most inspiring role models for omniplex thinking to have visited this planet in several centuries was R. Buckminster Fuller, who said of himself, "I seem to be a verb."

In the teaching traditions of the mystical Sufi culture, simple stories and fables can exemplify the themes of paradoxical or omniplex thinking. Many of them portray what we commonly think of as stupidity and wisdom at the same time, such as the following, one of my favorites:

"One day the Mullah Nasruddin was adjudicating a dispute between two neighbors. After listening to the first one's arguments, he said, 'I believe you are right.' But then the other neighbor argued his case, very persuasively. When he had finished,

Nasruddin said, 'I believe you are right.' A bystander, perplexed by his answers, protested: 'Wait a minute! They can't both be right!' The mullah looked at him, stroked his beard, and said, 'I believe you are right.'"

# THERE IS NO TRUTH—ONLY YOUR TRUTH, HIS TRUTH, HER TRUTH, THEIR TRUTH . . .

Ask any person who was born and raised in the United States, "Who was Betsy Ross, and what did she do that made her famous?" Most of them will probably tell you something like "Betsy Ross sewed the first official American flag for George Washington."

This little "fact," this "truth," is repeated countless times in class-rooms, in schoolbooks, and on websites all over America. However, it's very probably not true.

According to an entry on the website www.USFlag.org:

"Elizabeth Griscom Ross (1752–1836), was a Philadelphia seam-stress, married to John Ross, an upholsterer who was killed in a munitions explosion in 1776. She kept the upholstery shop going and lived on Arch Street, not too far from the State House on Chestnut, where history was being made almost every day. According to most historians, she has been incorrectly credited with designing the first Stars and Stripes. The story has enormous popularity, yet the facts do not substantiate it.

"This account of the creation of our first flag was first brought to light in 1870 by one of her grandsons, William J. Canby, at a meeting of the Historical Society of Pennsylvania. This took place *ninety-four years after the event [supposedly happened]*. Mr. Canby was a boy of eleven years when Mrs. Ross died in his home."

Some other "truths" of American history are equally shaky. The poet Henry Wadsworth Longfellow wrote a poem that became famous titled "The Midnight Ride of Paul Revere." It depicted Paul Revere's supposedly heroic ride through the New England countryside, as he warned the citizens of the approach of the British forces. Visitors to the Boston area quickly discover that, notwithstanding Longfellow's admiring story, Revere never completed his mission. According to the historical record, he accidentally collided with a British patrol outside the town of Lexington; they took away his horse and made him walk back to Boston.

According to the record, two other men, William Dawes and Samuel Prescott, completed the ride. *Ninety years later,* the poet Longfellow, in an act of literary license, probably decided that Paul Revere, a silversmith—who, although a devoted patriot, had earned no particular place in history—was the more interesting figure of the three. And, possibly finding it more difficult to come up with words that rhymed with "Dawes" or "Prescott," decided that "Revere" made for a better poem. Generations of American children have read and recited the "adjusted" version of the story.

"All truths are half-truths."
—Alfred North Whitehead

By the way, the famous "Battle of Bunker Hill," also a legendary part of American history, was not fought on Bunker's Hill, according to the historical record. And most of the "Founding Fathers" were not Christians, as is commonly believed to this day. As an exercise in Zen-learning, you might want to search the Internet and explore these "truths" yourself. Or shake your faith in what you know by reading Tom Burnham's enlightening book, *The Dictionary of Misinformation,* which calls into question a great number of accepted "truths."[4]

## An Exercise

Please gaze intently at the following word for a long time—long enough to imprint it into your visual memory.

# *"truth"*

Note the most important feature of the word as presented: it's surrounded by quotation marks, which typically indicate that a word is being used in some qualified way, or in a figurative sense rather than literally.

Please repeat this exercise many times, closing your eyes and seeing it as vividly as possible in your mind's eye. Turn your head at different angles and look at it. Trace it with the forefinger of each hand. Imagine seeing it in different colors. Imagine seeing it underlined. Say it repeatedly, silently and aloud, until it begins to sound strange and even peculiar. Take your pen and write it several times, taking care to include the quotation marks.

I ask you to train yourself, by whatever means you find effective, so that whenever you hear, say, read, or write the word truth, you get an immediate and vivid mental image of the word in quotations, as above. If you can train yourself to think of truth as "truth," you will have taken out an important insurance policy on your sanity.

Simplex thinkers tend to carry around a flawed notion of truth. At the deepest levels of conviction—their religious beliefs—they are utterly convinced that *their* truth must be true for everybody. They don't understand that their religious beliefs, moral codes, social values, and often their political convictions are largely an accident of space and time.

*All "truth" is local to the brains in which it resides.*

Had the fundamentalist Christian who's living in Kansas been born in Jakarta or Karachi, he or she would very likely be a fundamentalist Muslim. Had the fundamentalist Muslim living in Teheran or Riyadh been born in rural Tennessee, he or she would very likely be a fundamentalist Christian, adherent to a particular denomination that he or she had been taught is the "correct" religious belief system. Had either of them been born into a Jewish family, he or she would very likely see the world through the ideological lens of Judaism. If they had been born in parts of China or Japan . . . well, you probably get the point.

*Once you let go of your need to feel certain*
*about everything, you liberate your natural*
*intelligence, at all levels.*

People who torture and murder one another in the name of religion are basically fighting about who has the "real" truth. Presumably, the last one standing will be right. As Palestinian guerilla leader Yassir Arafat noted, "You're basically killing each other to see who's got the best imaginary friend."

"May the god of your choice bless you."
—Kinky Friedman (writer, musician,
aspiring politician)

There's another big problem with "truth": proving that *anything* is true. We human beings tend to be very, very sloppy with facts, evidence, and the things we believe as a result of them, or in many cases in spite of them. Psychologists who study these things have shown repeatedly in experiments that many people cannot reliably distinguish between a concrete fact, as reported, and an inference or an assumption based on that fact, particularly when the report of the fact uses somewhat suggestive language.

Once their minds form an association with a reported fact, they often treat the inference, or the assumption, or the conclusion as factual in itself. Attorneys, political consultants, and advertising copywriters know that merely placing two facts together in a chain, or associating them closely in some way, will entice many people to jump to a conclusion that is not necessarily supported by either fact. We'll explore the syndrome of inference-observation-conclusion in Chapter 6.

## The Tree of Knowledge: When Is a Fact Not a Fact?

Another very fundamental principle of practical intelligence is: *not all facts are created equal.* People who lack the capacity for dynamic, multiplex thinking, and who stay stuck at the simplex or duplex level, don't clearly grasp that some facts are less "factual" than others, that some truths are less "true" than others. For them, a thing is true or not true, rather than "true for me," "true to some extent," or "true under some circumstances."

Let's explore this very important and rather subtle concept using the analogy of a tree—the "tree of knowledge," as shown in Figure 4.1.

The most direct, intimate, and fundamental way we can "know" something is by our own personal, *sensory experience* of it, which occurs before we say anything about it or how we remember it. We experience it with our senses, before we begin to think about it in categorical terms. When you taste a hot-fudge banana split sundae, you "know" it at a direct sensory level. You might talk about it, marvel over the taste and mouth feel of it, try to describe it to someone else, even write a poem about it, but you'll never be able to capture the essence of the sensory experience in words. Another person who's also tasted such a dessert can share your sense of enthusiasm, but he or she will never know *your* experience of it. Others can describe their experience of their sundaes, but you'll never know as they knew it.

As the tree of knowledge figure suggests, verbal descriptions are only weak maps, or replicas, of the sensory reality a person has experienced, and some are a lot weaker than others. Perhaps the first part of the tree of verbal description—the trunk—is attaching a *label* to the experience—calling it something. *Descriptions* are further removed from the original sensed reality, as we begin to apply adjectives, judgments, and implications.

A *report,* as suggested by the tree diagram, is someone else's verbal map, or description of his or her experience, or perhaps even a second-hand description based on a third person's description.

## Figure 4.1.    The Tree of Knowledge

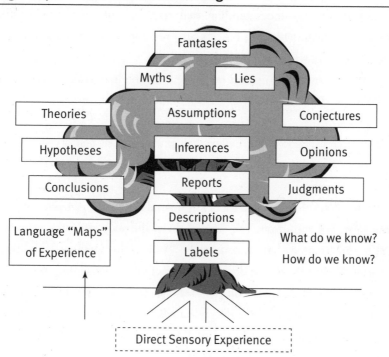

Can you sense, intuitively, that this progression of levels takes us in the direction of knowledge that is increasingly uncertain—that is, it becomes increasingly difficult to verify or validate it in our own experience?

For instance, assumptions and inferences are different from second-hand reports, which are different from first-hand reports, which are different from direct sensory experiences. Conclusions, judgments, opinions, hypotheses—these are all labels we use to characterize information according to its "distance" from direct personal experience.

Theories and conjectures offer *potential* truths, and they may be expressed in sufficiently abstract language that they can never be really "proven." Myths, lies, and fantasies are knowledge-packages that grow far out on the branches of the tree of knowledge.

The most important value of this tree of knowledge concept is the sanity-preserving understanding that truth is not only local to the brains in which it resides, but it's also relative to the original sensory experience on which it's supposedly based.

We can put it into street language with the line from a Creedence Clearwater Revival song:

> "People say, 'Believe half of what ya see, son,
> and none of what ya hear.'"

Here's another peculiar aspect of mental flexibility: *perception of cause and effect*. We commonly ask "Why?" "Why did such-and-such happen?" "Why did country A attack country B?" "Why is this species of fish disappearing?" "Why do kids in disadvantaged neighborhoods join gangs?"

We human beings compulsively seek "reasons" for what we observe. "A *causes* B." If we don't want B to happen, we have to make sure A doesn't happen. The temptation we fall prey to, so often, is to perceive only those cause-and-effect relationships we can easily understand. We don't like to overload our brains with complex relationships, so we often look for—and find—simple "A causes B" relationships. But much of what goes on in the great, wide world around us is *multicausal*: A affects B, which affects C, which affects J, which affects B, which affects R, which affects A.

Physicist David Bohm wrote and lectured about what he called the *implicate order*—an ever-unfolding cascade of relationships between matter, energy, and information, which he believed shaped all of reality. He referred to the *explicate order* as the "appearance" of cause and effect we perceive and believe to be "true." He and others have argued that the human brain, unable to grasp even the concept of the implicate order, not to mention understand it, willfully imposes its perception of cause and effect on what it thinks it understands.

Another of the charming Sufi teaching stories illustrates the subtlety of cause and effect:

"One of Mullah Nasruddin's students asked, 'What is fate?' Nasruddin answered, 'An endless succession of intertwined events, each influencing the other.' 'That is hardly a satisfactory answer. I believe in cause and effect,' retorted the student. 'Very well,' replied the Mullah, 'look at that,' pointing to a procession passing in the street. 'That man is being taken to be hanged. Is it because somebody gave him a silver piece and enabled him to buy the knife with which he committed the murder; or because somebody sold him the knife; or because somebody saw him do it; or because nobody stopped him?'"

## HOW I LEARNED TO STOP ARGUING WITH PEOPLE

During my college days I received an excellent education in how to argue. I never took a debating class or participated in a formal debate. But I participated in informal debates nearly every day. A group of my fellow fraternity buddies would gather every morning at a particular table in the student union cafeteria. The continuously running conversation over coffee and sweet rolls was a kind of intellectual bus stop. Some guys would drop by after class and some would depart for the next class. And some would cut class if they found the discourse more appealing than the prospect of attending a lecture on calculus or physics.

Having come from a country school in a small town, I'd had little opportunity to engage in stratospheric conversations about the meaning of life, but I soon became one of the most skilled debaters. Mind you, we never called it a debate; we thought of it as just a place to hang out. But most of the time it was a contest of wits, egos, and testosterone.

"Conversation, n. A fair for the display of minor
mental commodities, each exhibitor being too intent
upon the arrangement of his own wares to observe
those of his neighbor."
—Ambrose Bierce, *The Devil's Dictionary*

Looking back from many years later, I realized that, beyond learning to argue skillfully, I *failed to learn* a couple of other things:

- I won my share of arguments, but seldom sensed that I had really changed anybody's mind. Making another person look foolish, or uninformed, or mentally incompetent may have won points with the onlookers or with other guys who argued from the same position, but all it usually did was leave the other person angry and in need of revenge.
- Whenever I sensed that I was on the losing side of a debate, my priorities shifted from winning to *not losing.* Even if I sensed at some level that my opponent's views made more sense than my own, I couldn't give him the satisfaction of seeing me defeated. I might revise my views later, at my leisure and out of sight, but I usually felt compelled to defend them at all costs. I imagine my opponents often did the same.

Think about your own experience with arguments.

Have you ever had the experience of suddenly discovering, in the midst of a heated debate with another person, or worse yet, a group of people, that *you were wrong*—and in fact wrong at the top of your voice? Someone politely offers a fact or a question that demolishes the whole position you've been aggressively selling, and you know it.

It's quite a disconcerting experience, isn't it? It's as if your brain comes to a standstill: your thoughts go into chaos, you get that "trapped" feeling, and you're temporarily stunned. You lose your train of thought. You're suddenly transformed from a valiant warrior into a desperate fugitive.

What you do next says a lot about you, and a lot about the way you've learned to use your natural intelligence. You have several options: for one, you can bluff and bluster—trying to distract attention from the inconvenient truth. You can ignore it and keep talking; you can shout down the person who said it; you can argue that it's not true or not relevant; or you can attack the credibility of the person who said it, or the source from whence it came. Usually, in this type of a situation, the best outcome you can hope for is a draw, and it's very likely that the "audience" will still perceive the contest as a loss.

A second strategy is the "you got me" strategy. You can just stop, admit that the story you've been spinning doesn't hold together, and take your lumps. Most probably, the other party to the argument, or the audience if there is one, will enjoy seeing you brought down to size. Your embarrassment becomes a temporary entertainment for them. You get to provide a public service by being the butt of the jokes that follow. After the humiliating episode, life goes on.

There's also a third strategy, which I highly recommend:

*Don't set up win-lose encounters with people.*

Somewhere in my early professional career it began to dawn on me that getting into arguments with people didn't seem to be serving my interests very well. I suppose I unconsciously picked up cues from some people I encountered who seemed more "laid back," more prone to listen carefully, and more deft at redirecting the thoughts of others. I began to sense alternatives to the brute force approach.

Eventually I sensed a deep-lying evolution in my understanding of people and ideas. I began to realize more and more clearly, and to believe with ever-greater conviction, that arguing with people too often derailed me from achieving my objectives.

"A man convinced against his will
is of the same opinion still."
—William Blake, "Auguries of Innocence"

In my book *Social Intelligence: The New Science of Success,* I described an episode that may have been the final turning point in my understanding.

"'You're wrong. You're dead wrong, and I'll tell you why.'

"That statement, and a few others that came after it, may have caused the loss of several million dollars worth of business for a company I was employed with many years ago.

"The person on the receiving end was a high-ranking civilian technical expert working for the U.S. Department of Defense. The person on the delivering end was an associate of mine, Jack (not his real name), a young man with considerable technical knowledge but few discernible social skills.

"He and I were meeting with the government expert for the first time. Our mission was to begin building a relationship that would enable us to acquaint him and his colleagues with our technical capabilities as a firm, and by that means create a competitive advantage for our firm as a contractor for Defense business.

"The government expert had just voiced a rather strong—and largely unsupportable—opinion about the future prospects of a particular type of technology. My colleague Jack, apparently blind to the larger context for the conversation, could not let this act of technical blasphemy go unanswered. He had to set this man straight. In short order, they were engaged in a heated debate.

"Far from achieving our objective of starting a successful relationship, we were rapidly achieving exactly the opposite. Before I was able to shift the discussion back to neutral ground, the damage had been done. We never succeeded in getting another meeting with him or any of his colleagues."[5]

I began to realize, dimly at first and then ever more clearly, that *outcomes are important.* I realized that we can approach any conversation, with a stranger at a bus stop, a co-worker, a prospective client or customer, or an intimate partner, with a choice of possible intentions:

- *As a performance*—a way to show off; we may seek to impress others with how much we know, how wise we are, and how well we can express ourselves.
- *As a sport*—a battle of wits in which we seek to dominate or defeat others with our debating skills; to prove to them or to onlookers that we're mentally superior to them.
- *As a way to sell*—we may seek to induce others to change their views and accept an idea, a viewpoint, or a course of action we want to promote.
- *As a way to learn*—we may seek to discover, through discourse, useful information, new ideas, new points of view, or new possibilities that might be personally beneficial to us.
- *As a way to connect*—we may simply seek to enjoy the sense of community that comes from affirming our common interests and shared views, rather than from emphasizing our differences. "Small talk," for instance, is small because it avoids conflict and controversy in favor of ritualized agreement, which preserves empathy, rapport, and feelings of camaraderie.

Chronic debaters—people who turn most conversations into win-lose arguments—often defeat themselves by confusing means and ends. This, I realized, was what I had been doing, all too often.

> "The best captain does not plunge headlong,
> nor is the best soldier a fellow hot to fight.
> The greatest victor wins without the battle . . ."
>
> —Lao Tzu

Simplex thinkers and duplex thinkers often tend to treat a conversation as a sporting event. They may express a strong opinion on some topic and check to see whether they get any takers. Often, another simplex or duplex thinker may disagree with some part, or all, of the opinion. Then they square off and proceed to debate. And for many of them, it really *is* a sport. They enjoy—or believe they do—the stimulation of mock combat.

Anyone, of course, is entitled to treat a conversation as a contest of debating skills. At the same time, they cannot divest themselves of responsibility for the consequences—the outcome they get. Many chronic debaters will say, "I believe the best ideas come out when people have to argue for their opinions. They have to get clear about what they believe." It's more likely, in my view, that adversarial exchanges of opinions tend to encourage dishonest and distorted thinking, as people conjure up arguments to support fixed positions. And often, I believe, this rationalization is a cover story they use to justify their social aggression.

Again, it comes down to outcomes. If the outcome I want is a "sale"—to invite someone to agree with my "truth"—then presenting my "truth" in an aggressive, coercive manner doesn't seem to be an effective choice. If I find my emotional satisfaction in showing off or defeating others, I need to ask myself: "What deficit in my own sense of self leads me to want to belittle or defeat others?" And, "Is this behavior taking me closer, or further away from the outcome I'm seeking?"

In Chapter 6 we'll explore various verbal strategies and techniques for influencing others without building resistance in them.

## A NEW WAY TO THINK ABOUT OPINIONS

In a particular episode of the long-running TV series *Star Trek,* the ever-logical, ever-pragmatic Mr. Spock, played by actor Leonard Nimoy, calmly observed: "Change is the essential process of all existence."

Indeed, it is. And if each of us could stay in touch, at all times, and at all levels of our consciousness, with that profoundly simple truth, we'd be much saner creatures than we are. Unwillingness to acknowledge, accept, and embrace that all of what we call "reality" is in a state of constant evolution is at the root of most forms of craziness. Let's take a moment to reconnect with this simple truth and its implications.

Your body creates about 2.5 million red blood cells per second, which live, on an average, of about 120 days. Most of your other body cells die and get replaced in approximately the same time span. By that reasoning, you're not the same person you were three or four months ago.

In fact, you're not the same person you were a second ago; it just seems like it's the same "you." Consider that millions of your brain cells have just changed as a result of reading the last few paragraphs of this book. New information has altered the chemical patterns, connections, and signals that flow between and among your brain cells and the other cells of your body.

> "One can not step twice into the same river."
> —Heraclitus

From the level of molecules and subatomic particles, all the way out to the stars and galaxies, energy exchanges are constantly re-forming all matter. Movement is an all-pervasive constant of the universe. Your childhood home has changed since you grew up there. Your childhood friends have grown bigger, probably in various directions. Some of your friends and family members may have left the planet. Your favorite movie stars are getting older. You're changing every day, hopefully for the better, but possibly also in some ways you'd rather not.

The illusion that you're the same person you were a few seconds ago, and perhaps that you've "always" been who you are, exists only because of memory. Brain cells don't die and get replaced (with some interesting exceptions), so your memories connect your experience of the present with your experience of the past.

Here's the punch line of this discussion: if all things in the universe are constantly changing, *why do so many people seem to feel their opinions must be fixed, permanent, and final?* Why shouldn't opinions be works in progress, just as we humans are works in progress? Why not give ourselves permission to be imperfect?

*Opinions tend to turn off your curiosity switch.* "Arriving" at an opinion puts an end to a mental journey. After all, why keep looking for possible answers when you've found *the* answer?

On another hand (not "on *the* other hand," as duplex thinkers often say), keeping your opinions perpetually on probation tends to keep your curiosity channel more open.

Curing yourself of *opinionitis* requires letting go of the need to be right. It means detaching your ego from your ideas. It means allowing ideas to stand or fall on their merits, rather than emotionally owning and defending them. It means having enough confidence in your thinking processes that you can live with ambiguity and complexity.

Here's a sanity-enhancing recommendation:

*Retire the word "opinion" from your vocabulary.*

If we think of the word "opinion" as signaling a stopping point, a final conclusion that accounts for all of the "facts" in a situation, then calling something an opinion tends to signal that you've stopped thinking about the issue, question, proposition, or topic.

The alternative term "position" also tends to imply the same "closing of the book." To say "My position on that is . . ." sounds like one has taken up a fortified military position and is prepared to repel all attackers. In contrast, using a term that suggests that thinking is still underway serves as a cue to yourself and others that there is always more to know and more to consider.

Try replacing "opinion" or "position" with some other terms, like "my viewpoint," "my take," "my current understanding," or "my impression."

At this point some people will surely say, "But you can't be wishy-washy. You have to stand for something. How can you not have opinions?"

It's not about not having opinions—it's about *not being owned by our opinions*. It's about treating your opinions as works in progress, just as you think of yourself as a work in progress. Retiring the word "opinion" from your vocabulary doesn't stop you from forming work-in-progress viewpoints that can serve your thinking processes; it only makes it more difficult for you to attach them to your sense of self. And it can tend to make you more directly conscious of your opinion-making and concluding processes, as you require yourself to search for original ways to describe what you're doing with your mind.

## THREE PHRASES THAT CAN
## KEEP YOUR MIND OPEN

As we'll see more clearly in Chapter 6, language is one form of mental software, and changing your language can cause you to change the way you think.

As a mental down payment on a project to radically revise our language habits, let's consider just three simple but powerful verbal strategies that support and reinforce the key mental habit of Mental Flexibility:

> *Three keys to Mental Flexibility:*
> *"I don't know."*
> *"I made a mistake."*
> *"I've changed my mind."*

Think carefully about the implications of each of these key statements. They telegraph to ourselves, as well as to others, that we have the courage to change, to learn, and to grow. Using them fluently, skillfully—and appropriately—frees us from ego-defending. They enable us to assert our entitlement to be human.

## "I Don't Know"

For example, how do you react when someone asks you a question: "Are you familiar with the theory of psychocosmesis?" "Have you eaten at that great new place, Gizzardi's?" "Do you know how to calibrate a Franostat?" Do you react with alarm when you realize you don't know the answer to the question, or maybe that you don't even know what the questioner is talking about?

Does some inner voice, from somewhere below the level of consciousness, tell you that you "should" know—and that you mustn't let anyone find out that you don't know? Do you have the impulse to fake it—to answer evasively or conjure up some approximate answer? Or when you inform the questioner that you don't know the answer to his or her query, do you feel inadequate, embarrassed, or slightly inadequate?

From the standpoint of mental health and the liberating habit of mental flexibility, it's irrelevant whether or not you *should* know. The simple fact is that you don't. And by training yourself to say, "I don't know" simply, unapologetically, unashamedly, and in a matter-of-fact tone of voice, you avoid turning positive mental energy into negative energy. In so doing, you reserve and redirect your mental energy to the possibilities that the situation offers.

At this point, some people will certainly protest: "But if I go around saying 'I don't know' all the time, won't people think I'm incompetent?" Probably they will. There's no need to take it to extremes. We can just start by eliminating the flinch reaction—the "I must know everything" syndrome—and verbally affirming our right not to know, at least in those situations in which not knowing is reasonable.

"We don't know one-millionth of 1 percent
about anything."
—Thomas A. Edison

## "I Made a Mistake"

A similar value applies to the key phrase, "I made a mistake." For some people, acknowledging that they've made an ineffective or inappropriate choice or decision is equivalent to confessing that they're all too human. If they've invested a lot of mental energy into repressing their subconscious doubts about their competence, they may be tempted to try to fake themselves out as well as fake out others they feel are passing judgment on them.

Again, it's very helpful to train yourself to use the phrase—when appropriate—with an attitude of simple matter-of-fact disclosure. You're only saying that you can now see alternatives to the decision you made that you now like better. You're not a bad person, nor were you a bad person when you made the decision you'd now like to have made differently. By detaching your ego from your decision, you own your right to have a "batting average" or a "track record." You don't have to be "right" every time; you just have to get it right on a large percentage of the tries.

> "Mistakes are part of the dues one pays
> for a full life."
> —Sophia Loren

## "I've Changed My Mind"

Similarly, the simple expression, "I've changed my mind" affirms your right to change, learn, and grow. Many of our cultural messages and signals seem to convey the idea that one must be certain about things, and moreover that one must always make the "right" judgment on the very first try. Changing one's mind, particularly in a situation involving argument and adversarial relationships, is often condemned as an indication of incompetence or weakness of character. One of the most damning accusations aimed by political contestants against their adversaries is inconsistency—not having firm opinions and positions on every issue, or even worse, changing one's positions.

Don't confuse changing your mind with not making good decisions—they're not the same thing. What may have been an effective and appropriate decision or viewpoint at some point in time may no longer be effective and appropriate if the evidence changes or if you discover a better conclusion based on the original evidence. If you can't seem to come to confident conclusions about anything, then you probably need to work on your decision-making skills. But if you can't "unmake" a decision when better evidence or a better rationale is available, you're confusing rigidity with competence.

> "Faced with the choice between changing one's mind
> and proving there is no need to do so,
> most people get busy on the proof."
> —John Kenneth Galbraith

If the people you typically deal with are likely to perceive mind-changing as weakness or incompetence, you may find it helpful to explain it to them in ways they can tolerate and accept. For instance, you might say, "I've looked at that issue again, and I'm seeing it in a new way," or "The situation has changed; maybe it's time to re-think the decision," or "That decision hasn't panned out the way we hoped; I think it's time for a better approach."

The point of using these mentally flexible statements is not to invite others to see you as incompetent, but to remind yourself of your mental "civil rights"—the right to be human, the right to learn, adapt, and grow, and the right to continually update your thinking. By choosing your language effectively, you not only free yourself to think more clearly, but you probably cause others to perceive you as mentally flexible and confident in your own practical intelligence.

# Notes

1. Feldenkrais, Moshe. *Awareness Through Movement*. San Francisco: Harper, 1991.

2. Gardner, John. *Self-Renewal: The Individual in the Innovative Society*. New York: Norton, 1995 (reissue).

3. Zindell, David. *The Broken God*. New York: Bantam, 1994 (p. 110). Used with permission. I have modified the sequence of paragraphs slightly to support the flow of ideas in this chapter.

4. Burnham, Tom. *The Dictionary of Misinformation*. New York: HarperCollins, 2005.

5. Albrecht, Karl. *Social Intelligence: The New Science of Success*. San Francisco: Jossey-Bass, 2006.

# 5

## *MENTAL SOFTWARE UPGRADE 2*
### *Adopting Affirmative Thinking*

> "The three great requirements for a happy life
> are something to do, something to love,
> and something to hope for."
> —Joseph Addison

"I'm just your basic forty-year-old bag."

So said a woman as she introduced herself to about thirty other people in the first session of an evening course I taught some years ago. The sessions explored a range of life skills, and we had just assembled to get started. Each person gave his or her name and shared whatever personal information he or she felt was appropriate.

Most of her fellow members chuckled at her clever self-characterization, but the subtext of the comment was not lost. How we describe ourselves to others usually reflects how we define ourselves internally.

It wouldn't be surprising to discover that she used that same self-description in various other conversations. In fact, it had probably become a cute slogan in her conversational inventory. It might have served a number of purposes: as a social gesture of humility; as a bid for empathy with the group; as a self-message of resignation; or as an invitation to pity.

Maybe she didn't really "mean" it. Maybe it was just "something she said"—just a cute way to make conversation with strangers.

Whatever the explanation, one important fact remains: *she said it.* That means that *the rest of her heard it.*

## CLEANING OUT THE ATTIC:
## MENTAL DECONTAMINATION

The phrase "positive thinking" has been around for many decades. It has become so common, I believe, that it has lost most of its meaning. Slogans like "Think positively," "Have a positive mental attitude," and "Be a positive thinker" have become hackneyed, shopworn, and uninspiring. People tend to think of "the Norman Vincent Peale stuff," slogans and recitations based on Peale's famous book *The Power of Positive Thinking.*[1] Indeed, Peale did dramatize the concepts skillfully— at least at his time and for the social environment he was writing for—and it's difficult to refute any of the key points in his book. Nevertheless it seems very clear that more people talk about "positive thinking" than actually practice it.

This is the main reason that I've chosen a more contemporary phrase in favor of the older, hackneyed term "positive thinking." Some people may be firmly glued to that phrase, and if they prefer to keep using it, I have no objection. Throughout this book, however, I've chosen to substitute a phrase that seems to me more descriptive, more focused, more contemporary, and more actionable: *affirmative thinking.* Here's a working definition:

> *Affirmative Thinking: A pattern of selective attention and ideation that supports a high level of mental health.*

In Chapter 6 we'll delve more deeply into the part that language plays in making us mentally well or unwell, and we'll study some verbal strategies and patterns that help to create and maintain a healthy state of inner experience. Because much of our conscious ideation finds expression in language, we can improve the nature of that ideation by using our language more intelligently. In this chapter, we shall begin by dwelling somewhat more heavily on the first element of the definition: selective attention.

As described in the definition above, affirmative thinking involves two primary patterns of mental activity: *selective attention* and *selective thinking.* Selective attention involves actively "censoring" what you allow into your mind and proactively choosing what you direct your attention to. Selective thinking involves dwelling intently on the kinds of ideas, reasoning processes, conclusions, and intentions that are more likely to bring you positive results in your life than negative results.

> "Change your thoughts and you change your world."
> —Norman Vincent Peale

## "SENSORSHIP": CHOOSING WHAT YOU WILL ALLOW INTO YOUR MIND

In the month after Marilyn Monroe ended her life, suicide rates in the United States increased by 12 percent; rates increased by 10 percent in England and Wales.

Studies of teen-age suicide patterns in America between 1973 and 1979 showed an increase of an average of about 7 percent in the seven days following thirty-eight nationally televised stories of suicide. In 1933—before television—a nineteen-year-old Japanese student, Kiyoko Matsumoto, committed suicide by jumping into the thousand-foot crater of a volcano on the island of Oshima. The news of her death, and the story of her despair, sparked a bizarre fashion across Japan: in the next few months, three hundred children did the same thing.

Each day about eighty-six Americans take their lives (not the same eighty-six, of course) and over 1,500 attempt to do so. The suicide rate in Japan is over one hundred per day, in a country with less than half the population of the United States.

Although few of us are driven to commit suicide—the ultimate act of self-disapproval—almost all of us are much more susceptible than we think we are to the programming messages we receive from the surrounding culture every day. There seems to be little doubt that the least well-adjusted among us take their cues from the entertainment environment. A number of teen-aged mass murderers have modeled their life's drama after the news stories about others of their kind. *Social modeling* is a primary basis for learning how to behave in various contexts, and the media coverage provides plenty of models for those few deranged individuals who want to make the ultimate statement.

*But the rest of us aren't immune, either.*

A mountain of research data now shows that heavy TV watchers, for example, tend to have a generally skewed perception of life and society that aligns more with the synthetic reality of the TV medium than with the culture as it is. They estimate crime rates to be much higher than they are; they rate their own chances of being assaulted or otherwise victimized as much higher than they are; they tend to express a more pessimistic and cynical view of life; and they tend to report higher levels of depression, anxiety, and suicidal ideation.

Students who are heavy TV watchers tend to do less well in their studies than those who watch little or no TV; they tend to report that they cheat more; and they tend to express lower levels of social intelligence than their media-free counterparts.

Television addiction, or more broadly *media addiction,* is increasingly recognized by psychologists and sociologists as a serious problem that impairs the mental health and social effectiveness of more and more people.

Think of your brain as very similar to the browser on your computer—the software you use to scan or surf the Internet. The only difference is that you're always connected to your perceptual environment; you can't turn off your biocomputer as you can turn off the computer on your desk or your lap. Your "mental browser" is taking in information from your environment, even to some extent while you sleep. *And everything that comes in has an effect.*

You can, however, choose what you pay attention to. By favoring information, images, sights, sounds, experiences, and people that support affirmative thinking, you can increase your chances of feeling better, being more healthy, and living longer. Just as you can "point" your computer browser at any Internet resource you choose, and thereby "de-select" all others, so too can you deploy your mental browser for your own good. Let's coin a phrase and call it *"sensorship."*

> *Sensorship: The practice of consciously and*
> *consistently choosing what you will allow*
> *into your mind.*

Most of us are so continuously bombarded by the influencing messages of our daily environment that it's difficult to stop and become aware of them and to consider their effects on our unconscious thinking.

We understand that the "news" tends to portray a morbid view of life, but there are many other messages, including some we don't even think of as conveying positive or negative influences. Consider one of a number of more subtle examples of environmental messages. Here's one that's generally not considered particularly important, yet it tends to seep into our thinking, and maybe even our attitudes about ourselves and about life. To remind yourself how all-pervasive the media culture is, consider for example the lyrics of some of the most popular songs of the Western culture.

"You're Nobody 'Til Somebody Loves You," made popular by the famous American crooner Dean Martin, conveys an interesting message. Taken literally, this song presumably means that your sense of self-worth should depend on having a suitable romantic relationship with a suitable partner.

Another popular song goes: "When somebody loves you, it's no good unless she loves you *all the way.*" Presumably, you can become somebody if somebody loves you, but not unless she loves you all the way. If somebody loves you a lot, but not really all the way, then presumably you're a partial somebody—or maybe you're a partial nobody. If several people each love you a little bit, would that be enough to make you a somebody?

Another all-time classic, dating back more than fifty years, is "You Belong to Me." ("See the pyramids along the Nile". . ., etc.) The mate to that song, I suppose, is "I'm Yours." ("I'm yours, heart and soul, I am yours . . .") When we human beings think—and sing—about one another in terms of property rights, are we really capable of loving and being loved unconditionally? Do we equate loving others with owning them or being owned by them?

American country-western music has long been the object of jokes for its preoccupation with grief, self-pity, failure, infidelity, and unrequited love. A popular classic for many decades was "The Tennessee Waltz," about a woman who introduced her best friend to her boyfriend and they waltzed away together. "Tom Dooley," a hugely popular song in the 1950s, told of a man who killed a beautiful woman and was about to be hanged. In Johnny Cash's "Folsom Prison Blues," the protagonist—serving a life term for murder—is sad, not because he's remorseful, but simply because he'll never get out.

Spoofs of country song titles testify to the prevalent themes of despair, low self-worth, and alienation. Titles like "I Miss You a Lot, But My Aim's Gettin' Better," "She Got the Goldmine and I Got the Shaft,"

"If the Phone Don't Ring, It's Me," and "If I'd 'a Shot You Sooner, I'd Be Out of Jail By Now" play upon the bittersweet angst of hillbilly and western music.

One website even offered some classic Jewish-country-western ballads:[2]

- "Mamas Don't Let Your Ungrateful Sons Grow Up to Be Cowboys (When You Could Very Easily Have Taken Over the Family Hardware Business That My Own Father Broke His Back to Start and Your Father Sweated Over for Forty-Five Years, Which Apparently Doesn't Mean Anything to You Now That You're Turning Your Back on Such a Gift to Ride Around All Day On Some *Meshuggenah* Horse)";
- "I Was One of the Chosen People ('Til She Chose Somebody Else)";
- And, of course, the ever-popular "Stand by Your Mensch."

Certainly it's unrealistic to suggest that anyone's mental health might be seriously impaired by the lyrics of a song—other than very rarely, at most—and we human beings sometimes do find a kind of perverse enjoyment in lamenting about our lot in life. We occasionally like to horrify ourselves by riding roller coasters and going to scary movies, and sometimes it feels good to feel bad. We can identify with the themes and lyrics of sad songs. In some ways, perhaps, they may even validate our personal experiences and help us take them less seriously.

The broader point, however, with respect to the policy of sensorship, is to remember that our emotional state and our unconscious processes can be colored by anything and everything that we take in. That simple fact makes a case for diligently preferring positive, affirmative, uplifting, optimistic, and hopeful thought processes—and the inputs that tend to invite them—far more than we prefer negative thoughts and inputs.

I'm not suggesting that everyone stop listening to all sad music or reading sad poetry and tragic novels. I am suggesting, however, that each of us can do well to make a conscious inventory, many times each day, of what we're accepting into our minds. And even the seemingly mundane inputs like music and entertainment deserve scrutiny.

Let's go a step further. Sensorship includes not only the information environment, but the *people* in your world as well. Many of the people who inhabit your social "bubble" are there at your invitation, or at least as a result of your acquiescence. Some of them may not deserve to be there. You may be sharing social space with people who undermine your efforts to maintain a positive state of mind.

In *Social Intelligence: The New Science of Success,* I defined *toxic* and *nourishing* behavior as:

> "*Toxic behavior*: a consistent pattern of behavior that makes others feel devalued, inadequate, angry, frustrated, or guilty.

> "*Nourishing behavior*: a consistent pattern of behavior that makes others feel valued, capable, loved, respected, and appreciated."[3]

We have the right, so far as circumstances permit, to prefer the company of nourishing people and de-select toxic people from our lives. Here's a simple and important truth:

> *You can "fire" anyone from your life whom you find*
> *toxic and disaffirming to your personhood.*

Some people have allowed their personal environments to become populated with toxic individuals, who consistently undermine their sense of emotional well-being. They may complain about the petty atrocities these others commit against their self-hood, and yet can't bring themselves to think of issuing "pink slips" to those who don't belong in their lives.

"I can't 'fire' my mother!" they may say. Why not? What obligation does one have to one's blood kin, who after all are only related by genetic accidents? Does one have any special obligation or responsibility to suffer at the hands of toxic fathers, mothers, brothers, sisters, aunts and uncles, or cousins that one doesn't acknowledge toward toxic people who are not genetically connected?

Of course, we often have to make tradeoffs in dealing with toxic individuals. Leaving a job, a marriage, or an important relationship is seldom as simple as just issuing a pink slip; there may be other consequences to consider. But "firing" someone might not necessarily mean never seeing him again; you might decide to limit it to reducing your interactions with the person, or setting a limited context for interacting that makes it less easy for him to drain your psychic energy.

It may be advisable to try to improve relationships or persuade some toxic people to treat you humanely. Just as a boss would be advised to get a "problem employee" to change his or her ways, and to fire the person only as a last resort, we can do the same thing with people in our lives who are "problem friends." Presumably almost everyone—employee or friend—deserves a "fair warning" before getting a "pink slip." But ultimately, each of us gets to make choices about the people and experiences we will allow to influence our lives, and consequently to influence our thoughts and our mental state.

## An Exercise

Draw a sketch with yourself in the center of a sheet of paper (use a stick figure if you like; it's not an artistic exercise), and then draw the constellation of people you experience, at least occasionally, during the course of a few months of normal living. Write each person's name beside his or her figure.

Now write a numerical score beside each person, ranging from 1 through 5, to code your sense of that person's influence on your life and your mental state. Use a 5 for the people you experience as consistently nourishing, supportive, affirmative, encouraging, and affectionate. Give a score of 1 for any person you experience as consistently negative, critical, argumentative, unkind, or unloving. Score the others along the scale as appropriate.

While you're at it, add to your diagram any particular experiences or activities you typically engage in; then score each of them in terms of its value to your mental health and well-being. Add your job, groups of people you hang out with, and any organizations you belong to.

You can do several things with this diagram. For one, you can rededicate your energies to appreciating those you do find nourishing and affirmative. Make sure that you show by your behavior that you are grateful for having them in your life. And remind yourself to appreciate, at least mentally, the activities and opportunities that support your mental health and well-being.

Second, you can think carefully about the tradeoffs you've been making by continuing to have the toxic people, experiences, or situations in your life. De-selecting some of them from your social browser might be difficult—your boss or your spouse, for example. Ultimately you have three choices for dealing with a toxic relationship or a toxic situation: you can change it; you can accept it and adjust to it the best you can; or you can leave it.

Firing a person from your life need not be a hostile or aggressive act. It can be done calmly, politely, and even lovingly. If you haven't been able to improve the situation sufficiently, and you believe your immune system is ultimately at risk, you can simply say something like, "I've been thinking about my life lately, and I've been deciding what my personal priorities really are. I've decided that I only want positive relationships with positive people. I don't know how to build a positive relationship with you that serves my needs, so I've decided not to see you any more. I don't harbor any animosity toward you; I just find that there's no place in my life for this relationship any longer."

One can apply this sensorship policy to the whole of life. The first requirement, of course, is to become more fully conscious of what we're actually taking into our minds. Then we can make better choices that bring better results in our lives.

## RESISTANCE TO ENCULTURATION, A.K.A. "CRAP DETECTING"

In his provocative book, *Teaching as a Subversive Activity,*[4] New York University Professor Neil Postman quoted writer Ernest Hemingway as declaring: "To be a good writer you have to have a good, built-in, shock-proof *bullshit detector.*" Putting it much more politely, the humanistic psychologist Abraham Maslow cited the necessary skill of *resistance to enculturation.*

Postman, presumably shooting for the middle ground between the vulgar and the polite versions, coined the term "crap detecting." I find that term refreshingly offensive and very useful.

Hemingway, Maslow, and Postman—and many leading thinkers throughout history—have advocated the importance of the individual's ability to see past and through the curtain of culture. They believed that each of us has a responsibility to ourselves, and to our fellow human beings, to refuse to take what we see and hear at face value.

It's easy to become hypnotized by the swirl of messages that surround us: do this but don't do that; buy this, own that, wear this, drive that; eat this, drink that, smoke this; don't believe them—believe us; don't side with them—side with us; demonize this person and idolize that person; worship this or that celebrity. *We're much more the products of our cultural environment than we want to believe.*

Being skilled at crap detecting means not being gullible, but it doesn't mean being cynical. Not everyone is out to "put one over on you"—it's just that some people are, and if you're conscious of the possibilities, you can perceive and react appropriately.

Perhaps a practical definition of crap detecting is in order:

*Crap detecting: A non-gullible and non-cynical*
*habit of considering the potential motives and*
*purposes behind what people tell us.*

The temptation of human beings to mislead and manipulate one another probably goes at least as far back as our ability to use language— and maybe even to draw pictures. Masses of people have been incited to war, cowed into fear, and separated from their hard-earned yams by disreputable individuals who've learned to play upon their unconscious impulses and emotions.

Hermann Goering, Hitler's second in command and chief of the German *Luftwaffe,* spoke confidently of the ease with which people can be induced to go to war. Interviewed in his cell during the Nuremburg trials by Gustave Gilbert, an intelligence officer and psychologist, Goering was quite candid about his methods. Gilbert kept a journal of his observations of the proceedings and his conversations with the prisoners, which he published in his book *Nuremberg Diary.* He relates part of a conversation with Goering in his cell on the evening of April 18, 1946:

> "We got around to the subject of war again and I said that, contrary to his attitude, I did not think that the common people are very thankful for leaders who bring them war and destruction.
>
> "'Why, of course, the *people* don't want war,' Goering shrugged. 'Why would some poor slob on a farm want to risk his life in a war when the best that he can get out of it is to come back to his farm in one piece? Naturally, the common people don't want war; neither in Russia nor in England nor in America, nor for that matter in Germany. That is understood. But, after all, it is the *leaders* of the country who determine the policy and it is always a simple matter to drag the people along, whether it is a democracy or a fascist dictatorship or a Parliament or a Communist dictatorship.'

"'There is one difference,' I pointed out. 'In a democracy the people have some say in the matter through their elected representatives, and in the United States only Congress can declare wars.'

"'Oh, that is all well and good, but, voice or no voice, the people can always be brought to the bidding of the leaders. That is easy. All you have to do is tell them they are being attacked and denounce the pacifists for lack of patriotism and exposing the country to danger. *It works the same way in any country.*'"5

He was probably right.

In every culture, there are a few "deep thinkers" and a large number of "sheep thinkers." This may seem like an unkind assessment of the human condition, but it hardly seems arguable in the grand scheme. Totalitarian leaders know that their most dangerous enemies are the deep thinkers. Not only can they think clearly, but they can often encourage the sheep thinkers to turn on their crap detectors and rethink what they've been told. That's why virtually all dictators and demagogues try to silence the intelligentsia and inhibit the expression of political opposition in the media.

> "The men the American people admire most
> extravagantly are the most daring liars;
> the men they detest most violently are those
> who try to tell them the truth."
>
> —H.L. Mencken

What makes the sheep thinkers so easy to manipulate, as Goering observed, is the fact that they like having clear and simple answers, value having firm opinions, and are utterly convinced that they "think for themselves." They typically form their opinions and views of the world from "official" sources in the surrounding media environment. Whoever controls those media controls their opinions, for the most part.

Brainwashing works best when the washees are convinced that their brains haven't been washed.

*Case in point*: every year, the United States President is required by law to appear before a joint session of the Congress and report on the "State of the Union." And every year, virtually without fail, each President's public approval ratings increase by 5 to 10 percentage points in the opinion polls taken during the following two weeks. Professional pollsters know that opinion polls, in modern media-based cultures, mostly measure the impact of news coverage, not the thought processes of the masses.

Resistance to enculturation also includes what we think of as intellectual courage, or "having the courage of our convictions."

*Case in point*: Guglielmo Marconi, an Italian inventor and one of the early pioneers of radio and electronics, believed that it was possible to send radio signals over long distances, so that people would be able to communicate between continents. The weight of almost all reputable scientific opinion was against him; scientists in 1900 believed that radio waves, which traveled in straight lines, could never be used over long distances because of the limitations imposed by the curvature of the earth. Marconi decided to try it anyway. On December 12, 1901, he set up a specially designed wireless receiver in Newfoundland, Canada, and received a Morse-code signal—the letter "S," represented by three pulses, or "dots"—from Poldhu, Cornwall, in England. Just over a year later, on January 18, 1903, he sent a message of greetings from President Theodore Roosevelt to King Edward VII, who sent his reply. Several years later, scientists discovered the *ionosphere,* the layer of charged particles in the earth's atmosphere that have the effect of refracting or "bending" short-wave radio signals, causing them to follow the contours of the earth. Marconi's intellectual courage was rewarded: he received the Nobel Prize in physics in 1909.

Part of intellectual courage is knowing when to listen to the advice of others and when to trust your own judgments.

# CLEANSE YOUR MIND
# WITH A "MEDIA FAST"

Mohandas Gandhi, one of the most revered thinkers and thought lead-ers in history, made a habit of spending one day each week in silence. Usually on a Monday, he wouldn't speak, nor would he be spoken to. He used the time for reflection, reading, and listening to his own mind. Through silent work, meditation, and exercise, he attempted to redis-cover the center of his intelligence. Many of us could benefit from find-ing the wisdom of our own silence.

While many of us may think that such a practice would be com-pletely impossible in today's sensory-overload world, consider that in his later years Gandhi often met with political organizers, journalists, and high government officials, as well as the students at his *ashram*. His attention was in great demand, yet he found time to meditate, to spin cotton thread on his primitive spinning wheel, and to study the classics of religious literature. If Gandhi could do it, so can we—if we think it's important enough. The challenges are different for us, but no greater than those Gandhi faced.

Admittedly, so much conspires against our mental peace, tranquil-ity, and privacy. Almost everywhere we go in the modern commercial-ized culture, sights and sounds demand our attention. The radio in the car; the boom-box blaring in the hands of teen-agers walking by or from another teen's car; the television in the airport waiting area and the relentless security announcements over the public address system; the in-flight movie or the video news on the airplane; the rock music playing over the sound system in the coffee shop or restaurant; the per-son talking on the cell phone at the next table; the jarring sights and sounds of TV news; the raucous diatribes of political talk shows on radio; and of course the relentless hammering of the TV set at home.

Many of us spend vast amounts of our time imprisoned in environ-ments that include man-made sights and sounds almost exclusively. How often do we cast our eyes on scenes that contain no evidence of human activity, and whose sounds and smells are those of nature and not of "civilization"?

Audiovisual pollution has become so commonplace that many of us have lost all sense of our entitlement to peace and quiet. The "news" in particular, that strange combination of anxiety and amusement, has become ever more unreal, unrealistic, and surreal. In my book *Social Intelligence: The New Science of Success,* I described the "Only Ten Basic News Stories":[6]

1. *Shock and Horror*—the school shooting, for example.
2. *Tragedy*—hurricanes and other disasters are great for this category.
3. *Hot Sex*—celebrity porn always makes a good story.
4. *Scandal*—we love to see the rascals get found out.
5. *The Fall of the Mighty*—show us the rich and powerful getting knocked off their pedestals.
6. *Conflict*—always adds "juice" to a news story; people love to watch a fight, even if it's only a name-calling match.
7. *Worry*—tell me what to worry about this week: Hurricanes? Gas prices? Crime?
8. *Voyeurism*—show me something bizarre, sick, twisted, or lurid.
9. *Dilemmas*—abortion, capital punishment, euthanasia, gay marriage; irresolvable conflicts are easy to disguise as "balanced" reporting.
10. *"Gee-Whiz" stories* (change of pace)—give me something cute or fun now and then, so I won't think the news is all negative: the spelling bee, for example, or the dog who rescues the elderly lady from the fire.

Dr. Andrew Weil, one of the most highly respected holistic health practitioners, recommends a one-week "news fast" as part of his "Eight Weeks to Optimum Health" plan. Weil advises:

"I want you to discover and make use of the fact that you have choice as to how much news you allow into your consciousness, especially if it disturbs your emotional and spiritual equilibrium."

You can reduce the cultural noise level coming into your mind in stages. Consider making one day per week a *TV-free day*. (This is a movement that is gaining acceptance in the United States and other media-based cultures.) Leave the TV set turned off from midnight to midnight. You may need to negotiate with your family—or use your personal authority—to get them to cooperate. Simply staying out of the room while a TV is operating doesn't help much to free your mind if you can still hear it.

Once you can get through a full TV-free day on a regular basis, start locking other media channels out of your consciousness. Don't watch recorded video material and don't go to the movies on your media-free day.

Progress from there to leaving all radios turned off on your media-free day. That includes drive-time radio broadcasts and especially radio news. Leave the music turned off as you drive. Make a conscious effort to choose your activities so that you'll seldom be exposed to other people's media pollution.

Once you've become comfortable with turning off all broadcast and televisual media, progress to leaving newspapers and magazines out of your life on your media-free day. Don't even read the advertising material that comes in your mail on that day.

So: no TV, no movies, no videotaped or digital video watching, no radio, no music, no newspapers, and no magazines. For your next challenge, stay off of the Internet for the full twenty-four hours of your media-free day. Once you can do that, make it through the day with your cell phone switched off.

The first few times you experience a full-day media fast, you may feel rather strange, possibly somewhat disoriented, maybe even deprived.

You'll start to become conscious of how much of your time and attention are involuntarily confiscated by the passive consumption of cultural junk food. You may feel a sense of something missing—a familiar ritual that's been taken away. Your sense of time may seem less compartmentalized and less incremental.

Eventually, you'll probably experience a general sense of greater calm, a less frenetic sense of what's going on around you, and relief from a lingering, low-grade sense of urgency. You'll have no choice but to listen to your own interior monologue. Without the many distractions imposed on your consciousness, you may enjoy spending more time with your thoughts. Ask yourself: "What am I learning as I clear my mind of media pollution, and how can this special state of attention help me?"

After I removed all broadcast TV signals from my home about five years ago, I experienced a noticeable shift in my state of mind. I felt more placid, more optimistic, more open to new experience, and more charitable toward myself and others. It's no exaggeration to say that I felt my mind had been cleansed, to some extent. I still watch selected movies from time to time—particularly the old classics, musicals, and comedies, and I feel no loss in not having broadcast video material in my personal environment.

## RE-ENGINEERING YOUR ATTITUDES

Remember the fundamental principle: *we think with the whole body*. That means that what we call an "attitude" is a whole-body information pattern. The conscious ideation links to unconscious ideation, as well as to emotional patterns and even somatic, or visceral, patterns. Affirmative attitudes are positive information patterns and negative attitudes are negative information patterns—they have desirable or undesirable effects throughout the body.

Our cultural history abounds with stories that encode a very basic belief: attitudes can heal and attitudes can kill. A witch doctor or a voodoo priestess points a bone menacingly at someone and that person takes to bed and stays there until he dies. A person with advanced terminal cancer undergoes an emotional transformation and the cancer goes into remission. One person who seems to have much to live for takes his or her own life, while a person who is severely disabled decides that life is worth living and achieves a large measure of success and happiness.

Between the attitudes that kill and those that heal, there are attitudes that shape our health and well-being every day. Consider attitudes like jealousy, envy, or resentment. They can predispose us to react and behave antagonistically toward others, and often to our own disadvantage.

Attitudes are options. The motivational speakers and writers tell us that "the difference between success and failure (and happiness and unhappiness, by the way) can be summed up in one word: *attitude*." Cliché or not, they're basically right. The word "attitude" and the concepts behind it may seem somewhat vague at first thought, but the more you think about it the clearer the concept becomes.

Here's a simple definition:

*Attitude: A mental state that predisposes a person to think, react, and behave in certain ways.*

This definition is like the way pilots describe the attitude of an airplane in flight. The attitude of an aircraft or a spacecraft is its orientation at any one instant: its location at a point in space and time, the direction to which its nose is pointing, the angle of its wings to horizontal, and the angle of its fuselage—level, climbing, or diving. Its attitude is constantly changing—it must, or it will fall to earth—and where it goes in the next second is predicted by its attitude at this moment.

We humans are a lot like the airplane. What we think, say, and do in the next moment depends largely on the attitude we carry in our minds at this moment. A "defiant" attitude may predispose us to argue, to oppose the intentions of others, or to reject offers to cooperate. A "placating" attitude may predispose us to try to make peace; of course, it could also work against our own interests in some situations. An attitude of "contempt" may predispose us to discount what someone says or to refuse to acknowledge his or her rights or interests in a situation.

Some of our attitudes are transient, as we react to various situations. Others may be more durable, more lingering in their effects on our thoughts, reactions, and actions. Another term for a dominant, enduring attitude is a *mindset*. A mindset is a fixed management of ideas, beliefs, values, and conclusions that shape the way we perceive, react, and behave. Just as a table setting affects the way people share a meal, a mindset affects the way we think. Some of our mindsets may not be serving us well.

*Case in point:* consider the attitude of *vengeance*. In the form of an adjective, we describe it as being vengeful, as wanting revenge. We also refer to it as carrying a grudge, wanting to retaliate, or "get even." The effect of a vengeful mindset is twofold: it *causes* us to behave in certain ways and *prevents* us from behaving in some other ways. Conflict situations can easily draw people into vengeful attitudes. A bitterly contested divorce, the break-up of a business venture, or a political battle for control of a corporation can often lead people to become vengeful. Unfortunately, acting out of vengeance can often achieve exactly the opposite of one's overall purpose. Many people who get caught up in the throes of a bitter divorce are tempted to use legal procedures in hopes of inflicting injury on the other party. Divorce lawyers know that a contested divorce is much more profitable than an amicable one; many of them are tempted to help the protagonists fight rather than cooperate. *Revenge is often more costly, in the long run, to the revenge-seeker than to the presumed enemy.*

Here's one of the most important facts of life you can ever learn:

> *Aggressive attitudes are attachments—they shackle*
> *us to the people or objects on which we focus them.*

*Case in point:* you're driving your car in heavy traffic, when an aggressive driver cuts in front of you, causing you to have to hit your brakes suddenly. Depending on your state of mind—your attitude or mindset at the moment—you might become angry at this unprovoked injustice. You blow your horn at the delinquent driver, as if to punish him for this misbehavior. You follow closely on his tail and you glare at him in case he looks into his mirror. Your heart rate increases, your blood pressure rises, your hormones start pumping, and you forget the pleasant thoughts you were having just a few seconds ago. The reptilian circuits of your brain kick in and you're now bent on revenge. You note that the traffic in your lane is slowing, and the adjacent lane has picked up speed. You quickly shift over to the faster lane. As he increases his speed to try to jump in front of you again, you increase your speed to pass him and keep him boxed in. As the car in front of him increases speed, you move closer to the car in front of you, to make sure he stays stuck in his box. *You've temporarily set aside your sanity to engage in a battle of egos with a complete stranger.* And there's nothing to win; the best you can hope for is to trade one negative emotion—anger—for another negative emotion—the squalid glee that comes with making someone else become angry. And your immune system will register the effects of the stress.

It seems appropriate that we often refer to being angry as "being mad." Mad it is.

If you've ever experienced the case example we just reviewed, or something like it, consider that you've allowed the other person to inflict psychological discomfort on you, not once, but twice. The first event is when you become angry as a result of his misbehavior. The second event is when you go into the revenge mode. You've become *dysfunctionally attached* to this stranger. While you're trying to even the score, you're psychologically hooked to him—he's become your evil twin. While he may not know it, and probably doesn't think of it that way, you're allowing him to determine how you feel.

Suppose you could train yourself—and indeed you can—to diminish the strength of your reaction to this provocation, and all such similar provocations? Suppose that you hit the brakes, react with mild anger for a second or two, and then let the incident go. You let it fade into history. Recognizing that no valuable outcome is possible by continuing to interact with the person who has misbehaved, you simply abstain from blaming, criticizing, and retaliating. You go on with your life. Your emotional state returns to a healthy positive level within a few seconds or at most in less than one minute.

This may seem like an abnormal human reaction but actually it's a very wise one, and a very effective one. By not going into the anger and revenge mode, you actually free yourself from the other person's influence much sooner than you otherwise would. You needn't condemn nor forgive: you simply detach your emotional state from the event. Think of it this way:

*The best revenge is not needing revenge.*

In just about all cases, negative emotions cause us to become *uncentered*: we get disconnected from the authentic source of our ideas and reactions, and we begin to figuratively "orbit" the person or circumstance we're preoccupied with. Consider the liberating effect of letting go of a variety of negative, aggressive, or fearful attitudes that we human beings have built into our minds over the many thousands of years of our existence:

- *Envy*: when we envy others, our attention becomes negative rather than affirmative, and we attach it to those others rather than keeping it optimistic and affirmative and letting it flow toward the things we want and deserve.
- *Jealousy*: when we cause a state of jealousy in ourselves, we devalue our own worth; we try to compete with others for the approval of those to whom we've given power over our sense of self.

- *Greed*: when we pursue the acquisition of *things*—including money, which is a proxy for acquiring things—we make the things our masters; we make our self-worth contingent on having the things rather than being authentically who we are.
- *Guilt*: when we accept guilt, we allow the disapproval of others to control our emotional state; when we behave in self-compromising ways to avoid the guilt that others would impose upon us, we bargain away our self-esteem.
- *Contempt*: when we hold others in contempt, we emotionalize our perceptions of them in a negative way; we tie ourselves to them unnecessarily through the negative energy that flows from us to them.

In all cases, the liberation from negative attitudes toward people and experiences comes from letting go of our negative emotional connections to them, perceiving them in an emotionally neutral way—even if we're engaged in adversarial interactions with them—returning to our natural center point, and reclaiming our energy so that we can "recycle" it into positive form and redirect it toward positive ends.

## THE ATTITUDE OF GRATITUDE

Some years ago I had the distinct pleasure of meeting Dr. Hans Selye, who was one of the pioneering researchers in the medical study of stress and its effects on human beings.

I was in my hotel room in Monterey, California, preparing to leave to walk the one block to a conference center where Selye was to address a large meeting of social service and mental health experts. He had agreed to write an opening message—a foreword—for my book *Stress and the Manager,* which was due to be published shortly. I had informed him by letter that I planned to attend the conference and hoped to shake his hand and express my thanks for his contribution.

The telephone rang; it was Dr. Selye, inviting me to pick him up at his room and walk together to the conference center. I knocked on the door to his room and there appeared a small gnome of a man—he was nearing age seventy at the time—who was engaged intently in making an extra hole in his new belt with a Swiss Army knife. Gracious, engaging, elegantly humble, and with a twinkle in his eye, he took a few minutes to praise my book and to share some thoughts on a philosophical level.

One thing he told me has stayed with me for the many years since that meeting, and I believe I've been able to understand the depth of its meaning, perhaps a little bit more every day. It was a very simple, but ultimately profound idea.

"Karl," he said [I'm paraphrasing here, with literary license], we know that our state of mind has an inevitable effect on our health and well-being. By now this finding is irrefutable, and it's inescapable. What I've concluded so far is that the best way to stay mentally and physically healthy is to live our lives with an *attitude of gratitude*."

There wasn't time for him to elaborate much further on the idea; as we walked the few hundred feet to the conference center, he was beset by a series of admirers. "Are you Dr. Selye?" one after another would ask. With that trademark twinkle and a mischievous smile, he would say, with his charming Hungarian accent, "That is my tragedy." I suppose the fans assumed I was his bodyguard or some such person, considering that I had no equivalent face recognition at the time.

An *attitude of gratitude*: that poetic phrase, simple and yet subtle, started me thinking more seriously and diligently about the whole "mind-body" connection, and wondering whether we humans could actually learn to voluntarily find and sustain special states of mind conducive to healing and to maintaining mental and physical health.

Combining Selye's advice with findings from many other sources, particularly brain research, hypnotherapy, and information systems, I began to reflect on the nature of "moods." We use the term "mood" to describe an emotional state, usually connected with a particular set of ideas and reactions, which changes from moment to moment. Is it possible, I asked, to manage our moods voluntarily and deliberately, rather than simply allow them to be triggered and controlled by our experiences?

I've since come to believe, and to apply in my own life, the notion of finding a particular mood that's conducive to mental health and well-being.

Hans Selye and many other researchers have speculated that the special configuration of ideas, feelings, reactions, and intentions that are associated with certain particular mental states causes a chain of reactions throughout the body that support healing.

As we'll see in Chapter 11, your immune system is constantly listening in on your thought processes. Every thought you have gets expressed as a set of chemical messages and nervous-system patterns that flash throughout your body. Reputable research studies clearly show that the status of the immune system, including the number and types of immune cells and the concentration of various immuno-proteins, rises and falls in direct relationship to the ongoing mental process. The work of Drs. Carl and Stephanie Simonton with terminal cancer patients clearly supports the idea that states of mind can cause, aggravate, ameliorate—and even cure—cancer and other life-threatening diseases.

## THE ATTITUDE OF ABUNDANCE

One of the old clichés of "positive thinking" refers to "seeing the wine bottle as half-full versus seeing it as half-empty." Comedian George Carlin has an answer: "The #*$! bottle's too big!" My own view is: "It depends on who's been drinking the wine. If it's me, the other half is in my tummy." Actually, I only drink wine occasionally, so half a bottle is plenty for me.

What we're playing with in this little "mental riff" is the concept of *abundance*. Each person, through the complex and unique maze of personal experiences that shapes his or her view of self and world, evolves a sense of what it takes to survive and thrive in life. Each of us builds up an unconscious *complex*—a constellation of mental patterns and reactions, as psychologist Carl Jung defined it—associated with scarcity and abundance.

One person might evolve an unconscious belief structure around a sense of risk, loss, deprivation, and impermanence. "You can't trust anybody." "You have to fight for what you want." "Life is a battle; there are winners and losers." "Don't get too attached to anything or anyone, because you might lose it." At the extreme, scarcity-minded people can become overly conserving, unrealistically thrifty, pessimistic, ungenerous, fearful, risk-averse, envious, secretive, suspicious, and sometimes highly competitive. Many therapists believe that obesity, and chronic overeating in general, are often linked to an unconscious sense of scarcity and loss, sometimes acquired in childhood.

We get plenty of cultural signals that seem to sell a world view of scarcity. Many of our cultural norms suggest that people who compete fiercely are more deserving of admiration than those who cooperate. War making is far more popular than peace making. In recent years, Western business thinking seems to have moved toward a scarcity-based mindset, with hyper-competition evolving into a "zero-sum" mentality. "Business is war," the popular business writers tell us." The T-shirt slogan "Second place is just the first loser" telegraphs a win-lose, zero-sum principle of life, anchored in scarcity.

Abundance-minded people are less likely to view life though a lens of risk, loss, and winning versus losing, and more through a lens of shared fate and faith in unanticipated consequences. They tend to be less fearful, less anxious, less aggressive, more optimistic, more generous, and more willing to believe that "things turn out for the best if you know how to make the best of the way things turn out." They tend not to react enviously or resentfully to the success or good fortune of others. They can praise, appreciate, and affirm others without feeling that they're diminishing themselves. They can give of themselves generously without expecting a *quid pro quo* payback.

Interestingly, both abundance-minded people and scarcity-minded people tend to find the supporting evidence in everyday life to justify their beliefs.

Part of abundance thinking is letting go of the desperate attachment to individual outcomes. If I want to get A but I actually get B, I can grieve and get angry about not having A, but I may very well find that B turns out to be a fortunate outcome as well. If I stay stuck on wanting A, I may not appreciate the satisfaction that *not getting* A has bestowed upon me.

Buddhist teaching posits that most of human misery is caused by emotionalized desire. Letting go of anxious desire does not mean giving up on getting the results you want—or at least getting the results that may be feasible in a particular set of circumstances. It merely means not attaching yourself emotionally to a particular outcome. Letting go of the anxious attachment empowers you to work non-anxiously toward your desired outcome, and also to adjust your thinking and your strategies to your experience as it unfolds.

## PRACTICAL ALTRUISM

A good way to sum up a whole variety of life-affirming attitudes into one package—one mega-attitude—is to think in terms of *altruism*. It's a familiar word but not one that gets a lot of use in conversation. For some people, it seems to suggest a naïve tendency to do good things for people at the sacrifice of one's own interests. The really noble human beings, the real humanitarians, may be capable of thinking and behaving altruistically, but for the rest of us "normals," it seems a bit too much. An admirable trait, perhaps, but not a realistic way to live and function.

Certainly, not everyone is easy to love; in fact, some people seem to specialize in making it difficult for others to love them. Situations can often put people into conflict with one another. Neighbors can become enemies. People or departments in a business can get caught up into competition with one another. History, tradition, precedent, and habit can feed long-running conflicts and feuds. And, of course, there are people who like to cheat, manipulate, and use others for their selfish ends. Why should we be altruistic when others are behaving selfishly?

The answer is profoundly simple: *it's not about the others—it's about us.* It's about fully owning your emotional state, your frame of mind, your attitudes, and your reactions. It's about finding your center and disconnecting from the provocations of people and situations and behaving from a mentality of non-aggression, optimism, and even generosity.

In our saner moments, we realize that we tend to get better results in dealing with most people and most situations by approaching them in a positive, cooperative spirit rather than antagonistic spirit. But how often do we lose sight of that simple truth? Let's think of it as *practical altruism*—less idealistic and more realistic.

> "You can catch more flies with a drop of honey
> than with a gallon of gall."
>
> —Abraham Lincoln

If you subscribe to the principle of *karma,* as it has been Westernized, you can think in terms of the "karmic loop," which is the roundabout connection between your actions and your consequences. Some actions have immediate consequences, others have longer-term consequences, and some even have consequences after we leave the planet. If you insist that your good deeds be rewarded immediately, or at least sooner than you forget that you've done them, that's not altruism—it's paycheck psychology.

Dr. Albert Schweitzer, the revered physician and humanitarian who devoted his life to helping others, said:

> "No ray of sunlight is ever lost, but the green which it awakens into existence needs time to grow, and it is not always granted to the sower to see the harvest. All work that is worth anything is done in faith."

Dr. Milton H. Erickson, widely regarded as one of history's most gifted hypnotherapists, treated thousands of people in his long career and taught many therapists to facilitate the linkage between state of mind and well-being. He and others believed that a distinctive pattern of ideation, possibly uniquely different for each individual, could be the facilitating influence for virtually all self-healing.

The research and clinical practice of Drs. Carl and Stephanie Simonton rests upon this "healing state of mind" concept. For many years the Simontons have treated people diagnosed with terminal cancer in their Texas facility. Early in their work they concluded that a majority of terminal cancer patients carried around with them a distinctive unconscious complex—a belief system and a constellation of associated ideas that could actually weaken their immune responses and predispose them to growing tumors or not being able to reject them.

The Simontons discerned in their patients what they described as a "victim" mentality. Beyond the implications of their health problems, they seemed to view themselves as helpless failures in life. In one vernacular: they thought of themselves as being eternally *at effect,* rather than being *at cause.* They thought of themselves not as making things happen in their lives, but as being the perpetual victims of things that happened. This passivity, and its associated ideation of fear, doubt, and impotence, set them up for disease.

A primary element of the comprehensive therapeutic cancer intervention developed by the Simontons was an intensive process of re-education on the part of the patients. They learned, through cognitive therapy, counseling, and training in meditation and visualization, to reassert themselves as the causative agents in their lives. Following on from the re-engineering of their attitudes, they learned to use vivid mental images to counteract the development of their cancers. This combination of attitude and images has become a key aspect of a number of modern schools of therapy and personal growth.

In my investigation of various therapeutic concepts, particularly hypnotherapy and the developing field of *psychoneuroimmunology,* I believe

I've begun to perceive the features of a more or less generic mental state that could be associated with healing and well-being. As implied by this discussion, this ideational state seems to deserve a label something like altruism. Practical altruism seems to be its incarnation when we interact with the world. As we learn to acquire and hold onto a particular state of ideation—a whole-body complex of thought—altruism in general seems to be an appropriate label to capture the sense of it.

There's an old novelty song that explains how "the knee bone's connected to the thigh bone, the thigh bone's connected to the hip bone," and so on for many verses. Attitudes are like the parts in that song: the attitude of gratitude is connected to the attitude of generosity, which is connected to the attitude of abundance, which is connected to the attitude of optimism, and so the attitude song goes. By reflecting on and appreciating the various positive attitudes available to us, and letting go of the dysfunctional attitudes that don't serve us well, we can truly cleanse our minds.

## MEDITATION, MINDMOVIES, AND AFFIRMATIONS

In Chapter 13 we'll explore some of the more advanced methods of mental programming and affirmative thinking, particularly the use of meditation and visualization. We'll explore both *silent meditation,* which is using a "mantra-word" to quiet the mind and release the processes of relaxation and healing; and *active meditation,* which uses self-programming mental messages that contribute to healthier mental processes and greater well-being.

We'll also explore the effective use of *affirmations* and *recitations,* which are verbal self-messages that translate our intentions into messages to the unconscious levels of the biocomputer. As we'll see, many of the popular "positive thinking" slogans are limited in their effectiveness because they're not designed to match the software functions of the subconscious process. When we add audiovisual components to them—emotionally impactful language, auditory cues that hook into deeper levels of ideation, and mental images that match the way we want things to be—our affirmations and recitations can become powerful cues to reinforce affirmative thinking, motivation, and diligence in pursuit of our goals.

We'll also explore "mindmovies," which are vivid multisensory mental rehearsals of what we want to cause to happen. By building a clear and compelling "script" for the outcomes we want, and by repeatedly experiencing the desired sequence of events in our imagination, we have a greater chance of getting the results we want than by just hoping for them.

Meditations, mindmovies, and affirmations are important elements of a success-oriented mentality. Author and motivational speaker Richard Israel contends:

*"In life, there's no success and there's no failure:*
*You get what you program for."*

# Notes

1. Peale, Norman Vincent. *The Power of Positive Thinking.* New York: Ballantine, 1996.
2. Website of Pete Levin. www.PeteLevin.com.
3. Albrecht, Karl. *Social Intelligence: The New Science of Success.* San Francisco: Jossey-Bass, 2006 (p. 12).
4. Postman, Neil. *Teaching as a Subversive Activity.* New York: Delacorte, 1969.
5. Gilbert, G.M. *Nuremberg Diary.* New York: Farrar, Straus and Company, 1947 (pp. 278–279).
6. Albrecht, Karl. Social *Intelligence: The New Science of Success.* San Francisco: Jossey-Bass, 2006 (p. 12).

# 6

## *MENTAL SOFTWARE*
## *UPGRADE 3*
### *Adopting Sane Language Habits*

> "'When I use a word,' Humpty Dumpty said
> in a rather scornful tone, 'it means just what
> I choose it to mean, neither more nor less.'
> 'The question is,' said Alice, 'whether you can
> make words mean so many different things.'
> 'The question is,' said Humpty Dumpty,
> which is to be master—that's all.'"
> —Lewis Carroll, *Through the Looking Glass*

ABRAHAM LINCOLN ENJOYED POSING A RIDDLE to his associates: "If you call the dog's tail a leg, how many legs does he have?" Most of them would answer "Five." Lincoln would reply, "No, he has four legs. Calling a tail a leg doesn't make it a leg."

What's the difference between a "motorcycle club" and a "motor-cycle gang"? What's the difference between a "terrorist" and a "freedom fighter"? Anti-abortion activists say they're "pro-life," while pro-abortion activists say they're "pro-choice." Which one is "correct"? Are we saying something different if we describe a person as a "politician" rather than a "member of Parliament" or a "member of Congress"?

Let's think about words—*really* think about words. Words are much more than simple, inanimate symbols—just verbal "data." In the human biocomputer they have enormous power. They invoke meanings and emotional associations in those who use them and those who hear them. Words can be weapons, they can be tools, and they can be art. They can inspire, incite, inflame, soothe, inform, educate, mislead, manipulate, and confuse.

Many famous leaders have understood and capitalized on the psy-chology of language and have used this knowledge to arouse and mobi-lize people, for both good and evil. Poetry, literature, popular slogans, metaphors, and patriotic songs all have the power to move people in profound ways.

The study of *rhetoric,* for example, deals with the primal patterns of language, and how they convey meaning beyond the mere symbolic data of words. For example, at the time of the American Declaration of Independence from Britain, Benjamin Franklin reportedly made one of the most memorable statements of the time. When one of his fellow statesmen said, after the group had passed the Declaration of Independence, "Now gentlemen, we must all hang together," Franklin replied "Indeed, we must, or assuredly we shall hang separately."

## LANGUAGE AS MENTAL SOFTWARE: WHAT YOU SAY IS WHAT YOU THINK

Alfred Korzybski, a respected scholar and researcher who studied the psychology of language, proposed a kind of "theory of relativity" of knowledge, in his book *Science and Sanity,* published in 1933. He coined the term *general semantics* to describe his theory of how the structure of language shapes human thought, and particularly how certain language habits contribute to conflict, misunderstandings, and even psychological maladjustment.[1]

Korzybski asserted that there is no such thing as "universal truth" or "universal knowledge," and in contradiction to the teachings of a long line of philosophers starting with Socrates, Plato, and Aristotle, he believed that the structure and psychology of language made it impossible for any two minds to ever know exactly the same "reality." Speakers of English, he maintained, do not construct the same models of reality with their words—"verbal maps", as he called them—as speakers of Japanese, Swahili, or Spanish. Since different languages represent concepts in different ways, the structural differences of those languages impose unavoidable differences on our mental models of reality.

Korzybski believed that Aristotle, although greatly respected as an historical figure, was trapped inside a mental box he could not detect: the structure of his own native language. His attempts to define universal, abstract concepts such as truth, virtue, responsibility, and man's relationship to nature and God were, Korzybski argued, doomed to failure. They would always be bounded by the structure of the ancient Greek world-view as encoded in the Greek language. He referred to this view, disparagingly, as "Aristotelian thinking."

The Renaissance philosopher René Descartes compounded the problem, in Korzybski's view, by selling scholars for generations to come on the idea of a two-part reality, based on verbal dualisms. Korzybski referred to this compulsive dualism as "Cartesian thinking."

Even worse, Korzybski argued, any two speakers of the same language do not even share exactly the same reality, because each person grows up learning his or her own unique meanings for the many words in his or her native language. "Meanings," he pointed out, "are not in the *words*; they are in the *people*."

To state the theory of general semantics in its simplest terms: No two brains contain exactly the same "meaning" for any word, expression, or concept; therefore there can be no universal true-for-everybody meaning of any "verbal map."

Serious issues can arise from the dominating influence of language on thought and behavior. For example, arguments over the meanings of abstractions like "democracy," "capitalism," and "justice" are ultimately futile, because they have differing personal meanings for different people. Wars and ethnic conflicts often start as a result of, or in connection with, reckless use of highly charged language.

The "magical" use of language in some cultures, including supposedly modern ones, indicates a primitive state of psycho-semantic development. Spells, curses, oaths, prayers, and incantations have been part of virtually all human cultures.

Even numbers can take on a magical meaning and power for some people. One can still find hotels in major cities around the world without a thirteenth floor. The fact that the so-called fourteenth floor is actually the thirteenth floor doesn't matter. What matters is not having the number "13" on any elevator buttons or room-number plaques.

In some cultures, after a person dies, speaking his name is taboo, for various reasons. This prohibition may be related to a superstitious fear of death and dead people; or it may reflect a belief that the name has magical power to summon back the spirit of the deceased, derailing him or her from the journey to the next world.

> "Pray, n. To ask that the laws of the universe
> be annulled in behalf of a single petitioner,
> confessedly unworthy."
> —Ambrose Bierce, "The Devil's Dictionary"

A milder form of word-magic, often taken to comical extremes, is forbidding the use of certain words or expressions to prevent people from talking about—and presumably thinking about—"unauthorized" topics. In the nineteenth century, public figures referred to severe downturns as "depressions," but in the 1930s the term "recession" evolved to soften the distressing connotations.

In the 1970s, President Jimmy Carter scolded his chief economic adviser, Alfred Kahn, for scaring the public about the possibility of a recession, and actually forbade him from using the term. Thereafter, in his speeches and press interviews Kahn substituted the code word "banana" for "recession." "Well, if we *do* have a 'banana,' I think . . . ." Almost everyone who heard him knew what he was talking about, but he followed the letter of Carter's directive, actually calling attention to the comically inept attempt to pacify the public.

One of the foundation skills of practical intelligence is awareness of these deeper-lying psychological phenomena of language, which involves the ability to monitor one's own use of language patterns and the language patterns of others, and to avoid certain verbal pathologies that can cause misunderstanding, conflict, and even psychological maladjustment, both individual and collective.

> "Nobody goes to Waikiki Beach any more;
> it's too crowded."
> —Overheard on a plane bound for Hawaii

Therapist Wendell Johnson applied many of Alfred Korzybski's general semantics (GS) principles in his work with troubled people. In his book *People in Quandaries,* he posited that much of what we call insanity is really a head full of confused mental models, most of which are contaminated by the irrational use of language. Johnson reported that he seldom met with a new patient who was able to clearly articulate what was wrong with his or her life. This inarticulate blockage, Johnson concluded, was both a consequence and *a cause* of the maladjustment.[2]

Similarly, Johnson discovered, whenever a patient arrived at the point at which he or she could clearly articulate the dilemmas causing the distress, that person would almost always progress rapidly to a solution in a relatively short time. According to Johnson, many crazy people aren't really crazy; *they talk crazy* and that makes them think in crazy ways.

Consequently, Johnson devoted much of his therapeutic practice to *semantic re-education,* a process of helping people reframe and restate their life situations in language more conducive to sanity and effective problem solving. In recent years, the methods of *Neurolinguistic Programming* (NLP) have capitalized on the primary principles of Korzybski's GS theory.

Therapist Albert Ellis, whose ideas we'll explore further in Chapter 11, also applied this semantic sanity approach in his theory of Rational-Emotive Behavior Therapy, or "REBT." Often referred to as the "Lenny Bruce of therapy," because his frequent use of profanity calls to mind the iconoclastic and tragic comedian of the 1950s, Ellis taught his patients to reframe their problems, their worlds, and their ideas of themselves in what he called the language of sanity.

The basic idea behind general semantics and its usefulness for personal growth and therapy is so simple that it evades the mind. What Korzybski and his descendants were saying is: Language both expresses our thoughts and creates our thoughts.

Another way to put it is to say that, *not only do we say what we think, we think what we say.* The choice of words available to us—mental maps, as Korzybski called them—pre-determines how we can build the concepts we process in our minds and the concepts we use in communicating with others. A subtle change in the choice of language can make an important change in the meaning that arises in our own minds, and in the meanings that we evoke in the minds of others.

The psycho-dynamics of language can be very subtle. Consider the verbal behavior of *displacement,* in which a person shifts from the first-person "I" form to either the second-person or third-person form— "you" or "people" or "it." You can spot this semantic maneuver fairly often if you're alert for it.

*Case in point*: Julian Bond, formerly a very active member of the cadre of "new black" leaders who spearheaded the American civil rights movement in the 1960s and 1970s, made an unguarded public remark, implying that Asian business owners in inner cities were cheating and exploiting poor black people. When confronted with the implications of his remark, he apologized publicly. Note the switch from the first-person pronoun "I" to the impersonal third-person form "it," as he subtly side-steps responsibility for the remark:

> It's against everything I ever believed, and everything
> I ever stood for. *It should never have been said.*

Note that he didn't say, "I should never have said it." Instead, the most he could muster was a condemnation of the offending statement as if it were an inanimate object of some kind, separate from himself.

Verbal patterns such as displacement often play a part in *rationalization,* the process of explaining one's ignoble behavior in terms of socially acceptable reasons.

## HOW LANGUAGE "PACKAGES" YOUR THOUGHTS

In elementary drawing classes, art teachers sometimes help students learn to see more accurately, so they can draw more accurately, by having them overlay a grid pattern onto an existing picture. Each square in the grid encloses a small part of the total picture and becomes a miniature picture of its own, which is easier to study and copy. All the student has to do is copy what he or she sees in each grid square, put all the grids together, and the overall picture eventually emerges.

Just as the squares in the grid serve to subdivide the visual picture into separate visual packages, human languages subdivide the "reality" we perceive with our senses into *verbal packages*. The names we give to things, the names we give to categories of things, and the names we give to categories of categories mostly have the effect of subdividing our understanding of them.

> "Men imagine that their minds have the
> command of language, but it often happens
> that language bears rule over their minds."
>
> —Francis Bacon

The fact is that our words don't actually describe "the world." The best we can do is describe our *individual sensory experience* of the world—our perceptions—and even at that we're forced to choose from a limited palette of verbal tags that serves as a mental proxy for our sensory experience. Visually, for example, we think we "see" the world, but what we see is the pattern of neurons firing in the retinas of our eyes. We apply verbal tags to those patterns: "green car," "cloudy sky," or "narrow hallway," and we accept those retinal patterns and their verbal tags as indistinguishable from reality.

Anthropologists and other scientists who study human societies refer to *language communities,* which are distinctive groups of people who share a common set of verbal maps as necessary to their participation in a common cultural group. English speakers in various countries belong to similar language cultures, which differ from one another to various degrees. Asian language cultures differ even more widely from one another, and from English language cultures. Language both expresses community and creates community.

Certain language patterns such as slang and popular figures of speech can signal a person's self-identification with a particular language community, social group, or class-level. American teen-agers, to some extent, form a language community, united by the standard seventeen-word teen-age vocabulary—"teen-speak." With the repetitive use of terms like "like," "ohmigod," "I'm all. . .," "awesome," "totally," and "cool"—or "hot," depending on whether they're describing a thing or a person—they signal their identification with their peer group.

One person can simultaneously belong to several language communities. It may happen from time to time that the verbal behavior expected of a person in the context of one language community conflicts with the customary verbal behavior he or she learned as part of a different language community. In such a case, the person must adjust his or her verbal patterns to suit the situation by deploying those language habits characteristic of one particular community.

Schoolchildren who come from ethnic minority communities, for example, typically have learned certain language patterns, figures of speech, and grammatical forms unique to their parent cultures. In the United States, black children may have learned a version of "ghetto English," also known pejoratively as "Blacklish" or "Ebonics," which is considered backward and uneducated by the majority white community. Latino children often learn language habits unique to their individual cultures. When white or Anglo teachers scold these children for using "improper" English, the children may sense that their native language forms have been more or less outlawed by the school system and its culture. Some of them become unsure of themselves and reluctant to express themselves outside their private cultures. Some black people even accuse others of "talkin' white" when they try to use the standard forms of English that are accepted and enforced by the majority culture.

> "If the people don't wanna come out to the ballpark,
> how ya gonna stop 'em?"
> —Yogi Berra (American baseball player)

As expert users of our language, we become so fluent and so automatic in the process of packaging ideas into words—verbal maps, as Korzybski called them—that we're seldom conscious that our verbal maps only *represent* reality; they are not in themselves the reality we're trying to think about. Korzybski's fans in the general semantics field are fond of quoting his signature statement: "The map is not the territory."

Sometimes the human biocomputer malfunctions as it tries to form an idea verbally, particularly when two thought processes compete for its limited attention. For example, I was standing at the cash register of an electronics store, paying for a purchase. At the cash register next to me, the clerk was filling out a refund form for a woman who was returning an item. A split-second after my counter clerk asked, "May I have your credit card," her counter clerk asked her for her Zip code. Apparently his biocomputer combined the part of the phrase he'd just heard with the phrase he was assembling in his mind, and he said, "What's your Zip card?"

Slips of the tongue—sometimes referred to in popular discussion as "Freudian slips"—offer interesting glimpses into the biocomputer's language processing software. For example, a radio newsreader in California, after reading an item that reported on a government study that estimated that as many as twelve million Americans have serious drinking problems, went on to say, "and in local news, the city of Escondido won a bottle with . . . er, ah . . . make that a *battle* with the state of California over Proposition 13 relief funds."

We might think of words, phrases, and sentences as tools for dividing and subdividing our perceptions of reality into manageable chunks, sort of like cutting cookies out of cookie dough. The descriptive categories, or "cookie cutters," that a language user learns to apply have a profound effect on the way his or her biocomputer processes his or her unique reality.

*Case in point:* in his thought-provoking book *One, Two, Three . . . Infinity,* physicist and science writer George Gamow reported that the Hottentot of southern Africa used a counting system with only four numbers. They reportedly used words for one, two, and three, but had no means of distinguishing larger numbers, typically using a generic word that means "a large number." Apparently, to the Hottentot "four" and "infinity" mean approximately the same thing. This curious fact was apparently the metaphorical premise of Gamow's interest in scientific and cultural curiosities.[3]

*Case in point:* In the Japanese language culture, one uses a variety of different counting vocabularies to refer to various kinds of objects in groups, whereas English typically uses a single, standard form. For example, when an English speaker—or thinker—buys a couple of tickets, he or she typically says, "Two, please" to the clerk. However, a Japanese thinker would likely say, "Nimai, kudasai," using the special counting vocabulary for paper items like postage stamps, sheets of paper, or tickets. Counting liquid things that come in containers, such as bottles of milk or juice, or cans of soup, might call for the counting series *ippai, nihai, sanbai, yonhai,* and so on. Japanese people customarily use the series *ikko, niko, sonko, yonko,* and so on to enumerate small rounded objects such as eggs. To count cylindrical objects like sticks, pens, or pencils, the preferred cookie cutters would probably be *ippon, nihon, sanbon, yonhon,* and so on. The Japanese language tradition has unique sets of counting words for books; for tiny round edible food items like beans, peas, or grapes; and still others for things that come in bunches, like radishes, carrots, or parsley. It might seem strange to the Japanese that English has only one generic set of counting words, while English thinkers might consider the Japanese customer unnecessarily complicated.

*Case in point:* Modernized language cultures seem to make finer distinctions in describing—and perceiving—colors than so-called primitive cultures do. The Shona people of Zimbabwe (formerly Rhodesia) typically name only four colors, or ranges of colors, across the visible spectrum. Some tribes in New Guinea use only two terms for colors, roughly equivalent to "darker" and "lighter."

*Case in point:* Kinship terminology in particular reveals the kinds of perceptual differences that make various language cultures unique. While English speakers tend to use certain generic terms such as *uncle* and *cousin* to refer to members of one's family or clan, many other cultures have more specific terms to identify the gender of the person being described. For some cultures, it seems peculiar and inadequate to refer generically to a cousin without specifying whether the person being described is male or female, and whether this generic cousin is the son or daughter of one's father's brother or sister or one's mother's brother or sister. How can one understand a reference to a person's uncle without knowing whether he is the father's brother or the mother's brother? People who speak the Jinghpaw language of Northern Burma (also known as Myanmar) use some eighteen basic terms for describing kinship categories, and none of them translates directly into English.

Trying to translate an idea from one human language to another is analogous to trying to convert the information on one kind of a map—say, a street map—to another kind, such as an aerial photograph or a geological map. Each type of map does something different with the aspects of reality it supposedly represents. Neither type of map is wrong, and yet none of them is completely right. Korzybski emphasized that every map is a distortion of reality, and verbal maps in particular are conceptually distorted.

"What's in a name?" asked young Juliet in Shakespeare's famous play *Romeo and Juliet*. "That which we call a rose, by any other name would smell as sweet," she said. Well, not actually. Salespeople, advertisers and marketers, political leaders, and con artists have learned, all throughout history, that the name one attaches to a person or an idea can have a huge effect on the way people think about and react to it.

Repetitive brand advertising, for example, seeks to implant an expression, a slogan, or a jingle into as many brains as possible, so that it triggers the desired associations with the product experience. This "brain drool" reaction is so effective and so commonplace in the Western commercial culture that few people notice it or consciously object to it.

You're a fan of movie star Tom Cruise? Would you be just as keen about watching someone named Thomas Mapother, his real name?

Maybe you liked the classic films starring Norma Jean MacDonald, who was rechristened by Hollywood marketers as Marilyn Monroe.

Would you pay to see a movie starring Marion Morrison? You have, if you've ever watched a John Wayne movie.

Are you a fan of the old western movies, many starting Leonard Slye—sorry, that's Roy Rogers?

Do you enjoy the movies produced by Allen Konigsberg, a.k.a. Woody Allen?

Did you enjoy the vaudeville style of comedy by Nathan Birnbaum, otherwise known as George Burns?

Names have psychological power. In some native cultures, it is forbidden to speak the name of a member of the tribe who has died, lest his soul's journey to the next world be impeded. City leaders in India have reasserted local identity by replacing their British colonial names with the original names: Bombay went back to Mumbai; Bangalore went back to Bengalooru ("the city of boiled beans"); Madras went back to Chennai. In South Africa, the new black political leadership is replacing some old *Afrikaaner* city names with original tribal names: Pietersburg became Polokwane. Some leaders have advocated a change in the name of the national capital from Pretoria, named after an Afrikaaner hero, to Tshwane, the name of a local chief from pre-colonial days.

The inadequacy of language as a means for encoding thoughts became frustratingly obvious to early researchers working on the problem of computerized translation from one language to another. According to one early story, they presented the computer with the English figure of speech "out of sight, out of mind," had it translated into Russian, and had the translated version converted back into English. The machine came back with "invisible idiot."

Modern computer software does a fairly good job of language translation, but programmers still struggle with idiomatic forms such as this one: "Although the photographer and the art thief were close friends, neither had ever taken the other's picture."

# JUMPING TO CONFUSIONS:
# INFERENTIAL THINKING

Professor William V. Haney of Northwestern University devoted considerable attention and research to a particular semantic malfunction, which he believed played an important role in faulty thinking, incompetent decision making, and human misunderstanding and conflict in general. Haney studied the phenomenon he called *inference-observation confusion,* which is the inability to clearly separate conclusions from the information on which they're based.[4]

## The Inference Awareness Test

Here's a little test of your inference awareness. The following report gives some information that is acceptable as true. Read the account of the situation very carefully. Then read the statements that follow the report. Decide whether each statement is True, False, or Unverifiable from the information given in the story. Circle "T" if you can *prove* the statement true from the story; circle "F" if you can *prove* the statement false from the story. If a statement is not *definitely* true or definitely false, circle the "?" to rate it as unverifiable. Once you have answered a question, *do not change your answer.* You may refer back to the story as often as you like. After you've rated all the statements, check Appendix A for a discussion of the solution.

## THE INCIDENT

The safe in the cafeteria office of Apollo Company was found standing open. Company security has questioned three employees in connection with a sum of $1,500 which is unaccounted for. All three of the employees questioned knew the combination to the office safe. It has been determined that one of these employees, Joe A, was on vacation for the entire week during which the incident occurred. Another employee, Jane B, has refused to make any statements and has insisted on talking to a lawyer. The third employee, Jim C, has volunteered to take a lie detector test. Company security is considering calling in the police.

**Statements About the Incident**

1. All three of the employees questioned knew the    T    F    ?
combination to the safe.
2. All three of the questioned employees have    T    F    ?
denied taking the money.
3. Joe A did not take the money.    T    F    ?
4. Jane B has refused to cooperate with the    T    F    ?
investigation.
5. Joe A has volunteered to take a lie detector test.    T    F    ?
6. Only Joe A, Jane B, and Jim C knew how to    T    F    ?
open the office safe.
7. $1,500 was stolen from the office safe.    T    F    ?
8. Whoever robbed the office safe left it    T    F    ?
standing open.
9. The thief has not yet been identified.
10. Either Joe A, Jane B, or Jim C stole $1,500 from    T    F    ?
the cafeteria office safe at Apollo Company.

Now check Appendix A for a discussion of the solution.[5]

# Text and Subtext: Listening on Four Channels at Once

Screenwriters, novelists, and others in the fantasy trade routinely manipulate what they call the *subtext* of a story. Subtext is the text that isn't there: it's the implied message, what's "between the lines," what could be said that isn't. It's the part that we're supposed to fill in with our minds as we watch or read. In many dramatic scenes, the subtext conveys more information, more powerfully, than the text.

In the film *Fiddler on the Roof,* for example, Chaim Topol plays the character of the philosophizing milkman Tevye, who often has rather insubordinate conversations with his God. In one tragic scene, after Russian soldiers have rampaged through the village, destroying homes and property in order to deliver a message to the Jews living there,

Tevye walks through the village, looking around at the effects of the senseless destruction. He pauses, looks skyward, raises his hands slightly, palms up, shrugs his shoulders painfully, and we can interpret his expression as one of confusion, disbelief, and questioning. He says nothing, but he has communicated what we need to know through the subtext of his gesture.

Text and subtext are not specialized dynamics reserved to the theater. They're present in our lives all the time. We always mean something more—and sometimes something different—from what we can say with words. We all use subtext, and we're all influenced by subtext as we talk with, to, at, and around one another.

Whenever a person is saying anything, he or she is actually transmitting messages on four key channels at once, as illustrated in Figure 6.1. These channels are:

1. *Facts*: the verifiable content, information, or evidence he or she offers. Assumptions, inferences, and speculation, if clearly identified as such, can qualify as part of the "factual" content, because they are offered explicitly rather than obscured or disguised by manipulative language.
2. *Feelings*: the emotional orientation (anger, aggression, dominance, fear, guilt, and so on) that the speaker conveys or seeks to induce you to feel. Advertising messages, for example, often arouse

## Figure 6.1.   Four-Channel Listening

certain emotional responses connected with attributes of a product. Appeals to patriotism, religious fervor, or class identity can cloud and contaminate the meanings of what's being said.

3. *Values*: judgments or evaluations the speaker is making or seeks to induce you to make. The use of *high-affect language,* that is, terms with strong emotional associations, can imply value judgments. Sarcastic language usually signals an attempt to sell a value judgment.

4. *Opinions*: decisions about how to interpret the information the speaker is offering and what conclusions you "should" reach about what needs to be done in a certain situation.

To the extent that the message comes heavily loaded with feelings, values, and opinions, you can reasonably suspect that the speaker has chosen the "facts" carefully to support the messages on the other three channels. By decoding what you hear in the media, editorials, talk shows, political discourse, propaganda, and all forms of persuasive conversation in business, you can usually separate the messages into these four key channels. Remember also that various nonverbal patterns, such as tone of voice, facial expression, and other subtle cues, can support or diminish the impact of the messages on any of the channels.

> "If dogs could talk, we'd probably have
> as much trouble getting along with them
> as we do with people."
>
> —Karel Capek

You can also contribute to greater clarity of understanding in business situations by training yourself to present your views more honestly, with less manipulation, and by clearly identifying your own feelings, values, and opinions.

## "CLEAN" AND "DIRTY" LANGUAGE: STRATEGIES FOR SEMANTIC SANITY

We can think of the difference between semantically primitive language, which often signals archaic thinking, and semantically sophisticated language, which tends to signal adaptive, dynamic thinking, in terms of the metaphor of "clean" language and 'dirty" language. We're not referring to obscenity when we refer to "dirty" language. What we mean is language that tends to contaminate, corrupt, pollute, and obscure understanding and cooperation. Clean language, of course, is the alternative pattern to dirty language.

### "Dirty" Language: The Seven Semantic Sins

Dirty language tends to express certain semantic malfunctions, which arise from malfunctions in thinking, as exemplified by these Seven Semantic Sins:

1. *Blanketing*—declaring one's opinions, beliefs, or judgments as if they were true for everybody, without acknowledging that they belong to the one speaking or that others are entitled to hold other views. Example: "The best Italian restaurant in town is X." Alternative: "My favorite Italian restaurant in this town is X."

2. *Aggression*—belittling a person by describing him or her in demeaning, critical, judgmental, accusative, or sarcastic language, usually for the purpose of diminishing the value that others perceive in his or her character or ideas. Example: "He's a soft-headed liberal with neo-communist leanings and a chocolate addiction." Alternative: "I disagree with his overall political ideology; I don't believe the ideas he's espousing will work very well in this situation."

3. *Directiveness*—pressuring a person indirectly with "should" language, which can sound coercive and can cause a person to

feel his or her autonomy is being encroached upon. Example: "If you're smart, you'll diversify your investments" or "You should join the such-and-such professional association." Alternative: "I think it's important to diversify investments these days" or "The such-and-such professional association might suit your needs."

4. **Attribution**—attaching a motivation, often an ignoble one, to a person's behavior, which implies that we've discovered his or her despicable reasons for disagreeing with us. Example: "You're just being obstinate because you don't want this project to succeed." Alternative: "I wonder if you fully agree with the course of action the team seems committed to. Would you please explain your view of the project?"

5. **All-ness**—generalizing so broadly as to obscure important differences, variations, or alternatives that might be relevant to the interpretation or conclusion being offered. Example: "People don't like change." Alternative: "Some people find change uncomfortable and some actually prefer it. How can we make the changes we plan to make appealing for as many people as possible?"

6. **Dogmatism**—a strong, unconditional, declarative statement or value judgment that does not acknowledge the validity of alternative views. Example: "Kids these days have far too many electronic gadgets." Alternative: "Some kids seem to have a lot of electronic gadgets. I think there are negative side effects for some of them."

7. **Polarization**—framing an issue, problem, or disagreement in terms of only two mutually exclusive possibilities, also known as *dichotomizing* issues. Example: "You're either with us, or you're against us." Alternative: "To what extent are you willing to support us in this venture?"

## "Clean" Language: Updating Your Language Habits

The antidote to dirty language is, of course, clean language. Clean language is a pattern of discourse that is psychologically neutral and that honors the entitlement of others to think and speak for themselves.

Point for point, we can substitute clean language patterns for the seven semantic sins, as follows:

1. Verbal cues such as "to me," "in my experience," and "so far as I know," remind us and others that we acknowledge the self-locality of our "truth."

2. We can substitute *non-aggression* for *aggression*. Scrubbing out attacking, critical, judgmental, sarcastic, and accusative terms from our statements may make it more difficult to express our anger, but they also tend to minimize hostile responses by others.

3. We can substitute *non-directiveness* for *directiveness*. Limiting the use of "push-language" such as "should's" and "ought's" and implied coercion tends to make people feel more comfortable with our ideas and more likely to accept our suggestions.

4. We can substitute *non-attribution* for *attribution*. Limiting the use of accusative or condemnatory language, acknowledging that we can't really know another person's motivations, and referring to the *behavior* we find difficult instead of the presumed motivations, can help to resolve disagreements respectfully.

5. We can substitute *non-allness* for *allness*. Verbal cues like limiters and qualifiers—"It's possible that . . .," "In some situations . . .," and "To some extent . . ."—remind ourselves and others of the limitations that over-generalizing can impose on our thinking.

6. We can substitute *non-dogmatism* for *dogmatism*. Verbal cues that acknowledge the relativity of truth, and that remind us and others to consider multiple options, multiple causes, and multiple possibilities, can help others to express their ideas without feeling they have to do battle against our ideas.

7. We can substitute *non-polarization* for *polarization*. Limiting the
use of dichotomizing statements like "win or lose," "succeed or
fail," and "us and them" tends to open up the range of thinking
and discussion and to admit more options and possibilities into
our thinking.

## A Code of Intelligent Discourse

Appendix D provides, for easy reference, a Code of Intelligent Discourse
that incorporates these semantically sane strategies.

> Wag more, bark less.
>
> —Bumper sticker

## EXPRESSIONS YOU CAN REMOVE FROM YOUR VOCABULARY

If, by this point, you've become comfortably attached to the concept of
semantic sanity, you may be ready for the step of sorting out your
semantic tool kit: eliminating certain terms, expressions, and figures of
speech from your vocabulary.

Think of your usage vocabulary—the words you commonly
deploy—as consisting of three subsets of words, as illustrated in Figure 6.2.

You have lots of terms in your vocabulary that are emotionally *neutral*. They have little or no emotional charge: words for common,
everyday items; experiences; articles and prepositions; numbers and
various other "utility" words.

Then you have terms with mostly *positive* emotional influence:
words like love, peace, friendship, joy, and chocolate.

And you have terms that tend to conjure up relatively *negative*
emotional associations: words like hate, enemy, pain, sick, cancer,
and taxes.

The theory of *semantic filtering* is very simple: you train yourself to
minimize or eliminate the use of emotionally negative words to the

## Figure 6.2.    Connotations of Vocabulary Words

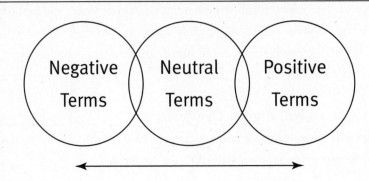

Minimize These Terms        Favor These Terms

greatest practical extent, leaving the emotionally positive words, phrases, and figures of speech to shape the way you think and express your ideas.

In my "Brain Power" seminar, business and professional people learn to "pre-hear" what they're about to say, and choose more positive ways of expressing their ideas. Here's a starter list of expressions you may want to filter out of your vocabulary, as you form ideas in your mind and as you speak your mind to others:[6]

1. I can never do anything right.
2. I can't (get a break, find a job, stand to. . .).
3. I dread (an experience, impending event, outcome).
4. I hate (you, him, her, this, to do. . .).
5. If it weren't for (you, my health, my kids, my mother, my job), I could (succeed in some way).
6. If only (any statement that agonizes over the past).
7. I'm (dumb, stupid, lazy—any negative adjective).
8. I'm a (failure, loser—any negative label).
9. I'm afraid (that, of—anything that might happen or be true).

10. I'm dead (tired, on my feet, brain-dead, etc.).
11. I'm dying to (know, meet, try).
12. I'm sick of, sick and tired of (any unpleasant experience).
13. I'm wiped out.
14. Nobody likes me.
15. That just blows my mind.
16. That drives me crazy.
17. That kills me.
18. This is awful (terrible, stupid, etc.).
19. Why do these things always happen to me?
20. With my luck, I'll probably (negative prediction).

You might think of others to add to my list. Review your complete list carefully: are there some things you regularly say—or think? Once you start monitoring your habitual speaking patterns, you might be surprised at how many of them you use. Initially, you might find that some part or parts of you, a non-conscious mind module of some type, resists giving up the privilege of expressing your feelings in negative, self-critical, defeatist, or cynical terms. Maybe it just seems "too nice." But with time and practice, I'm willing to bet that your self-talk patterns, as well as the language you use with others, will migrate further and further toward the affirmative end of the spectrum.

## THE SELF-CONVERSATION: CLEANING UP YOUR INTERNAL DIALOG

Sixties philosopher and cartoonist Ashley Brilliant offered a quintessentially self-sabotaging line in one of his many cartoons that commented on the challenges of living. He portrayed a very stressed-looking individual, with the caption: "Once I wanted total happiness; now I'll settle for a little less pain."

*Self-talk* includes anything you say to yourself about yourself, either aloud or in the privacy of your mind. Just as your overall vocabulary is composed of the three sub-vocabularies shown in Figure 6.2—positive, neutral, and negative terms—so you can think of self-talk in the same three categories. Try making a careful review of the things you say to yourself. Start tracking your silent conversations, as well as the things you mumble to yourself occasionally. Listen for terms such as those listed in the preceding section. Also make a note of the things you say whenever you describe yourself to others, whether seriously or in jest.

Here are some candidates for expressions you might banish from your self-conversation:

- Negative nouns, such as clod, coward, dimwit, dingdong, dumb-bell, dummy, failure, fool, idiot, jerk, klutz, loser, nitwit, old bag, old bat, slob, and any others you might have adopted.
- Negative adjectives, such as clumsy, crazy, disorganized, dumb, fat, inept, klutzy, lazy, neurotic, old (when said with a negative connotation), schizy, spacey, spastic, stupid, ugly, and any others you might have adopted.
- Emotional "dead-end" words, which can derail your thinking with negative or pessimistic emotions, such as: this is awful, this is terrible, I hate it when this happens, I don't know what to do, I'm screwed again, I have no choice, it's all your fault, it's not my fault, you made me mad, you can't fight City Hall, if only. . ., see what you made me do, and any others you might have adopted.

Filtering these and other types of negative self-talk out of your mental and spoken vocabulary might seem like quite a challenge, especially if you've been using them for many years. And some of your mindmodules might be disappointed if you deprive them of their right to feel defeated, victimized, and self-pitied. However, if you make a continuing and diligent effort, you might be surprised to discover how extensively you can change your pattern of discourse, and how much better you feel as you do.

## SNAPPY COME-BACKS:
## THE LANGUAGE OF FUNNY

In the well-loved and long-running American TV comedy *Cheers,* one of the characters who sat around the bar, Norm Peterson, had a talent for the "snappy come-back" based on a clever turn of words. Consider the following excerpts from various shows, in which the bartender of the evening would greet him as he sat down on his customary stool.

**Woody:** "Hey, Mr. Peterson, what's up?"
**Norm:** "The warranty on my liver."

**Coach:** "What would you say to a beer, Normie?"
**Norm:** "Daddy wuvs you."

**Coach:** "Can I draw you a beer, Norm?"
**Norm:** "No, I know what they look like. Just pour me one."

After you've enjoyed the humor—assuming you did—then ask yourself, what's the basis for each of these verbal gags? Look for the one comedic premise that runs through them.

Did you spot it? It's very simple: in each case the bartender phrases his question with a commonplace figure of speech or a familiar metaphor, and in every case Norm answers from the *literal* meaning, not the *figurative* one.

For example, the figure of speech "Can I draw you a beer?" is commonly understood to mean "Shall I open the tap and pour some beer into a glass for you?" Norm's off-beat response *literalizes the metaphor,* suggesting comedically that Coach was offering to draw a picture of a beer for him.

Another metaphorical reversal Norm could have used in reply to the question is "I sure hope so, I'm thirsty." This would be a comedic "mistake" of the term "Can I," which is a commonplace variation on "Do I have your permission to."

I enjoy collecting and creating "mental jelly beans"—snippets of humor based on the clever turn of words or offbeat concepts that throw the mind out of gear. Here are some examples of mental jelly beans offered by comedian Steven Wright:

"I went to a bookstore and asked the saleswoman, 'Where's the self-help section?' She said if she told me, it would defeat the purpose."

"If someone with multiple personalities threatens to kill himself, is it considered a hostage situation?"

"If you shoot a mime, do you have to use a silencer?"

"Is there another word for synonym?"

And a few contributed by comedian George Carlin:

"Why is there an expiration date on sour cream?"

"Why is the alphabet in that order? Is it because of that song?"

"If you try to fail, and succeed, which have you done?"

"In California there's a hot-line for people in denial. So far, no one has called."

Creativity researchers report a close three-way relationship between sense of humor, particularly clever use of language; positive thinking; and the ability to think creatively and generate new ideas. Test this in your own experience: do you find that sour, sullen, gloomy, and pessimistic people seem to have fewer good ideas and less of a novel outlook on life than the ones who laugh, smile, and like a good joke? How about your own mental habits: do you keep a positive frame of mind, appreciate humor, and come up with new ideas?

# Notes

1.  Korzybski, Alfred. *Science and Sanity: An Introduction to Non-Aristotelian Systems and General Semantics.* Boston, MA: Colonial Press, 1933.

2.  Johnson, Wendell. *People in Quandaries.* San Francisco: International Society for General Semantics, Reprinted 2000.

3.  Gamow, George. *One, Two, Three. . . Infinity: Facts and Speculations of Science.* New York: Dover, 1988.

4.  Haney, William V. *Communication and Interpersonal Relations* (5th ed.) Homewood, IL: Richard D. Irwin, 1986.

5.  The Inference Awareness Test is adapted from seminar materials included in the "Brain Power" seminar, developed by Karl Albrecht International; used with permission.

6.  This inventory of terms to be minimized is adapted from seminar materials included in the "Brain Power" seminar, developed by Karl Albrecht International; used with permission.

# 7

# MENTAL SOFTWARE
## UPGRADE 4
### Valuing Ideas

"There is one thing stronger than all the armies of the world,
and that is an idea whose time has come."
—Victor Hugo

CHARLES F. KETTERING WAS AN INVENTOR, an engineer, a teacher, and an advocate of social change who made a significant impact on the development of American society in the early part of the twentieth century. Born in 1876, Kettering departed the planet in 1958 with more than 140 patents to his credit and having received honorary doctorates from nearly thirty universities.

Kettering and his collaborator Edward Deeds developed an electric generator for automobiles, named the "Delco." They also pioneered electric auto-ignition and a self-starter for automobiles, which first appeared in the 1912 Cadillac. Kettering later developed the spark plug. The Delco evolved into a company of the same name, which was acquired by General Motors and became one of the leading producers of automotive electrical parts and systems.

Kettering's other inventions included the electric cash register, Freon as a coolant for refrigerators and air conditioners, leaded gasoline, quick drying paint for automobiles, safety glass, the portable electric generator, four-wheel brakes, the automatic transmission, the electric railway gate, the first synthetic aviation fuel, the World War I "aerial torpedo," an incubator for premature infants, and applications of magnetic fields to medical diagnosis.

His residence in Dayton, Ohio, was reportedly the first air conditioned home in America.

Kettering became vice president of General Motors Research Corporation in 1920 and held the position of GM's head of research for twenty-seven years. The organization was later renamed Kettering University as a tribute to his creative leadership.

In 1945 Kettering and Alfred Sloan established the Sloan-Kettering Institute for Cancer Research in New York City, which remains one of the pre-eminent medical centers in the world.

Kettering had this to say about the fate of ideas:

"Human beings are so constituted as to see what is wrong with a new thing, not what is right. To verify this you only have to submit a new idea to a committee. They will obliterate 90 percent of rightness for the sake of 10 percent of wrongness. The possibilities a new idea opens up are not appreciated, because not one [person] in a thousand has imagination."

I believe Kettering may have been a bit too harsh on his fellow human beings. My estimate is that about one person in a hundred has imagination. On some days I'd even argue for one in ten.

# DO YOU HAVE LOTS OF GOOD IDEAS?
## (ALMOST EVERYONE DOES)

When I lecture to groups of business people, I like to ask, "How many of you have lots of good ideas?" Then I wait a few seconds to see how many of them raise their hands to acknowledge their mental productivity. Typically, about 40 to 50 percent of the audience will raise their hands. I also usually notice that about half of those who do raise their hands seem to have difficulty in deciding to do so. They probably haven't thought about it, because they've never been asked about it. This question usually starts some wheels turning in their heads.

Then I usually coach them with the "correct" answer. "Actually," I may say, "there is a 'correct' answer to that question. The correct answer is that all of you have lots of good ideas, every day. So let's repeat the question and let's make sure everyone answers correctly— let's see 100 percent of the hands in the air, please." Most audiences will amiably oblige me and show all hands.

Anyone who has a normal brain and nervous system has lots of ideas, and usually some very good ones, every day. The main reason why many people don't appreciate their idea-having capacities is that *they allow their ideas to escape from their minds,* to evaporate into the mists of time as events move along.

Ideas are like butterflies—they're transient, fleeting, and often incompletely formed. Unless we invite them to stay, they tend to wander off.

Skilled "idea people" tend to be very possessive about ideas; not that they want to hoard them or keep others from having them—quite the contrary. They want to make sure they don't get away. Consequently, they typically have some kind of a personal system that enables them to capture fleeting ideas when they first appear. Some people write notes to themselves, some recite an idea several times with the hope of imprinting it in memory, some carry around a capture device such as a PDA or a voice recorder. But very few of the most productive thinkers around us just rely on their memories to keep ideas from escaping.

When Albert Einstein died in 1955, at the age of seventy-six, he left behind, in addition to the volumes of his published work and scientific papers, a collection of over two thousand pages of personal notes, ramblings, calculations, and musings.

One might readily protest, "But I'm not an Einstein. I'm an ordinary mortal; I don't have the mental horsepower he and other geniuses had." Here's the counter to that counter: If one so brilliant as Albert Einstein found it necessary to capture his ideas on paper, doesn't that serve as a hint to the rest of us?

## "IT SLIPPED MY MIND . . ."
## (ALMOST EVERYTHING DOES)

Most people seriously over-rate their memories. I've sat in countless staff meetings, planning meetings, and operational review meetings and heard one person ask or direct another to take care of some task. "OK, sure. I'll take care of that." The person making the promise doesn't write anything down; he or she just "makes a mental note of it."

Actually, that's a strange figure of speech: *a mental note.* It seems to imply that the brain has a kind of "scratch-pad" memory on which we can jot notes and later look them up. Actually, this mental scratch pad *is* imaginary; it doesn't exist. Maybe the person doing the promising actually scribbles a note on the back of a file folder, the top of a memo, or the bottom of the agenda. Then he or she immediately lets go of the idea. Chances are it will get lost in the jumble of other information.

Two weeks later, the person requesting the action asks, "Did you take care of the 'X' matter for me?" Then comes the forehead-smacking moment: "Oh, darn! It slipped my mind. I'll get right on it. Sorry about that." This little episode is probably repeated millions of times a day in human interactions all over the world.

I "made a mental note of it," but it "slipped my mind." I call it the Short-Term Memory Delusion. The point is:

*There is no such thing as a mental note.*

This flawed concept of mental notes betrays a near-universal misunderstanding of the way the human biocomputer organizes its memories. Here's how it actually works.

As you've probably heard countless times, your memory system has two separate departments—*short-term memory* and *long-term memory*. Your short-term memory holds onto information for a matter of seconds up to a few minutes—seldom longer. You meet someone at a party, a business meeting, or a social function. Someone tells you the person's name, you may repeat the name as you introduce yourself, and then you probably forget the name within seconds—unless you have a strong enough motivation to remember it. A friend recommends a book you think you'd like to read. You make a "mental note" of the title, and within a few minutes you've forgotten it completely. Moreover, you've forgotten that you've forgotten it.

You ask someone to take care of some small matter for you; he cheerfully agrees and promises to do it. A few minutes later, he's probably forgotten it completely—unless you've given him a motivation to remember. Later, both of you may have forgotten that you asked and the other person promised. If some event causes you to focus on the desired action or favor again, it might come back to mind. What can be more frustrating is if you later remember the favor you were promised, but the other person has no recollection at all of having promised.

Your so-called mental note is doomed: the only way it will survive the next few minutes is if you *copy it into long-term memory*. Long-term memory is the biocomputer's database: the assorted collection of ideas, facts, figures, experiences, emotions, sights, sounds, movements, rhythms, bodily sensations, slogans, skills, and knowledge that make you unique. And it's pretty unreliable, just as short-term memory is unreliable.

Most of our ideas and intentions never make the leap between short-term memory and long-term storage. If you like computer analogies, imagine that you've created a document of some kind on your computer and you turn off your computer without saving it in a file. You've forgotten to tell the computer to remember it. Now imagine that your computer occasionally fails to save your work products, even if you tell it to. For some unknown reason, it might save some files and not others, even if you click the "Save" command every time.

Actually, your biocomputer is quite a bit like the misbehaving electronic computer in that particular respect. Sometimes it remembers and sometimes it doesn't. And more often than not it remembers part of the message but not all of it.

Your biocomputer even has a "Save" button of sorts, although you can't "click" it directly. In a primitive area of your brain known as the *limbic system,* located just above the roof of your mouth, a minute blob of brain tissue called the *hippocampus* plays a key role in shifting selected short-term memories into long-term storage. The hippocampus seems to act as an agent—possibly one of several—that saves those memories that it deems worthy of keeping. It apparently reads the general level of arousal connected with various thoughts as they flow through, and it tags the ones that have high survival implications or high emotional importance to the owner of the brain.

The influence of the hippocampus and related neurologic structures helps explain why we may quickly imprint either a shocking experience or a joyful one into our long-term memories without even trying, while we struggle mightily to remember the mathematical equations we need to know for the exam. Shock, fear, and joy have arousal value. In simple terms:

*We remember best the things that arouse us the most.*

This is a simple and familiar truth, which most of us utterly fail to capitalize on most of the time. Exciting experiences, exciting news, exciting ideas tend to stay with us because the hippocampus—our brain's "Save" button—detects the threshold of arousal and copies the message into long-term storage.

In this sense, most of our memory is accidental and involuntary. When we strongly intend to remember something, we may or may not create a state of arousal sufficient to trigger the hippocampic save function. By reciting information repeatedly, telling ourselves that it's important, and wanting to remember it, we often can. And we often do not.

Memory experts tell us that we can manage our hippocampuses— or hippocampi—in such a way as to improve our storage and recall. One simple trick they teach is to activate as many senses as possible, which increases the stimulus to the hippocampus. See it, say, touch it, hear it, draw a picture of it, explain it to someone else, relate it to something else you know. All of these methods can help us save the important things we want to recall.

Other memory tricks include creating a vivid mental image or choosing a visual metaphor, possibly with a humorous element, and associating the idea we want to remember with it. The legendary Greek orators of the Classic Age could lecture extemporaneously for hours after memorizing a series of familiar objects or images associated with the topics they wanted to expound. A typical method was to form a mental image of a familiar place, such as a public square, which had lots of walls, steps, pedestals, or other platforms on which they could place the associated objects in their imaginations. As they lectured, they would mentally "walk" around the location in a fixed sequence, seeing the symbolic object they had placed there and using it as a trigger for the next topic.

## A "Bookmark" for Your Memory

Here's a simple and easy method to keep an important piece of information circulating in your short-term memory longer than it otherwise would.

Suppose you're in a lively conversation with several people, and you're all passing the conversational "ball" back and forth quickly. An important point or a good idea or a question pops into your consciousness, and you're keen to share it with the others. However, just as you open your mouth to speak, someone else speaks up and the conversation moves along quickly. You still believe your idea, question, or factual input is worth sharing, and you don't want to let it "slip your mind" before you get a chance to speak. If you're closely engaged in the flow of the discussion, you know that by the time you can get some air time for yourself, you may well have forgotten what you wanted to say. This happens routinely in conversations.

Here's the technique: as you keep following the flow of the conversation with your conscious mind, you use your motor memory to create a "bookmark" that will remind you later that you have something else to say. Just take your brain "offline" for about three seconds, and cross your fingers at the same time that you focus your mind closely on the idea you want to remember. Link the physical sensation of crossing your fingers with the mental image of sharing the idea with the others when it's your turn to speak.

If possible, keep your fingers crossed until your turn comes. (If not, cross them again when you're ready.) As you get the group's attention and they look at you to speak, sense your crossed fingers and use the feeling as a memory cue to recall what you wanted to say.

So we can indeed improve our ability to recall what's important by various means. However, I wish to present for your consideration a much simpler and much more powerful way to capture and value ideas.

## THE GREATEST THINKING TOOL EVER INVENTED

OK—maybe the title for this topic is somewhat exaggerated, but not by much. I'm just a bit apprehensive that the thinking tool I'm about to describe is so utterly simple that you might underestimate its value and its importance unless I present it with appropriate fanfare. I think it needs a build-up—I have to "position" it in all of its importance; to create a sense of anticipation, almost a craving to know what it is. Are you getting curious? Are you?

This thinking tool is elegantly simple, easy to use, cheap to acquire and replenish, versatile, very portable, and highly effective. It has no moving parts, uses no batteries, never crashes, requires no training, and is usually worthless if stolen.

This thinking tool completely solves the problems of forgetting your best ideas, forgetting key bits of information, forgetting to do things, forgetting to follow up with others, and believing that you "never have good ideas."

What is this magical tool? It's *the index card.*

The first cave person who made some marks on a wall started humanity's long march to the index card and the Post-it® note. The human brain seems to be deliberately wired for language—both speaking and writing. The vast majority of people in developed countries can write easily and fluently; *yet very few of them write at the right time.* Because of the Short-Term Memory Delusion, most people allow their best ideas, important facts or bits of information and "things to do," to evaporate right out of their heads.

Utterly convinced that they can remember whatever has just popped into their minds, they disprove it countless times every day, and yet never reconsider their unshakeable faith in their short-term memory. Call it mental laziness, self-delusion, or simply a lack of interest, they muddle along allowing their idea-butterflies to flit away one after another.

I consider the index card—or "three-by-five card" as they're known in the United States and other countries that measure things with the so-called "English" system of measurement—to be a near-perfect idea-capturing system.

If you like historical trivia, you might like to know that Melvil Dewey, the inventor of the revered "Dewey Decimal System" used by libraries, invented the index card some time around 1876. He standardized the dimensions of the card at 75 millimeters by 125 millimeters—about three inches by five inches. His simple invention has been around ever since.

Technically speaking, we must consider the index card as one part of an idea-capturing system. You also need a pen, pencil, or something similar to write the ideas on it. So let's think of the pen and the index card as a combination made in heaven—an ideal way to invite those idea-butterflies to stay around.

*I'm never more than ten feet from a supply of index cards and a pen.* They're in my car, my kitchen, living room, dining room, all bathrooms, and the garage. They're on the night table next to my bed. They're on my desk, on my conference table, and in my briefcase. My staff all know that I expect a supply of index cards and pens to be within reach anywhere within our office area. And, of course, I usually wear shirts with a pocket, so I can carry a supply of blank cards, as well as keep the idea-cards I've been writing and thinking about lately.

I use an average of about a hundred index cards in a typical week, unless I'm outlining a book, a journal article, a client report or proposal, or a project plan. Then I may use lots more. When I'm out walking for exercise, eating a meal, talking with friends, driving my car, in the bathroom, on a plane, waiting for a plane, in a taxi, in a hotel—almost any waking activity—I'm constantly "listening" to the flow of ideas through my head. I listen to things other people say to pick up the bits of a new idea, maybe by associating with the words, phrases, or figures of speech they use. When I read magazines, I read for ideas or for "trigger" elements that bring up new ideas. When I watch movies or recorded videos, I look for ideas or bits of ideas, whether intended by the producers or not.

I've also used the method of *card planning,* or *affinity diagramming,* for many years; it's a simple procedure of itemizing all of the tasks or activities in a project, one per card, and then sticking them to a large wall with tape or putty. It's easy to move them around to form logical groups of related cards—hence the name affinity diagram. Once I see the total picture of the project I'm planning, the design of a book I'm writing, or the layout of a report or proposal I'm preparing, I can organize it most effectively. Sometimes it helps to keep the cards up on the wall and refer to them as a living project plan. In other cases it may be necessary or convenient to transcribe the plan into a written outline.

Whenever I think of some task I need to do or ask a staff member to do, out come the pen and an index card. I write a quick note and tuck it back into my pocket. When I arrive at my office in the morning, the first thing I do after switching on my computer is to pull out the batch of cards from my shirt pocket and see which ones need immediate action. Some of them I can assign to a staff member; others I've promised myself I will take for action. If there are many of them, I sort them in priority order and put them on my desk.

*I've simply come to the understanding that short-term memory can't be trusted.*

*If you want the idea-butterflies to stay with you,*
*you have to write them down.*

This system isn't perfect, of course, as no system is. Once I woke up in the deepest part of the night with a terrific idea that came to me in a dream. It seemed like a very interesting idea for a book. I fumbled in the dark for the pen and the stack of cards, and I scribbled the idea as best I could in my soporific fog. In the morning, I remembered that I'd had a great idea for a book, and—not remembering what it actually was—I immediately retrieved the card and read it. It said "Great idea for a new book."

*I've been trying to make a sale here.* I've been trying to sell you, the reader of this book, on adopting the behavior of keeping index cards handy and writing things down. My guess is that I've probably achieved approximately the following:

- Five percent of you already write things down, diligently, either using index cards, Post-it or similar slips, or scraps of paper. I've probably reinforced your conviction of the value of the habit.
- Twenty percent of you probably write things down occasionally. Approximately half of you may be induced by this book to make a more diligent practice of it.
- Fifty percent of you are probably thinking, "It might be a good idea to make a habit of writing things down." Possibly one in five of you will actually adopt the practice. The others will likely "make a mental note of it" and forget all about it as soon as you've put down the book.
- The remaining 25 percent of you will probably think, "I don't have any trouble remembering things—I don't need to write everything down," or even "I don't really have that much to remember." You'll go on believing that your short-term memory works just fine, and so your idea-butterflies will continue to escape. For some people, "good enough" is good enough.

It's intriguing to me how many adult people, including professionals in knowledge occupations, living in today's modern society, can't lay hands on a ball-point pen at a moment's need. I'll be standing in the passport line in an airport and someone will ask, "Can I borrow your pen, please?" For less than one dollar, this person could have in his or her pocket or purse one of the most important inventions of the human race, and has chosen not to.

## THINKING IN PICTURES

Here's a little exercise in *visual thinking*.

*Step One:* first, try to solve the following problem in your mind, without writing anything down, and before reading further. Then go to Step Two.

A three-volume set of history books is sitting on a bookshelf, having been shelved there in the customary manner, arranged in volume order from left to right. A bookworm starts at the first page of the first volume and eats his way through to the last page of the last volume. All three books are the same size: the front and back covers are each one-eighth of an inch thick; and each "page block"—the stack of pages inside—is one inch thick. Your task is to calculate the distance the bookworm travels in his journey.

When you think you have the correct answer, write it down on an index card. (It's important to write it down, otherwise you'll probably forget it by the time you finish the second part of the exercise.)

*Step Two:* now check your visual thinking process by using your pen and an index card to draw a sketch of the books as they would be arranged on the shelf.

Draw the three books as you would see them looking down from above. Volume one is on the left, followed by volume two, followed by volume three. Put a mark where the bookworm started, at the first page of volume one. Then draw a line from there to the last page of volume three. Next, add up the thicknesses of the parts of the books the worm ate his way through, to get the total distance of his journey.

When you're sure you have the correct answer, check the solutions in Appendix A to see if you're right.

*Step Three:* compare the result you got by working the problem only in your mind with the result you got by drawing the diagram.

Maybe you got the correct answer both ways. Or maybe you didn't quite picture the three books as they would normally be arranged. Did you allow the verbal description of the problem—traveling from the first page of the first book to the last page of the last book—to create a *mental set*: the expectation that the bookworm would have to travel through all three page blocks and all but two of the covers?

A very useful feature of the pen-and-card tool, as demonstrated here, is that it enables you to bring your thinking process outside of your head, capture your results while you're solving a problem, and organize all of the information into one scheme. And, obviously, it provides a useful communication device when you're discussing the solution to a problem with another person.

## ARE YOU A YES-PERSON OR A NO-PERSON?

A dozen people are sitting around a conference table, having a meeting to discuss a procedural problem that's been causing frustration in their department. The conversation turns to a search for possible solutions. Susan says, "Maybe we could ask the staff members for their ideas. They might come up with some possibilities we haven't thought of."

Whereupon John immediately replies, "No, let's not go through all of that. It's our responsibility to solve the problem. Let's just get on with this, and come up with something we can take to the boss." The other members of the group react with silence, their eyes scanning back and forth between John and Susan. A few of them nod vaguely, and the conversation moves on. Susan sits back in her chair, folds her hands in her lap, and tunes out. She thinks, "If they don't want my ideas, then to hell with it. I'll just let them do their thing."

Later in the meeting, John offers an option for solving the problem: "I think we could create a form for this. [Person A] can fill out part of it and pass it on to [Person B]. Then. . . ." Susan sits forward, raises her hand in a "stop the traffic" gesture, and says, "Not another form! We've got too many forms now—they're coming out our ears. We need less paperwork, not more." In the back of her mind she's thinking, "Now I've evened the score, you S.O.B. You shot down my idea, and now I get to shoot yours down."

Some of the other people around the table nod their agreement with Susan's position, and John sits back with a sullen expression coming over his face. The score is "Susan: 1, John: 1." Both ideas have been shot down. But there's a third, invisible part of the score: "Ideas: 0."

This kind of idea-killing exchange happens countless times a day, in offices, classrooms, homes, and lots of other settings. Truly, we'd have to consider it "normal" human behavior—not necessarily desirable or constructive, but basically normal. Most people do it routinely and unthinkingly.

As with the proverbial iceberg, the idea-killing impulse usually lurks below the water line of consciousness. It often happens spontaneously and habitually, before the person who does it considers the consequences of what he or she is about to say. It may be triggered by a feeling of envy or resentment: "Uh-oh! She's just come up with a promising idea; maybe that will make everyone think she's smarter than I am. How can I show how smart I am?" The primitive unconscious logic says: *"If I can show everybody that her idea's no good, maybe they won't think she's smarter than I am."*

Some people are habitual idea zappers, some less so. Sometimes a person is just in a cranky mood, or not feeling very well. They may have recently had an adversarial experience and their practical altruism program may not be fully operational. Some people are generally fearful, and don't feel comfortable with the ambiguity that comes with the creative process. A few may be downright malicious, and killing the ideas of others provides an outlet for their aggression. And many—perhaps most—simply don't know any better. They're acting out what they've been taught by the social modeling they've experienced so far in their lives.

Oliver Wendell Holmes, the American jurist and Chief Justice of the Supreme Court, said:

"The true test of any concept is its ability to survive in the marketplace of ideas."

And he might have added:

*The true test of any thinker is his or her ability to
see the potential in new-born ideas.*

The mental habit of valuing ideas means saying a tentative "yes" to every new-born idea, with the confidence that giving it time to breathe may enable it to evolve into something truly valuable.

A very few people, as inventor Charles Kettering characterized them, are idea lovers. I call them "yes-people," who affirm, nurture, and support new-born ideas, however strange, peculiar, unrealistic, or even offensive they may first seem. They see ideas as precious assets, as intellectual wealth. They realize that not all ideas eventually sell themselves, but they see no value in killing them off prematurely.

No-people tend to contaminate their perceptions of new-born ideas with all manner of fears, failure fantasies, apprehensions, ego-defenses, emotional reactions, and aggressive motives.

Valuing ideas calls for much more emotional and intellectual courage, and a basic faith in the value of ideas, than idea-killing requires. Ultimately, faith in the value of ideas equates to faith in our own selves and in our own thinking processes. Award-winning *National Geographic* photographer DeWitt Jones likes to say, "There's usually more than one 'right' answer."

## THE P.I.N. FORMULA: PROTECTING IDEAS

While riding on a plane between Sydney and Canberra, Australia, I happened to notice an item tucked into the seat-pocket in front of me that seemed rather interesting. It was an envelope about four inches wide and about six inches long, with an adhesive closure tab on one end. The brightly printed outside of the envelope seemed, at first glance, to be designed as a mailer for having film developed. One could write the various specifications in the appropriate boxes, write one's

address, insert a roll of film and some cash, and mail it to the processing lab. Presumably they would receive the pictures to the address
given. This seemed like a fairly useful item to find on a plane.

Then I studied the envelope a bit further and discovered that it had
a secondary function: the label told me it was also designed to serve as
an *air-sickness bag*. The plasticized insert and the expandable side panels
seemed well-suited for that mission also.

I mused for a moment at what seemed to me a fairly imaginative
product. I surmised that the film lab provided the envelopes to the
airline at no charge, for use as "barf bags," as the flight attendants call
them. Here was a product that could perform double duty, and which
served as a marketing tool at virtually no cost to the film lab.

Then I had some third thoughts. I found myself thinking, "If I were
an employee working in that film-processing lab, I'd sure be hoping that
the person who mailed the next envelope I picked up clearly understood the instructions."

I love playing with oddball ideas; I always have. And I eventually
came to understand that playing with ideas, especially partly baked
ones, is not only fun but it's ecologically valuable. If we make a habit of
saying yes to ideas at first, and protecting them for at least a short
while, we can vastly increase the number of "good" ideas available to us.
This principle works in personal life, in education, in business, and in
public service.

Over the years I've evolved a handy method for protecting ideas,
one I've taught many times in executive seminars and modeled for
others during my activities as a business consultant. It's called the
"P.I.N." formula, and it's a three-step process for reacting to ideas.
The P.I.N. formula works for individuals, for two or more people in
conversation, in meetings, and in creative sessions involving design or
complex problem solving. It allows us to suspend judgment—at least
negative or critical judgment—long enough for ideas to grow on us.

A person, a group, or a team using the P.I.N. formula agrees to express reactions to an idea in three distinct steps, *in a required order:*

P = Positive aspects of the idea.

I = Interesting, or intriguing aspects of the idea.

N = Negative aspects of the idea.

I sometimes call the method a "safety pin" for ideas. Ideas are like infants in diapers, and the safety pins have to protect their tender selves from trauma during their formative period.

As we'll see in Chapter 12, when we study the "High Speed Problem-Solving" process, invoking the P.I.N. rule or formula allows people to toss around partly baked ideas without fear of ridicule. Group leaders can use the method to get lots of possibilities for solving a problem. A person who proposes a provocative idea can ask for a "P.I.N. reaction" as a way to entice other participants to engage the idea long enough to see its implications. And every one of us can make it our "default" reaction to ideas as we encounter them.

> "I always know when I've encountered a really
> great idea, because of the feeling of terror it
> causes in me."
> —John Franck, Nobel Laureate

## USING YOUR MAGICAL INCUBATOR

The noted nineteenth-century German chemist Friedrich August Kekulé reported a remarkable experience that led directly to an important discovery in hydrocarbon chemistry in 1864. Kekule had been trying to figure out the structure of the benzene molecule, one of a number of compounds he and his contemporaries had been studying.

According to his account:

"I was sitting writing on my textbook, but the work did not progress; my thoughts were elsewhere. I turned my chair to the fire and dozed. Again the atoms were gamboling before my eyes. My mental eye, rendered more acute by the repeated visions of this kind, could now distinguish larger structures of manifold conformation; long rows sometimes more closely fitted together all twining and twisting in snake-like motion. But look! What was that? One of the snakes had seized hold of its own tail, and the form whirled mockingly before my eyes. As if by a flash of lightning I awoke."

When he awoke, Kekulé instantly realized that his unconscious mind, in its dreamlike state, had presented him with the solution: the hydrogen-carbon pairs in the benzene molecule *must be arranged in a ring formation*—a hexagon, to be exact, which he recognized as the snake biting its tail. His research immediately confirmed what his unconscious ideation had figured out.

Scientific history abounds with similar examples of the "flash of insight" discovery that follows on from hard work and diligent thinking. These insight events happen more often than most of us realize, and it's possible to invite them to happen more often than they do. One way to make them more likely is to notice them when they do occur, cherish them, and optimistically expect that more of them will come.

Dr. Sidney Parnes, one of the pioneers of creative education, who helped give birth to the Creative Education Foundation and the Creative Problem Solving Institute at Buffalo State University,[1] tells of an episode involving his young daughter, who was trying to solve a problem. The drawstring had come out of the waistband of her pajamas, and she couldn't figure out how to get it back in. She tried various approaches, but none of them seemed to work without a long, tedious effort to thread it through the channel. As Sid tells it:

"She had temporarily given up on the problem, but apparently another part of her mind hadn't. Later, as she was opening the refrigerator to get some ice for a cold drink, she suddenly thought of the solution. She soaked the drawstring in water, put it into the freezer, and when it had frozen solid she took it out and threaded it easily into the waistband of her pajamas."

Creativity researchers refer to this idea-priming process as *incubation*. It's a pretty good metaphor, actually: it conjures up the image of eggs parked in an incubator, allowed to develop and suddenly spring to life.

The incubation "light bulb" experience—the "Aha!" event—often seems to happen as a result of two ideas or idea-fragments bumping into each other below the level of consciousness. Probably some mind-module recognizes the relevance of the connection and sends up a mental flare signal into conscious awareness.

For example, an Austrian woman named Hedwig Kiesler—more popularly known as the actress Hedy Lamarr—won a patent from the U.S. government for an electronic device, which came to mind while she was singing at the piano. Having escaped from Nazi Germany as World War II got underway, Lamarr was in the process of building a new career in America. Apparently rather technically minded as well as musical, she had been toying with the idea of using radio signals to control anti-submarine torpedoes. The idea was not generally considered viable by technical experts, because enemy forces could easily jam the control signals with interfering transmissions.

As she stood practicing vocal exercises beside the piano, with her friend playing various scales and melodies, the answer suddenly flashed into her mind. If the frequency of a radio signal were to change rapidly in some controlled pattern, known only to the sender and the receiver, a would-be enemy receiver would not be able to track it or jam it. The unconscious source of the idea seemed clear: if both the singer and the accompanist always know what the next note will be, they communicate perfectly as a musical team. The same principle should apply to radio communications.

Working with her friend, she sketched out a diagram of a piano-roll device that could change the frequencies to create an electronic "melody." She received a patent in 1942 for a "Secret Communications System," assigning the rights to the U.S. government. She never profited from her invention, which today is widely used in applications such as cell-phone technology to prevent interference between simultaneous conversations. Technicians know it as frequency-diversity, or spread-spectrum technology.

Some creative figures in history have claimed to have gotten their best ideas while under the influence of alcohol, psychedelic drugs, or even medications—a novel type of incubator, I suppose. My colleague and many-years friend Frank Ball, who heads the media division of a global financial services firm, reports having conjured up a novel and useful idea while under the influence of medical morphine. As he relates the experience:

"I was lying in a hospital bed recovering from an emergency surgery. The staff had given me a dose of morphine to help alleviate the intense pain I'd been experiencing. Despite the stress of such an experience, I was pondering intensely about a business problem I'd been trying to solve, with a very short deadline looming up at me.

"Morphine has a rather subtle effect on one's mental processes, even though the effect on the pain is significant. I found myself musing, pain-free for the moment, about how I was going to solve this pressing problem. I could see and hear fragments of ideas floating by as I faded in and out of this dreamy state. It was almost as if I'd opened the door to my incubator and was looking inside to see what was incubating there.

"My problem was to come up with a fairly clever 'opening number'—a video segment—to be used to kick off the annual partners' meeting for the firm. These annual meetings are a big deal.

"This particular meeting had one thing in common with most of the previous ones: the partners had to fly in—to Chicago, in this case—from all over the world, and the ones who had to travel the greatest distances always grumbled about the location. 'I just left Paris, France, to come to . . . Washington! In June!!' Or, more typically, 'Why Boston?' 'Why Miami?' In this case, it was going to be 'Why Chicago?' So we were asked by the firm's chief operating officer to come up with an opening number as a spoof on the perpetual complaints about where the thing was held.

"The day before my unexpected surgery, I'd been involved in two fruitless meetings and an hour-long conference call trying to come up with something that would work. As I lay there in my morphine-induced semi-coma, I was turning over the question in my mind: 'Why Chicago?'

"Then, in a moment of clarity, I sensed that the vocal cadence of the phrase 'Why Chicago?' matched that of the familiar 'Hallelujah' of Handel's 'Hallelujah Chorus.' I heard the new chorus in my mind: 'Whyyy Chicago? Whyyy Chicago? Why Chicago? Why Chicago? Why Ch-ihh-ka-go?' The comic irony made it click.

"Somehow I managed to remember the idea after the morphine wore off, and when I could function properly again I got my staff working on it. We created music tracks and recorded studio singers belting out custom lyrics that poked fun at the partners and introduced the charms of Chicago. Then we videotaped dozens of the partners lip-synching to the music. Cut together, it had a real MTV edge, and was very hip. We showed it as the opener for the meeting and it went over big. We heard no more complaining about the venue for the meeting."

Many good ideas result from the chance conversations between neurons. The process of incubation has three steps:

1. ***Preparation.*** You've been wrestling with a problem, a difficult decision, an exciting opportunity, or a dilemma of some kind, and you're feeling blocked. The harder you try to concentrate on the problem and the more energy you put into trying to solve it, the more it seems to elude you. You haven't been wasting your time or your energy: you've been getting ready to incubate.

2. ***Submersion.*** After spending some period of time thinking about the problem, you simply need to give your mind a rest and turn your attention to other things. You may not consciously realize it, but you've turned the problem over to other "minds" that go to work on it. Scientists have very little idea how the biocomputer does it, but it seems to allocate a certain number of its "processor cycles" to various things you've been thinking about.

3. ***Insight.*** This is the accidental part of the process. We don't know—yet—how to cause the unconsciously circulating bits of information to come together into a new formation. Maybe we'll figure that out some day soon. What we know now is that diligent effort in the first phase, preparation, sets up the problem so that the unconscious mind can go to work on it. Turning your attention to something else entirely seems to help, possibly by taking away the interfering signals from the conscious level and allowing the data to be processed in a new way.

"Chance favors the prepared mind."

—Louis Pasteur
(developer of the germ theory of disease)

Here's a simple method that can help make your magic incubator work for you:

1. First, give the problem, the issue, or the objective a name. *Call it something*: the "career blockage" problem; the "family feud" problem; or the "impossible schedule" problem, for example.

2. Next, review the various elements of the problem, refresh them in your mind, and particularly dwell on the tricky questions you haven't found answers for. Pack the problem up for incubation.

3. You may want to visualize the incubation process. Imagine taking an egg, writing the name of the problem on the shell of the egg with a felt-tip marker, then opening up the door of your mental incubator, and gently placing the "problem egg" into the warm, nurturing environment with the other problem eggs. Imagine and expect that, when the problem egg turns into a "solution egg"—it hatches, in other words—it will make itself known to your conscious mind.

4. Then, ask your "other minds" to go to work on the problem. You can even vocalize this request (preferably when no one else is nearby): "I want to find a solution to the 'X' problem. I've been thinking about it, and now I'll put it aside for the time being, and maybe an answer will come to me." Say and think this with a child-like sense of trust, believing that one of your other minds already knows the answer.

5. Just be sure you *let go of the problem* and find other things to give your attention to. If you keep obsessing about the problem and keep trying to grasp for solutions, then you're not incubating— you're just worrying. Genuine incubation requires that you let go of the problem for the time being.

6. Keep a pen and some index cards handy so you can write down the ideas as they bubble up to your conscious mind. The answer, or answers, might not come in a magical flash; you might not see visions or hear celestial music. You might get various bits and pieces or small insights that help you solve it with your conscious processes.

# "METABOXICAL" THINKING:
# BREAKING THE BOUNDARIES

"Imagination is more important than knowledge."

—Albert Einstein

No discussion of creative ideation could be complete without reference to the famous "nine-dot" problem. This ancient visual puzzle is probably the source of the well-worn cliché about "thinking outside the box." As a demonstration of the self-limiting effects of our mental patterns, it has few equals, and that's one reason why so many teachers and trainers use it in courses that dwell on creativity, innovation, and problem solving.

For those readers who've seen the nine-dot problem countless times: an apology in advance. Surprisingly, however, a large number of people who've already seen the nine-dot problem, and the solution—in some cases, repeatedly—still can't remember how to solve it. That's a good illustration of the power of patterns. And, considering that many people—possibly including you, the reader of this book—haven't encountered it, I would be remiss as an author in not presenting it.

## The Famous Nine-Dot Problem

Here's the famous nine-dot problem. Refer to Figure 7.1, which shows an array of nine dots. The objective of the exercise is to draw no more than four straight lines without lifting the pen from the paper, and without retracing any part of the line, in such a way as to connect all nine dots.

Use your pen and an index card and try to work it out before you look up the answer in Appendix A. Once you see the solution, you'll immediately see how it illustrates the effects of mental patterns.

## Why the Nine-Dot Problem
## Is So Challenging for Most of Us

The first reaction many people have after seeing the solution is: "Oh, you have to go outside of the square—the box."

## Figure 7.1.    The Nine-Dot Problem

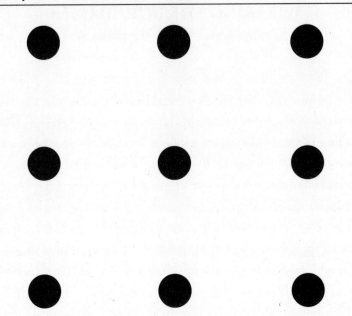

Of course, there's no box or square in the picture—just some dots. The brain, being a compulsive pattern-maker and pattern-recognizer, detects *what it believes to be a pattern* in the picture. We perceive what psychologists call a *subjective contour*—a familiar pattern that's suggested by the arrangement of the elements and that matches a memory pattern in the brain.

Once we "see" the pattern, it takes control of our thinking process. We substitute our memory-model of reality for reality. Much of our mental process falls into this pattern of "rectangular" thinking— unconsciously confining our perceptions to fit familiar patterns.

If you solved the nine-dot problem without seeing the answer previously, you probably felt a sense of liberation, of breaking through some kind of restraint and being free to do something new. This "break-out" strategy can be learned and strengthened with practice and motivation.

This kind of *pattern independence* is a hallmark of people who are skilled problem solvers, innovators and inventors, designers, and entrepreneurs. They've learned to see through, over, under, around, and beyond their own mental patterns—and the patterns that imprison others—to find different arrangements of the elements of a problem or situation.

Pattern independence, or the ability to think outside the various self-imposed boxes of our knowledge and experience, needs a better name than the worn-out cliché "thinking outside the box." Therefore, we'll invent a new one. Let's coin the term:

> *Metaboxical Thinking: The ability to detect*
> *and escape from the unconscious boundaries*
> *imposed by our perceptions of a problem.*

Metaboxical thinking has two parts: thinking *about* the figurative mental boxes we can put ourselves into and then thinking *beyond* them. We first need to recognize the mental patterns we're being tempted to apply and then liberate ourselves from them.

One might ask, "How can we consciously identify these mental boxes we put around the problems we perceive if they're *unconscious* patterns?" Actually, it's not quite so difficult as one might think.

The British philosopher and mathematician Alfred North Whitehead reportedly said, "It requires a very unusual mind to undertake the analysis of the obvious," and that's exactly what we learn to do in metaboxical thinking. We question the most obvious aspects of our so-called "knowledge" of the problem we're trying to solve, and we question the most obvious elements of the approach we're taking to try to get to solutions.

In my occupation as a management consultant, I frequently work with senior executives of various types of organizations as they re-think their businesses. Some of the questions I typically pose are: "What are the most fundamental 'truths' of your business? Your market? Your customers? Your competition?" "Are these 'truths' still true?"

"What assumptions are you making about the future of your business?" "What happens if those assumptions don't hold true?" "What assumptions might you be making that could be limiting your perceptions of your opportunities?"

Metaboxical thinking can help us get un-stuck when we get stuck trying to solve a challenging problem. It can help us "jump the track" and switch to a very different line of thinking. Professor Edward deBono, a noted authority on creativity, referred to what he called "lateral thinking." In his definition, lateral thinking—as contrasted to the more "normal" process of "vertical" thinking—involves letting go of an unsuccessful attempt at solving a problem and coming at it from a new angle. Another useful term for vertical thinking is "monorail" thinking. deBono's classic book *Lateral Thinking: Creativity Step-by-Step,* while somewhat dated, remains a highly respected reference for the topic.[2]

Lateral thinking, as Professor deBono described it, is one type of metaboxical thinking. It deals with changing the sequence of steps, abandoning the sequence, substituting a new sequence, or perhaps leap-frogging the sequential thinking process altogether. In Chapter 10 we'll explore the special combination of intuitive thinking and logical thinking—"intulogical" thinking—and we'll explore the connections to lateral thinking, incubation, and skillful problem solving.

Another interesting example of a thinking problem that calls for metaboxical thinking is the *anagram*—that tricky little word puzzle that requires one to rearrange a series of letters to make a familiar word. Anagrams are typically rather difficult to solve for one primary reason: They're constructed so as to suggest an acceptable word—that is, to match up with a mental pattern that makes them seem already "correct."

As an example, consider rearranging the following sequence of letters to make a known word:

m i n t e y

It has the look and feel of a real English word, even though we sense that it is not. When challenged to rearrange the letters to make a "better" word, many people find themselves somehow tethered to the existing form, and unable to think of alternatives. The existing pattern imposes a kind of structural tyranny over the mind—a set of invisible boundaries on the perception of what's possible. (*Hint:* the solution to the anagram above is a word meaning a state of animosity, constructed by moving the "e" and the "n" to the beginning of the series.)

According to historical accounts, England's Lord Melbourne challenged Queen Victoria to solve the following anagram, which reportedly kept her awake the whole night:

## t e r a l b a y

Inasmuch as this collection of eight letters can be rearranged in almost 40,000 ways, brute force and persistence are not particularly appealing as an avenue to a solution. One needs a mental strategy, a more productive way of designing a solution.

Before you look up the answer in Appendix A, try the following mental strategies that might lead you to the answer.

Mainly, you must find a way to break the tyranny of the comfortable pattern presented by the letters. One way to do this is to completely *deconstruct* the present arrangement. For example, take eight small scraps of paper, or bits of an index card, and write one of the letters on each scrap. Then scatter them out before you on your desk or table. Start shifting them around, trying various combinations of two and three letters, allowing your intuitive radar to search for other possible patterns. When you think you have the answer, or if you don't and you feel you've worked at it long enough, check the answer in Appendix A.

Anagrams, as simple as they seem, can be very effective exercises for expanding your divergent thinking skills and your skill of reframing situations or ideas. Here are a few more to solve (they're fairly easy), as part of your mental calisthenics:

r u n g h y

f l y m i a

m u l c i c a

d o r n e v

l e n d r a c a

The strategy we used to solve the anagram problem applies, in some form or another, to many problems we face in life, in relationships, and in business. To think metaboxically, we first have to *de-construct* our current conception of the problem we're trying to solve. What are the elements of the problem? What are some of the elements we can see for the solution? What constraints or restrictions are we accepting? By identifying the parts of the problem and potential solutions and rearranging them, just as we did with the letters of the anagram, we can open up mental doors that can let us out of the boxes we've constructed or accepted from others.

Magic tricks are an excellent example of the influence of mindsets and expectations, challenging us to think metaboxically, which we often do inadequately. The skilled magician leads us to lock into a mindset—an expectation of what's about to happen. The power of the "trick," and the amusement we get from it, come from the magician's clever exploitation of the mindset he or she has helped us to form.

> "Miracle, n. An act or event out of the order of nature
> and unaccountable, such as beating a normal hand
> of four kings and an ace with four aces and a king."
>
> —Ambrose Bierce
>
> *The Devil's Dictionary*

Incidentally, most magic tricks are engineered within the first few seconds; most of the theatrical moves, maneuvers, and conversational patter serve only to increase the strength of the expectation. Once the magician has "set up" the trick, which we typically do not notice, he or she is basically home free; he or she just has fun pumping up our expectations, which intensifies the impact of seeing the expectation completely contradicted.

Metaboxical thinking can also involve an important element of chance, or even accident, that guides our internal conversation about a problem. In fact, some of our best ideas come from fortunate accidents. Consider, for example, the way humor works. A good joke or a witty comment about some topic is a kind of re-framing: we suddenly see things in a different way.

Irish comedian Hal Roach tells a story that illustrates the limitations of thinking patterns—the boxes—and makes the failure to think metaboxically quite amusing:

"The parish priest was sitting at his kitchen table one afternoon, working on his sermon for the coming Sunday.

"It had been raining heavily for several days, and the dam up the river from the village had given way, flooding the town and driving all of the parishioners out of their homes.

"He looked out the window and saw the waters rising to the edge of his window sill. He saw people swimming about in the flood waters, rowing boats, and clinging to anything they could find that would float.

"Just then two people in a boat came by his window. 'Father, jump into the boat with us and we'll get you to safety.'

"The priest waved them on. 'No, no thank you. I'll be fine. Just be on your way and look after yourselves.'

"'Father,' they implored him, 'do come with us. It isn't safe to stay here.'

"'No, no,' said the priest. 'Off you go—I'll be fine.'

"'Well, please yourself,' they said, and they rowed away.

"As the water continued to rise, the priest gathered up his papers and moved upstairs to his study.

The water continued to rise menacingly. As he looked out his window, several more people came by in a large rowboat.

"'Father, please—get in the boat with us. We'll take you to safety.'

"Still quite calm, the priest said, 'No, my children. God will look after me. You go on and save yourselves—I'll be fine.'

"He'd have none of their pleading, so they finally gave up and went off in their boat.

"The waters kept rising to the point where he had to climb up onto the roof. There he was, holding onto the weather vane, when a third boat came by.

"'Father, you must come with us. This is a very dangerous situation; please get in the boat and save yourself. It's your last chance!'

"With great calm and magnanimity he waved them on. 'No, no—I'll be fine. I have my faith in the Lord. He will save me from the flood.'

"Distraught but unable to dislodge his unshakable faith, they went on.

"Unfortunately, his strategy didn't work. He drowned, and the next thing he knew he was standing at the Pearly Gates. St. Peter spotted him and called out, 'So, there you are!'

"The priest, looking astonished, raised his hands in confusion and disbelief. 'What happened?' he implored. 'Why did God not save me from the flood? I've lived a virtuous life, I've devoted my whole life to the service of the Church—I thought God would save me!'

"St. Peter shrugged his shoulders and said, 'What do you want? We sent three boats for you.'"

I often think about that little story and its implications for the opportunities and options that life presents to us. Several of my colleagues and I often use it as a metaphorical shorthand when discussing potential business opportunities: "Do you think this might be a 'boat' we're looking at?"

## Notes

1. Website for the Creative Education Foundation is www.Creative EducationFoundation.org.
2. deBono, Edward. *Lateral Thinking: Creativity Step-by-Step.* New York: HarperCollins, 1973.

# 8

## MEGA-SKILL 1
### *"Bivergent" Thinking*

"Not all who wander are lost."
—J.R.R. Tolkien

MANY YEARS AGO WHILE TRAVELING IN JAPAN, I met an executive of a Japanese textile firm over breakfast in a Tokyo hotel. When he discovered that I was a management consultant, we got to talking about Japanese and American business practices, and I expressed a particular interest in the Japanese approach to making decisions. He invited me to visit him and his fellow executives on my way through Nagoya, and I enthusiastically accepted.

During my brief visit, I met with him and his colleagues over coffee for an interesting discussion. During the conversation I inquired about their typical decision-making processes. How, for example, would they approach the question of adding a new line of textiles to their catalog?

My host, "Shiggie" (short for Shigeru), offered his perceptions of the difference between the Japanese custom of making decisions and what he understood to be the typical Western pattern. He had worked extensively with Western firms and observed what he felt were some important differences. He shared his accumulated observations [paraphrased here]:

"I think the typical Japanese method of making decisions is quite different from the Western or American method. We tend to arrive at decisions by a slower, more deliberative process, whereas Western executives tend to favor a faster, somewhat more aggressive process. Both processes can work, of course; however, our method has certain advantages which we like.

"Take, for example, the decision about whether to expand the product line in some way. It's generally understood that certain people would be involved in that decision. We get together for a meeting, have some coffee or tea, and talk it over from various angles. Usually the team members don't come to the meeting with their minds already made up. We talk at great length, and a consensus eventually emerges. When everyone realizes what the consensus is, we get up and leave. [He smiled politely.]

"Here is where one difference comes in, I think. Even though we don't usually specify the decision in great detail, everyone involved is bound by the mutual understanding of what was decided. There can be no 'nit-picking' or 'hair-splitting' later on; the decision is the decision, and everybody is obligated.

"The Western style, as I understand it, is usually to start the meeting with everybody offering their opinions, which they've often decided on before the meeting. There tends to be more debating and less questioning in the Western style of deciding. In a way, the Western-style meeting seems to be a contest of opinions rather than a search for a consensus. Somebody 'wins' the meeting, in other words.

"The difference in these two different ways of deciding— I believe—shows up in implementing the decision. In the Japanese way, anyone who is unsure of the decision or not comfortable with the course of action is expected to signal his concerns by his questions. We don't necessarily argue; we ask lots of questions. When the questions are all answered, we're at agreement. Of course, not everybody may be 100 percent enthusiastic about the decision, but once a person has had an opportunity to have his concerns heard and considered, then he is utterly obligated to do his part to make sure the decision is successful.

"The Western style, I believe, is often more adversarial. One person, or one faction, tends to win the meeting, by convincing the boss or by pushing the other factions into going along. Unfortunately, people who feel they've been pushed into going along, and haven't had a chance to express their concerns, may not feel much loyalty to the decision. Later on, they may be inclined to sabotage the course of action when things get difficult. So, I think the Western-style decision is more likely to get 'un-made' afterward if the consensus is not strong."

As with all generalizations, my Japanese colleague's characterization of the differences in the two ways of deciding has its limitations. One must imagine that not all Japanese or Western decisions necessarily follow these same patterns. However, it struck me at the time as an intriguing general proposition.

## THE DIVERGENT-CONVERGENT POLARITY: THE D-C AXIS

I began to reflect on my own observations of decision making in various situations, and I started to become very conscious of *one critical element* of the process. This element, I believe, lies at the heart of all decision processes, or problem-solving processes, regardless of culture, customs, or personalities. It's fundamental to the human thinking process, even though it unfolds differently in different situations.

The key element of the deciding process, I realized, was the *transition point* between two distinctly different types of thinking, as recognized by cognitive psychologists: *divergent thinking* and *convergent thinking*. I began to diagram decision processes I found myself involved with in terms of this key psychological or mental turning point, or change-over point in every decision.

Let's review the elements of divergent and convergent thinking, and analyze the role of the transition point in the process. First, some definitions:

> *Divergent Thinking: A thinking process that branches out from one idea to others, associated ideas.*

> *Convergent Thinking: A thinking process that reduces a large set of ideas or options to a select few.*

I began to see these two distinctive mental patterns as parts of the same spectrum, a complimentary polarity that we can recognize and capitalize on. For this discussion we'll refer to the spectrum as the *divergent-convergent axis,* or "D-C axis," and we'll refer to the skill of navigating across the whole D-C spectrum as one of four key "mega-skills" of practical intelligence. Let's coin another term in the lexicon of PI— "bivergent thinking":

> *Bivergent Thinking: A thinking process that integrates both divergent and convergent patterns of ideation into a synergistic combination.*

Figure 8.1 may help to illustrate this polarity—or perhaps we can also think of it as a *duality*—and the special role of the shift between the two patterns, which in my experience often takes place without the

## Figure 8.1.    The Pivot Point in Decision Making

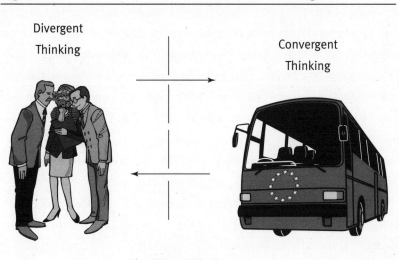

Divergent
Thinking

Convergent
Thinking

The "Pivot Point"

conscious recognition of the people involved. Somewhere in the progression from the first recognition of the problem or decision issue to the final decision and the course of action that follows from it, there must be a transition between these two distinctly different patterns of thinking. I've found it very helpful to characterize effective decision making as a process of consciously *managing the transition* between divergence and convergence. I call it the *"pivot point"*—the moment when the mind, or a group of minds, begins to shift from one of the two patterns to the other.

We can think of effective decision making or problem solving, in just about any situation, context, or culture, as an appropriate combination of three key skills:

1. The skill of divergent thinking;
2. The skill of convergent thinking; and
3. The skill of managing the pivot point, or transition, between the two processes.

Conversely, I'm convinced, after years of studying many decisions by many business leaders, ranging from the abysmally incompetent to the spectacularly brilliant, that *incompetent decision making can almost always be diagnosed as a failure of one or more of these three key elements.*

In a way, we're just acknowledging what common sense tells us: the ineffective decision makers didn't adequately consider the various key elements relevant to the problem; they didn't effectively narrow the range of potential solutions and converge to one that could work; or they couldn't figure out how to guide the thinking process to get from the divergent phase to the convergent phase.

We'll explore both divergent and convergent thinking skills more fully, after we examine several cognitive pathologies that often afflict decision makers in business and other organizations.

## PROCESS CONSCIOUSNESS: MANAGING THE "PIVOT POINT"

Imagine that you're sitting in a meeting with a dozen people who are trying to agree on a course of action to solve some problem—say a big schedule slip on a project or increasing crime in their neighborhood. You switch into your observer mode and pay attention to the struggles they go through as they try to get to agreement. Never mind the "content"—the various facts and figures, ideas, opinions, questions, and proposals; focus your attention closely on the "process"—the "how" of the way they try to get there. It may help to call to mind several meetings you've participated in or observed, to give you a rich sense of the kinds of thinking processes that go on.

Understanding the difference between *content* and *process,* particularly in a group situation, is one of the simplest, most powerful, and least understood secrets of practical intelligence. At least 95 percent of humans are utterly distractible by the information that arises in a discussion and quite oblivious to the process that's going on. When group meetings get confused, derailed, or deadlocked, or they fall into conflict, the cause is more likely to be a failure of *process consciousness* rather than not having the needed information or not having the intelligence to make use of it.

> "There's no right way to do the wrong thing."
> —Aldous Huxley

If you have a highly developed sense of *process consciousness,* you can think on both levels at the same time: you can observe, react to—*and guide*—the process and its content at the same time.

*Case in point:* some years ago I was asked by a colleague, who was teaching a university course on organizational behavior, to substitute for him during one session. The mission, he assured me, was simple. The group, about a dozen adult professionals, was working on a team project and all I had to do was be available to them for coaching or idea inputs if they felt the need. As the meeting got underway, there seemed to be some confusion about what they were to accomplish, and the discussion seemed to wander aimlessly. The elected group leader didn't seem to know how to bring it to a focus. The only woman in the group offered a suggestion: "Craig, I think it would be a good idea to take a few minutes and figure out an agenda for the meeting; what do we need to accomplish in the time we have?" The others glanced in her direction for a few seconds, someone else threw out an opinion related to the topic they had just been arguing about, and the discussion immediately veered off again into never-land. After wasting about thirty minutes of the three-hour session, they seemed to be totally flummoxed. I had said nothing so far. Finally the group leader turned to me and said, "Dr. A, it looks like we're stuck. What do you suggest?" I said, "I think it would be a good idea to take a few minutes and figure out an agenda for the meeting; what do you need to accomplish in the time you have?" "Good idea!" "That's it—what are we trying to accomplish?" All around the table I saw knowing nods, thumbs up, and approving fingers pointing toward me. As the group leader stood up to guide the process of building the agenda, and all eyes turned toward the whiteboard, I exchanged conspiratorial winks with the woman who'd made an accurate "process call" fifteen minutes beforehand. Sometimes people pay consultants to remind them of their common sense.

Now let's return to the hypothetical problem-solving meeting you've been observing. (You haven't lost track of the process we were just engaged in, have you?)

As you observe the meeting's process, here are some interesting dynamics to look for:

- Is the group skillfully led? Is there a clearly recognized leader, either formally appointed or accepted by the group? Are any other members trying to push the leader aside and take over the "alpha" role?
- How do the group members signal, detect, and respond to differences in rank, status, and entitlement? Is the group highly egalitarian, rigidly authoritarian, or somewhere in between?
- Which members seem to be entitled to do most of the talking, thinking, and deciding? All of them? Only the chief? A few people in an in-group?
- How does the group use the information it has available? Do they show respect for evidence and logic or do they decide based on emotions and opinions? Is an effective solution more important to them than making a decision without controversy?
- How well does the group make use of the knowledge and skills of all the members?
- How "process-aware" are the individual group members? Do they seem to understand the flow of the thinking process? Can they keep track of where they are, on the way to the decision? Do they seem to be aware of when they're diverging and when they're converging? Do they share ownership of the process?

Now imagine that your hypothetical group is moving along in its process, that it has avoided falling into conflict or confusion, and that a solution seems to be emerging from the discussion. Your next challenge is to *learn to detect the pivot point.*

How do you sense that the exploration phase—divergent thinking—is being superseded by the closure phase—convergent thinking—when the group members seem to be getting on the same bus, so to speak? What conversational cues can you detect that signal the increasing willingness of the members, or most of them, to embrace the developing course of action:

- "Option A won't fly. Neither will option C."
- "Well, if option A doesn't work, and option C won't work, I guess we're left with option B and option D."
- "It looks like the best way to go is. . . ."
- "Option X looks like it's the least of the evils."
- "Are we all in agreement with this?"
- "I guess that pretty much settles it."
- "That works for me."
- "Boss? What do you think?"
- "I don't think we really have any other choice."

Once you begin to look for the signals of *closure,* you'll find them very easy to spot. Sometimes a single statement or an exchange of comments signals the pivot point clearly; it may be obvious. In some cases, you have to judge for yourself whether the group has crossed over the line into convergence. At some point you become aware that most of the participants are buying into an emerging consensus.

Now imagine that you've been observing the group's process and you believe that they've moved into convergence too rapidly—you believe that they haven't identified some possible solutions that seem fairly obvious to you. Or you may believe that they've rushed through the process of choosing the favored option from the set of options that have emerged. Can you intervene constructively to help the group go back past the pivot point and return to a divergent pattern?

How would you, as a participant or an adviser, encourage a group of people who seem to be moving toward a favored course of action to go back to the "west" side of the pivot point and open up their thinking again?

*The answer*: you do it with statements that invite—and then model—divergent thinking. Some examples:

- "I'm wondering if we've overlooked some options that might be important."
- "Before we finalize the decision, I have a couple of questions."
- "Before we settle on this course of action, would it be worthwhile to see if anyone has any serious reservations about it that we haven't discussed so far?"
- "I'm a bit confused. I don't understand how we got from the definition of the problem to this particular solution. Could someone explain it to me?"
- "Could I bring up an aspect of the problem that we haven't discussed?"
- And even a simple cue like "May I ask a question?"

I've found the last example—"May I ask a question?"—especially effective as a way to invite people to think about their process. It's an innocent enough thing to say: presumably everybody has the right to be curious and to ask questions that can contribute to better thinking. It also seems, in my experience, to convey a sense of ambiguity, some unresolved aspect of the thinking process that deserves attention. I've found that many people react to this simple question by immediately preparing their minds for a return to divergence.

Now, let's add one more feature—perhaps the most important one—to our understanding of this hypothetical meeting we've been analyzing. Here's the most powerful possibility of all: *suppose all the people who are participating in the meeting have been trained in the methods of bivergent thinking?* Suppose they all understand what divergent and convergent thinking are; they all understand what the pivot point is and know how to spot it; and they all can consciously monitor the thinking process and share in managing it intelligently? That's the real potential of practical intelligence.

When the members of a group can consciously observe and manage their own thinking process, they can usually arrive at better decisions, more quickly, and more humanely than they otherwise would. If nothing else, simply paying attention to divergence and convergence as identifiable stages of the thinking process, and knowing how to spot— *and manage*—the pivot point enriches the process enormously.

Further, process consciousness enables a group to focus their mental energies more effectively. What happens in a group meeting when some of the members have already crossed over into convergence? They've passed the pivot point in their own thinking, regardless of whether the others have. What happens if, at the same time, other members of the group are still trying to think divergently—to understand the problem more fully and to consider some creative alternative? Many groups waste their time and energy in this mish-mash state of thinking. Some of them have already decided, some are still trying to state the problem, some are asking for information, and some may be completely confused.

An important rule, or at least a policy, of bivergent thinking is:

> *Get the whole group doing the same type*
> *of thinking at the same time.*

In Chapter 12 we'll explore the methods of "high speed problem solving" or "HSPS." Again we'll see the power of having everyone in the same "mindzone" at any one time, and of moving skillfully from one mindzone to another as the thinking process unfolds. Bivergent thinking is one essential part of HSPS, and we'll see again and again how much more effective people can be when they know how to observe and manage their thinking processes.

## GROUPTHINK: THE COLLUSION TO FAIL

When a lone person makes a decision without the need for input or participation by others, then decision making is mostly an isolated *cognitive process*. But the moment two or more people have their hands—or minds—in the decision-making process, it becomes as much a *social process* as a cognitive process. Collective decisions that fail are almost always both social and cognitive in their pathology. Some of the most famous failed decisions in history have displayed plenty of both.

The late Professor Irving Janis was a research psychologist at Yale University and a professor emeritus at the University of California, Berkeley. Janis spent many years studying the psychology of decision making. He was particularly interested in some of the historically disastrous decisions such as the failure to prepare for the attack on Pearl Harbor; the Bay of Pigs invasion debacle that permanently tarnished President John Kennedy's legacy; the "default" decision of Lyndon Johnson and his cabinet to Americanize the war in Vietnam; and the flawed engineering decision that led to the explosion of the Challenger space shuttle in 1989 and the death of seven astronauts.

Professor Janis proposed the term "groupthink" to describe the socio-cognitive malfunctions that led to those disasters and others. In his book *Victims of Groupthink,* he offered a psychological profile of the factors that could conspire to drive a group of people into a pathological state of false consensus, sometimes even in defiance of common sense.[1]

*Albrecht's Law: Intelligent people,*
*when assembled into an organization,*
*will tend toward collective stupidity.*

Groupthink has found its way into the business lexicon, although it's difficult to say that very many executives, military officers, elected officials, managers, or group leaders understand its effects very well or know how to counter them. Janis' psychological theory does not seem to have been skillfully transferred to business or everyday life situations, although it's often cited as a post-mortem cause of decision failure. I've observed the groupthink effect very often in the course of business activities, and I've evolved a somewhat less "psychological" view and a more sociodynamic model of it.

## The Nature of the Pathology

First, a definition:

> *Groupthink: An irrational pattern of group thinking*
> *and behavior that imposes artificial consensus and*
> *suppresses dissent.*

An advanced case of groupthink, according to Professor Janis' research, involves some or all of a number of features:

- A group leader, or an in-group of a few aggressive individuals within the group, or both, who've made up their minds about a prospective course of action and who have strong motivations— of various kinds—to sell the other members on it.
- A condition of uncertainty or ambiguity about the relative merits of the course of action. Typically, the group is not permitted to freely discuss the merits and drawbacks. The members get a strong message, either overt or covert, that they are expected to agree with the preferred course of action.
- A mentality within the group, either imposed by the leadership or shared by the members, or both, that ranks consensus and avoidance of confrontation higher than rationality and intellectual honesty.
- Lack of group competence in effective problem-solving methods; few or no members who can function as thought leaders, facilitators, or devil's advocates.

- In some cases, external pressures, forces, or risks that lead the group members to become defensive and seek a sense of solidarity or cohesiveness in the face of a "common enemy."

For any particular group that's highly susceptible to the groupthink effect, it may be *episodic*—occurring only in some situations with certain particular kinds of issues; or it may be *chronic*—a dysfunctional pattern of thinking and behaving that becomes a hallmark of the group's ineffectiveness. Just about all groups can fall into a groupthink pattern at times; unfortunately, some groups make it a pathological aspect of their culture.

Episodes of groupthink often evolve in fairly recognizable stages:

1. *Uncertainty, ambiguity, or confusion.* The group faces a situation, problem, issue, challenge, or crisis, the solution to which is not immediately clear.
2. *Early advocacy.* For any of a variety of reasons, including possibly ulterior or disreputable motives, a small core of individuals converges to agreement around a course of action they intend to put into effect. They may arrive at consensus by ordinary conversation, by collusive "back room" discussions, or even unconsciously by reading one another's signals. This core advocacy group may or may not include the formally appointed group leader.
3. *Pre-emptive decision making.* The in-group members push their preferred course of action upon the other group members, positioning it as obviously the "right" way to go, and virtually a foregone conclusion.
4. *Suppression of dissent.* Sometimes the other group members— even high-ranking executives—will meekly go along with the consensus, especially if it's presented confidently and persuasively. If any members express doubts, the advocates press their

case aggressively, usually pressuring the doubters into submission. If several strong individuals persist in disagreeing, the episode might degenerate into open conflict instead of drifting into groupthink. Here, the actions of the group leader may be pivotal.

5. *Punishment of deviance.* Any last holdouts find themselves on the receiving end of increasingly intense social pressure from the "enforcers," ranging from subtle cues like offhand comments ("You'll feel better about this approach once you understand it better") to overt bullying ("X, I've always thought of you as a team player. You know how important this effort is. I hope you'll put the interests of the team ahead of your personal concerns.") to downright ostracism. In extreme cases, the formally appointed group leader may actually threaten a recalcitrant member with punishment or expulsion from the group.

6. *Continuing rationalization.* As the preferred course of action unfolds, it may become increasingly clear how grotesquely ineffective it is. At this stage the coerced consensus and the human needs of the group members usually lead them to rationalize the failing solution. Groups and individuals can be remarkably resourceful in explaining away bad news, inflating the significance of good news, and maintaining an increasingly pathological state of utter denial of the likelihood of failure. The rationalizing becomes ever more skillful as a way to continue to suppress dissent on the part of those who have doubts; and it may play an important part in the group's defense of itself to its detractors in the wider world.

As a groupthink episode develops, the members of the group tend to find themselves locked into some distinctive social roles, in relationship to the group at large and to the preferred course of action, as illustrated by Figure 8.2.

## Figure 8.2.    Roles in a Groupthink Situation

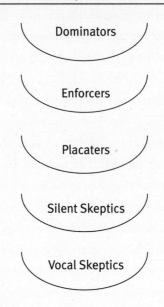

- *Dominators*: the in-group members who are driving the process of coerced consensus.
- *Enforcers*: some members who may take up the cause and assist the dominators in selling the course of action to the others. They may contact the holdouts individually, trying by subtle or not-so-subtle means to bring them around. They may be motivated by the desire for cohesion, belief in the preferred course of action, or the desire to gain favor with the dominators.
- *Placaters*: some members who may play the role of peacemakers, in some cases to ease their own discomfort with the prospect of conflict, or possibly out of a genuine desire to promote group spirit. They might try to placate the dominators and the enforcers, hoping to induce them to behave less aggressively or they may try to placate the holdouts, hoping to gently herd them into the corral.

- *Silent Skeptics*: members who disagree with the preferred course of action, or who are offended by the manner in which it was imposed, and who've been coerced into silence. They may pretend to be on board, or they may simply remain quiet and not call attention to themselves.
- *Vocal Skeptics*: members who refuse to shut up, and who must be dealt with by the group's methods for suppressing dissent. If the dominators and enforcers do not succeed in transforming the vocal skeptics into silent skeptics and more extreme measures do not succeed in disabling them as functioning group members, then the group may degenerate into a conflict state.

In recent years, the news media have given increased attention to "whistle blowers"—people working in dysfunctional organizations who make their malfunctions public. Quite often, the whistle blower is a competent, sometimes highly placed individual who has been unable to persuade the management to correct a condition perceived as improper, illegal, or immoral. The all-too-typical response of the organization that has been exposed in this manner is to regress to a defensive posture in which groupthink sets in with a vengeance. All of the classic stages and all of the classic roles just defined typically come into play. Honesty and openness seem to be the very last resort of the organization that is under scrutiny for its internal pathologies.

## Is There a Cure for Groupthink?

I've observed and worked with many teams, departments, and organizations that have learned to think effectively in a collective manner and that have relatively seldom fallen victim to the groupthink effect. Just as groupthink has a distinctive set of characteristics or patterns, "organizational intelligence" also has well-defined patterns.

Using a "mirror-image" analogy to the groupthink roles illustrated in Figure 8.2, we can define a complementary set of roles for the members of a collectively smart team.

- *Liberators*: an enlightened group leader, as well as any highly influential members who value effective problem solving and intellectual honesty and can promote and reward it on the part of the members.
- *Thought Leaders*: members to whom the others tend to look for new ideas, clear perspectives, good judgment, challenges to complacency, and metaboxical thinking.
- *Thinkers*: members who have the skills of practical intelligence that enable them to participate fully in the key thinking processes that shape the group's mission and determine its effectiveness.
- *Drifters*: members who, while loyal and willing to work, lack the skills to participate actively in the mental give-and-take of a smart team. They typically take their cues from others who behave more proactively. With training, coaching, and encouragement, some of them can become more skilled thinkers.
- *Saboteurs*: members who, for their own individual reasons, are alienated from the group, unable or unwilling to connect socially and mentally, and who don't feel they have an important contribution to make to the mental process of the group. They may even be antagonistic or destructive to the open-minded atmosphere that's a hallmark of a smart group. They may be well-suited for other kinds of jobs.

This view of team smartness as the inverse of team dumbness and groupthink has many implications in business, education, government, military organizations, and even in the informal organizations or groups that are common in our lives. A thorough exploration of the application of these models is unfortunately beyond the scope of this book, but it certainly seems to warrant development by others who may be qualified to contribute.

# BRAINSTORMING: MORE OFTEN TALKED ABOUT THAN DONE

Once per hour, at least, somewhere on the planet some executive or manager tells someone: "You guys get together and 'brainstorm' this problem and come up with a solution."

Most of the time the people to whom the mission is assigned understand what the boss really means. Occasionally, however, someone makes the mistake of taking the boss at his or her word: they get a group together and use the method of "brainstorming" as it was defined and designed by the late Alex F. Osborn, one of the creative leaders of the advertising industry in its early days. They spin out lots of ideas, not censoring any of them, until they have a huge list of possibilities. As a normal part of the generative process, they freely associate ideas with ideas, generating some that are outrageous, some that are comical, some that are far-fetched, and many of which that are only partly baked. A few may seem obviously practical at the outset.

If the boss happens to peek into the meeting at the point when the group is in the mass production mode, his or her credibility might be sorely taxed. The reaction may be—and I have personally observed it a number of times—"What are you people doing? I asked you to come up with a solution to a problem, not go off into outer space. Now get down to business and give me something that's realistic."

That's what the boss actually meant, in most cases. Most employees, receiving such a commission from the boss, either don't understand what brainstorming is, or they know but realize the boss isn't really asking for it. The poor benighted souls who don't read the signals accurately may go off and try to do something creative.

Alex Osborn developed and pioneered the method of brainstorming precisely because he had seen so much "narrow-band" thinking, so much idea-killing, and so little creative courage, that he believed people in business needed a specific method that gave them permission to break away from routine thinking.

Osborn was a very accomplished executive, advertising expert, and thought leader. He co-founded the firm of BBD&O, originally called Batten, Barton, Durstin, and Osborn (a name which, some wag immediately noted, "sounded like a trunk falling down a flight of stairs"). For many years he was the "O" in BBD&O.

Osborn wrote a landmark book, *Applied Imagination,*[2] in 1953, in which he laid out a conceptual basis for deliberate creativity, a learnable skill and process. In the same year he began teaching creativity seminars for business people and sending several of his colleagues to teach a course on creativity at the University of Buffalo. A year later he teamed up with Professor Sidney Parnes to set up the Creative Education Foundation there. The foundation hosted the first Creative Problem Solving Institute—the "CPSI"—which continues to this day as one of the most respected forums for education and training in creativity.[3]

After Osborn's death in 1966, Sid Parnes continued to provide the leadership for CEF and the CPSI programs until his partial retirement in 1984. Many of the methods Osborn pioneered are mainstays of creativity training programs all over the world.

Osborn's concept of brainstorming was very simple, although perhaps disconcerting and sometimes even stressful to people with a low tolerance for ambiguity. His method was based on the same basic principle of bivergent thinking that we've just reviewed: separate the divergent thinking process—idea production—from the convergent thinking process—evaluating ideas, choosing the favored ones, and implementing them. While disarmingly simple, this concept still seems to elude many, if not most, people in the business world.

The generally accepted rules of brainstorming are:

1. Suspend all judgments about what the "right" solution should look like.
2. Generate as many ideas as possible.
3. Do not evaluate, censor, favor, or disapprove of any idea during the production process; that comes later.

4. Go for quantity; use free association to generate as many ideas as possible, with no concern for which ones might be "good" or "bad." At this stage, all ideas are equal.
5. Capture the ideas in some way for later evaluation.

Osborn introduced a number of methods for proactively stimulating the idea-production process. Once the first batch of fairly obvious ideas comes out, the brainstorming process tends to slow down and taper off. At that point, using specific stimulus methods usually generates more and more successive rounds of options. It's like a nuclear chain reaction, in which one idea triggers other ideas, and the whole process gathers speed.

It's often advisable to conduct the brainstorming process in a separate meeting from the evaluation process. Combining both processes into one meeting tends to keep the notion of "being practical" hovering in the backs of the minds of the members. What we want at the brainstorming stage is the most *impractical* thinking we can get.

One very noticeable hallmark of the brainstorming process is humor: the "popcorn" effect by which one idea triggers other ideas seems to lead inevitably to comical possibilities. I've never observed, participated in, or led a brainstorming process that didn't have people in tears of laughter at various times. Indeed, some creativity experts believe that idea fluency and comedy—a sense of humor—may come from the same place in our biocomputers. Other researchers point to the health effects of humor, laughter, and creative ideation, all of which seem to affect the immune system and various other subsystems in a positive way.

But perhaps the most important aspect of understanding the brainstorming method is not in the technique itself—that's extremely simple—but in knowing where, when, and how to apply it to the opportunities that arise. It seldom seems advisable to have a formal brainstorming process to figure out where to go for lunch. At the other end of the spectrum, however, when we're considering the really big, high-consequence decisions or problem solutions, the time invested in a thorough search of the "idea space" associated with the issue may be well rewarded.

## SYSTEMATIC CREATIVITY: THE BALANCING ACT

Divergent and convergent thinking are two essential, valuable, and complementary processes; we need to marry them effectively in appropriate measure according to the demands of the situation. In the divergent stage we need to free our minds to explore an appropriate range of possibilities, relationships, and perspectives. In the convergent stage we have to apply logic skillfully and make good choices. Every problem situation presents with its own unique set of circumstances, information elements, constraints, and criteria for success.

Some problem-solving situations seem to invite lots of divergent thinking: sometimes we just need to find great options to consider. Other situations may demand a more disciplined, logical process of crafting a solution from the available knowledge. Expert problem solvers have learned to manage this creative balancing act to get the outcomes they seek. Consider an interesting example.

In 1967 the government of Sweden decided to make a major change in the everyday lives of Swedish citizens. After having driven their vehicles on the left side of the road for decades, Swedes would now be required to drive on the right. This change came about as a result of an increasing consciousness of Sweden's relationship to Europe and the need to become more integrated into the European pattern of living and doing business. As the number of motor vehicles in the country steadily increased, making the change sooner rather than later seemed to make sense.

Clearly a change of such magnitude and significance presented a challenging problem. How to get thousands of drivers to stop their cars—all at the same instant—change lanes, and continue on their way, without killing one another? Most of the population supported the change, but how could they do it with minimum damage to life and property?

The government set Sunday morning, September 3, 1967, just after midnight, as the instant for the change. For months prior to the switchover, educational campaigns ran throughout the country, reminding people to drive on the right side after the appointed time. The big event became the topic of news stories, radio shows, and daily conversation. Jokes abounded: maybe it could be done in stages, starting with trucks and buses, then going to cars, and later motorcycles. Maybe everyone should stay home for the first week, to minimize the casualties.

The government also ran a contest to choose a novelty song, or jingle, to promote awareness of the change. The winning song, "Håll dig till höger, Svensson!" ("Keep to the right, Svensson!") played relentlessly on radio stations for weeks in advance of the change.

At the appointed instant, traffic wardens along the main roads pulled the cover-bags off of the right-side traffic signs, ran across to the other side, and put them over the now obsolete left-side signs.

Reportedly, not a single traffic accident or injury was attributed to the change. After a short period of adjustment, Swedes became comfortable driving on the right side, and have ever since.

## Notes

1. Janis, Irving L. *Victims of Groupthink.* New York: Houghton Mifflin Company, 1972 (pp. 197–204).
2. Osborn, Alex F. *Applied Imagination: Principles and Procedures of Creative Problem Solving.* New York: Charles Scribner's Sons, 1953.
3. The web address for the Creative Education Foundation is CreativeEducationFoundation.org.

# 9

## MEGA-SKILL 2
### "Helicopter" Thinking

"I want to know how God created this world.
I want to know His thoughts. The rest are details."
—Albert Einstein

TWO OLDER CHICKENS were strolling around the barnyard, discussing the affairs of the day. Abruptly, one of them stopped and looked off into space, as if deep in thought. She turned to the other chicken and said, "You know, I've been wondering about something." "What's that?" the other chicken asked. "With all the eggs we've been laying," said the first chicken, "shouldn't there be a lot more chickens around here?"

That, in its most basic form, is *conceptual thinking,* and it's a fundamental dimension of practical intelligence. It seems to be in short supply across much of the popular culture, and not highly valued by the general populace or the popular culture.

Part of the evolution and progress of so-called "advanced" societies—those that have figured out how to manipulate their environments in favor of their own self-interest—is the development of *abstract conceptualization*. They've developed systems for preserving and transferring the collective knowledge that has enabled them to partially rise above the constraints of space and time. They've discovered, developed, or designed more sophisticated tools than the primitive ones all cultures have acquired. They've learned to harness, control, and allocate energy in great quantities.

It's interesting to note that most of the indigenous peoples in various areas of the world who were pushed aside by the invading European populations *did not have written languages*. The aborigines of Australia; the North American Indians; the Hawaiians; the Eskimo, Aleut, and Inuit peoples; the Indian tribes of Latin America; and most of the African tribes—all lacked the means for preserving and deploying abstract information. Aside from very simplified symbols and signal systems, they had no effective way to *encode knowledge*.

Without an abstract technology—*a symbolic thinking process*—it's virtually impossible to do things like design and construct huge buildings like pyramids, build ocean-going ships, cut canals through deserts, create gunpowder and advanced weapons, and of course fight off well-armed invaders who've taken a fancy to your ancestral homeland.

The cultures that have prevailed in the long term, for better or worse, have mostly been those whose leaders, at least, have acquired the faculty of abstract conceptualization.

## THE ABSTRACT-CONCRETE POLARITY: THE A-C AXIS

For the record, it might help to clarify the distinction between *abstract ideas* and *concrete ideas*. A concrete idea is one that *engages the physical senses,* or at least the memory of the senses. It's about something we can see, hear, feel, smell, or taste.

An abstract idea is *symbolic*—it's about a category or a characteristic or a collection of concretes. When I'm thinking of a tomato, a particular tomato, namely the one I'm eating at the moment, I'm thinking rather concretely. If I'm thinking of "tomatoes," that is to say tomatoes as a type of food, I'm thinking somewhat more abstractly. If I go further and think of "food," which is a category that contains the category of tomatoes, which is a category that contains the tomato I'm eating, I'm thinking of something even more abstract.

It's helpful to think in terms of a *ladder of abstraction,* which is a progression of categories, each contained within a more highly abstract category. I can shift the focus of my ideation from my next-door neighbor, as a specific person, to the more abstract idea of "a neighbor," which I have in common with many other people, to the idea of getting along with neighbors, to the idea of getting along with other people in general, to the idea of people getting along in general, to the idea of people in different nations getting along together, and so on *ad infinitum.*

> "Love is an ideal thing. Marriage is real. Confusing
> the real with the ideal never goes unpunished."
> —Wolfgange Goethe

Conceptual fluency, obviously, calls for the ability to freely shift the focus of our attention and our ideation among these various levels, or rungs, on the ladder of abstraction. Another useful metaphor, also a spatial analogy, for the ability to move up and down the scale of abstraction is the "mental helicopter." Just as we think of a helicopter as enabling us to move between ground level and various physical altitudes, we can use the notion of helicopter thinking as the process of navigating skillfully up and down the scale of abstraction. Hence, the definition:

*Helicopter Thinking: A thinking process that*
*integrates both abstract and concrete patterns*
*of ideation into a synergistic combination.*

The higher we take our mental helicopter—and the higher we invite others to go with us—the more "territory" we can see. The view from 10,000 feet includes more terrain, but enables us to discern less detail. The view from ground level gives us a very direct experience of the terrain but deprives us for the moment of the perspective that's available at 10,000 feet.

*Skilled thinkers must be skilled pilots of their*
*mental helicopters.*

## VISIONARIES AND ACTIONARIES:
## WE NEED BOTH

R. Buckminster Fuller was a Renaissance man—a philosopher, an inventor, and a writer, one of those people we like to describe as visionaries. He believed that simple but powerful concepts—the big ideas—can change the world if one knows how to use leverage in applying them. Fuller used a mechanical analogy from aerodynamics to explain his view:

> "Something hit me very hard once, thinking about what one little man could do. Think of the Queen Mary: the whole ship goes by and then comes the rudder. And there's a tiny thing at the edge of the rudder called a trim tab. It's a miniature rudder. Just moving the little trim tab builds a low pressure that pulls the rudder around. Takes almost no effort at all. So I said that the little individual can be a trim tab. Society thinks it's going right by you, that it's left you altogether. But if you're doing dynamic things mentally, the fact is that you can just put your foot out like that and the whole big ship of state is going to go. So I said, call me Trim Tab."

Many scholars who've studied Fuller's contributions would indeed refer to him as one of society's trim tabs. His remarkable pattern of conceptualization made him one of the most admired and revered thinkers of the twentieth century.

Many of the legendary leader figures of history have been trim tabs—people of vision who could articulate and sell a proposition of achievement that others could sign on to. They could see, not only beyond their noses, but beyond their immediate circumstances; beyond the prevailing views of their contemporaries and their culture; and even beyond the times in which they lived.

Many of them faced aggressive opposition from influential people who, for various reasons, could not or would not accept the possibilities they offered. Galileo, of course, was threatened with death by the Catholic Church when he lectured and published his view of science that contradicted 1,800 years of unquestioned belief in Aristotle's explanations of the world.

> "Toward no crimes have men shown themselves
> so cold-bloodedly cruel as in punishing
> differences in belief."
> James Russell Lowell

At the same time that we need trim tabs—the big thinkers—we also need skillful and dedicated doers. We need both *visionaries* and *actionaries* to make big things happen. As the late Dr. Peter F. Drucker, the dean of business experts, often said, "Somebody has to turn the great ideas into crude deeds."

Relate Fuller's expression of his view of the world with the tone of that expressed by Theodore Roosevelt:

> "It is not the critic who counts; not the man who points out how
> the strong man stumbles, or where the doer of deeds could have
> done them better. The credit belongs to the man who is actually in

the arena, whose face is marred by dust and sweat and blood; who strives valiantly; who errs, who comes short again and again, because there is no effort without error and shortcoming; but who does actually strive to do the deeds; who knows great enthusiasms, the great devotions; who spends himself in a worthy cause; who at the best knows in the end the triumph of high achievement, and who at the worst, if he fails, at least fails while daring greatly, so that his place shall never be with those cold and timid souls who neither know victory nor defeat."[1]

A few leading thinkers have been both visionaries and actionaries. Thomas Edison comes to mind, as does Henry Ford. In modern times scientist Robert Goddard, who in 1929 developed and proved the basic facts of rocket propulsion that formed the foundation for the exploration of space, was ridiculed in the pages of *Scientific American* magazine. The editors declared his ideas "too far-fetched to even consider."

Goddard was vindicated only after his death: when reporters asked Dr. Werner von Braun, the chief scientist of NASA's moon landing project, what words he'd recommend that the first astronaut say as he stepped onto the moon, Von Braun is said to have replied: "He should say, 'Goddard, we are here.'" When he left the planet, Goddard had 214 patents to his credit. NASA's Goddard Space Flight Center now bears his name, as does Goddard Crater on the moon.

One of the biggest scientific and engineering developments in modern history, the famed Manhattan Project, had two leaders—one a visionary and the other an actionary. The conceptual leadership of physicist J. Robert Oppenheimer galvanized some of the best minds on the planet to achieve a series of breakthroughs that resulted in the first atomic explosion. His co-leader, U.S. Army General Leslie R. Groves, managed the logistics, administration, finances, security, and the various other "practical" elements needed to bring the project to completion.

Teaming visionaries with actionaries often seems like a sensible thing to do. Synergy between the two kinds of thinkers requires that the visionary understand something of the world inhabited by the actionary, and vice versa. We can see some interesting examples of successful and unsuccessful combinations of visionaries and actionaries.

In politics, visionaries and actionaries can often team up effectively. The roles of president and vice president in American politics, for example, could well be made more synergistic than they've been in many administrations. Not many presidential administrations have developed an effective pattern of transforming the big ideas into plans of action.

Similarly, many universities will have a president who's expected to provide the conceptual and philosophical leadership, and an officer called the *provost,* who's supposed to manage the day-to-day affairs of the institution. Again, much of the success, or lack of it, enjoyed by the institution depends on a healthy and balanced combination of visionary and actionary thinking.

> "To make a great dream come true, you must first
> have a great dream."
> —Dr. Hans Selye
> (pioneer of the medical concept of stress)

Many corporations will have both a chief executive officer—the "CEO"—and a chief operating officer—the "COO." This does not always guarantee that they will work harmoniously. Some CEOs can't resist meddling in the details of the operation, and they may tend to over-control. At the same time, if the CEO neglects his or her conceptual leadership role, the ship tends to drift as he or she goes below deck and tries to fix the engines.

In the business world, having lots of ideas doesn't necessarily translate into moving higher on the organizational totem pole. Occasionally a mid-level executive will get a rocket ride to the board room as a result of inventing, discovering, or pioneering a new product or a new concept for the success of the business. More often, however, it's the ability to mobilize others who have ideas that leads to executive success.

As with the other polarities or dualities of practical intelligence, we can ask: why not be skillful at both? A person who's challenged to fulfill the role of a visionary can still benefit by knowing how to think and perform like an actionary, so long as he or she doesn't try to push the appointed actionaries aside and take over the controls. Conversely, a person who's challenged by an actionary role can still contribute his or her knowledge, experience, and judgment to the big-picture process of which he or she is a part.

## CONNECTING THE DOTS: YOU HAVE TO SEE THEM TO CONNECT THEM

One of the key elements of helicopter thinking is *relational thinking*—commonly referred to as "connecting the dots"—a metaphor that probably grew out of the children's books that present patterns of dots, which the child must connect with lines in order to see a picture. Skillful helicopter thinkers not only connect various bunches of "dots" more effectively than most other people do, but they tend to *notice more dots*—key elements and connections in a situation—than most other people do. The fact that we can only connect the dots we know about means that dot-finding is a key part of dot-connecting, and a key element of big-picture thinking.

As an example of an unusual collection of dots, consider a slice of history that's perhaps stranger than fiction.

*Australia has more camels than any other country—by far—including African and Middle Eastern countries.* In fact, Australia in recent years has begun exporting camels and camel meat to other countries, particularly those with Islamic populations.

How could this have come about?

The answer emerges from an interesting historical event that, when connected with other events and trends, becomes perfectly clear. But without seeing the other elements of the story and the connections, the fact of Australia's role as the biggest exporter of camels would make little sense.

Here's the story that connects the dots.

The first camels reportedly were brought to Australia from the Canary Islands in 1840. Australia was a very large and sparsely populated continent, and it still is. The early settlers needed animals for transportation and carrying cargo over long distances, and camels provided an excellent option. They were strong, sturdy, durable, resistant to most diseases, and they were fairly easy to domesticate.

Historians estimate that more than 10,000 camels were imported, from as far away as Palestine and India, up until the turn of the twentieth century. Most of them were the one-hump dromedary variety. Camel farms sprang up to breed and sell them all over Australia, particularly in the "outback," the remote rural areas.

But by about 1920, when motor vehicles became widely available in the farther reaches of the bush, demand for the camels nearly disappeared. Thousands of them were released into the countryside, to wander freely. They continued to breed, of course, and having no natural predators, their numbers grew to an estimated 200,000 to 300,000 by the turn of the twenty-first century.

So now, after nearly a century, camels are a business again. Camel hunters, abattoirs, and exporters are capturing and slaughtering them or loading them onto ships and sending them live to countries all over the world. They're abundant and cheap, and the export trade may not even be sufficient to keep their numbers under control.

Connecting dots often involves tracing or looking for the hidden connections—the subtle cause-and-effect relationships that may lurk behind the seemingly simple situation. In some cases these relationships are so subtle and intertwined with others that causes and effects are difficult to separate.

For example, many Westerners think of the veil, or the *abaya*—the head-to-toe garment that modest Islamic women wear—as merely symbols of repression forced upon Islamic or Arab females. Yet when they are viewed in the complex context of family and clan relationships, as in Iraq, for example, they are not isolated elements. The veil is an integral part of a larger *gestalt* of social rules and symbols, which many Westerners fail to grasp or appreciate. It cannot simply be abandoned or abolished without overturning other, centuries-old social dynamics connected to it.

In Iraq, for example, and in many Arab countries, at least 50 percent of marriages are between first or second cousins. One effect of the veil, or any other form of modest attire, is to remove young women from the kind of social circulation that poses competition to their male cousins—the "marriage market." Not only does the veil have practical benefit for young men seeking wives, but many young Iraqi women are firmly committed to marrying within the clan, and arranged marriages are still very common. Many of them see the modesty dynamics as perfectly natural and appropriate to the patterns of close kinship that shape their lives. The view of veiling as simply a form of oppression is largely a projection of Western social values onto the members of a very different culture.

Professor Robin Fox of Rutgers University, author of *Kinship and Marriage,* says:

> "Americans just don't understand what a different world Iraq is because of these highly unusual cousin marriages. Liberal democracy is based on the Western idea of autonomous individuals committed to a public good, but that's not how members of these tight and bounded kin groups see the world. Their world is divided into two groups: *kin and strangers.*"[2]

This lack of understanding of Arab cultural dynamics, particularly by American political leaders who believed they could "install" democracy in Iraq at gunpoint, had disastrous consequences for the occupation of Iraq and the struggle to suppress the insurgency. American leaders largely ignored the traditional socio-political hierarchy, which runs from the family, to the extended clan, to local religious leaders, and to the Islamic sect to which individuals belong. The idea of a national or local government, to Iraqis, seems to be an abstract and distant part of reality, a kind of necessary evil, perhaps. What Americans and other Westerners consider patriotism, namely a loyal attachment to the abstract idea of a native country, seems to make little sense in the locally based clan-oriented social structure of Iraq.

The spectacular failure of the American attempt to forcibly install democracy in a country like Iraq, with its uniquely different sociopolitical substructure, raises not only the question of whether those who attempted it really understood the Arab culture, but also the question of how well they understood democracy itself, and how it actually worked in the cultures of their own birth.

## PAINTING THE BIG PICTURE: MINDMAPPING

How about using big pictures—*actual big pictures*—to think about the big picture?

Here's a simple and useful method for organizing ideas, which might seem rather strange and unusual to you at first, but which can grow on you very quickly. It's been around for a long time, although it hasn't become as popular as it deserves to be. I use it every day, as do many of my professional associates. The method goes by various names, including mindmapping, idea mapping, concept mapping, thought mapping, cluster diagramming, and idea-gramming. The most popular handle for the method seems to be mindmapping.

Some readers may already be very familiar with mindmapping, and if you're one of those I solicit your patience for the following explanation, with the hope that something in it may help to extend, clarify, or re-energize your interest in the method.[3]

One glance at Figure 9.1 tells you just about all you need to know.

This mindmap, created by design guru David Kelley, founder of the IDEO design firm and the Hasso Plattner Institute of Design at Stanford University, shows his thinking process for the design of a presentation at a conference.[4]

## Figure 9.1.    An Example of a Mindmap

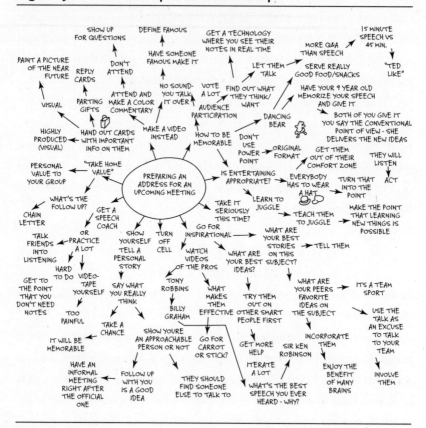

Figure and text adapted from a mindmap from IDEO's David Kelley. *Business Week,* September 25, 2006.
Used with permission

Kelley described his thinking process this way:

"When I want to do something analytical, I make a list. When
I'm trying to come up with ideas or strategize, I make a mindmap.
Mindmaps are organic and allow me to free associate. They're great
for asking questions and revealing connections between seemingly unrelated ideas.

"I start in the center with the issue or problem I'm working on and then as I move further away I get better and better ideas as I force myself to follow the branches on the map and in my mind. The cool thing is that you allow yourself to follow your inner thoughts, which is different than making a list where you're trying to be complete and deal with data."

Some users of the method like to call it *radial thinking,* to emphasize the outward-moving, divergent process as it unfolds.

There are also some software products that enable a person to build mindmaps on the computer screen and to work with them in various ways.[5]

The first time I used this radial idea mapping process, or mindmapping, in my professional work as a management consultant was many years ago during an executive retreat, in which the members of the top team of an energy company in the U.S. Southwest wanted to think through some fundamental strategic issues. I had often used the method for my own thinking and with small groups at various times, but had never used it with a group of tough-minded, operationally focused male executives. The method worked so effectively that I've been a devoted fan of it ever since.

As we opened the meeting, it wasn't clear where we might best begin to unravel the tangled strategic issues facing the team. I had covered almost a whole wall of the meeting room with a blank sheet of engineering drawing paper, about four feet high and about ten feet long. I gave each member of the team a colored felt marker and proposed a rule that anyone could write anything they wanted anywhere on the chart at any time.

I offered to kick off the discussion by writing a single word—"Strategy"—in the very center of the chart. Then I invited the team members to "Say any words that come to mind in connection with this word." Very quickly came the responses: "customers"; "profitability"; "planning"; "competition"; "positioning"; "strengths and weaknesses";

and many more. For each new connection I drew a radial line outward from the central idea. After a few moments, the team members began further associating ideas with the secondary "branching" ideas; each of these new ideas led to another branch, and then to more and more branches and sub-branches as the ideas poured out.

This particular management team had been described to me as a rather argumentative group, but I quickly discovered that the radial pattern of harvesting ideas caused the process to move too fast for debates to set in. Whatever anybody said just got put up as another element of the picture. No one had the right to argue about whether anything should go up on the map. If somebody said it, it was included. In less than an hour, we had exploded the key issues they wanted to deal with into a constellation of interrelated sub-issues and their sub-issues, all visible at a glance. Here we had a visual "group memory" device—a way to capture what everyone knew and make it available whenever needed.

Next, we flagged the "blockbuster" issues—the ones that seemed to the executives to be driving, or at least shaping the options for, the other issues. Using that list of a half-dozen mega-issues, we assembled an attack agenda for the remainder of the three-day retreat. Then we transferred the main mindmap, the "mega-map," to another wall for ready reference, re-plastered the working wall with a new sheet of paper, and proceeded to apply the same mapping method to the main issues, one at a time. As we resolved each issue, we moved the mindmap to the history corral and went on to the next one.

I've been using variations of this simple but effective method in my consulting work for over two decades.

Mindmapping, or radial thinking, is a method for *divergent thinking*, which we explored in Chapter 8. The method allows you to branch out from one "seed" idea to many other related ideas—the *divergent* direction—and it also allows you work back to the place where you started. It's both explosive and implosive, bidirectional as well as bivergent.

Another very useful feature of the mindmap is that it enables you to *trace the connections* between ideas all along the various branching chains. The question arises: "How did we get onto the topic of employee satisfaction, when we came here to discuss the strategy of the business?"

The answer is: "We decided that delivering outstanding value to our customers had to be a key element of our competitive strategy. Then we recognized that [someone points to the mindmap on the wall] the kind of personalized customer experience we want to deliver depends on having well-trained and well-motivated people. That led us to the realization that attracting and retaining them has to be a key aspect of our organizational culture. And we recognized that we can only attract and retain great performers if this is a great place to work. That means we have to measure, monitor, and continuously improve employee satisfaction."

Now that's what I call connecting the dots.

## EXPLAINING THE BIG PICTURE: USING THE LANGUAGE OF IDEAS

Do you remember this famous line from William Shakespeare's play *Julius Caesar,* with which Marc Antony addressed the Roman throng at Caesar's funeral:

> "Friends, Romans, countrymen—
> I got sump'n I wanna tell ya."

You don't? I didn't think so. What he said was:

> "Friends, Romans, countrymen, lend me your ears;
> I come to bury Caesar, not to praise him. The evil
> that men do lives after them; The good is oft interred
> with their bones. So let it be with Caesar."

Powerful leaders throughout history, and especially thought leaders, have understood how to use the language of ideas to move people.

This patently obvious truth—or "truth"—seems to have eluded most of the people on this planet, including a majority of the so-called "educated" ones. It's remarkable, to me at least, how few people truly value the vocabulary of ideas and have learned to use powerful verbal patterns and figures of speech to influence others. Why couldn't we all learn to use the magical power of language to our best advantage—not to con or manipulate people, but to capture their attention and help them appreciate our truth?

The language of ideas is not necessarily lofty, academic-sounding, or abstruse. During the darkest days of World War II, Winston Churchill made history with the statement: "I have nothing to offer but blood, toil, tears, and sweat." Novelist Victor Hugo said, "There is one thing more powerful than all the armies of the world, and that is an idea whose time has come." President Franklin Delano Roosevelt famously declared, "We have nothing to fear but fear itself."

Children growing up in any modern culture have an opportunity to learn to become conceptually fluent by becoming *verbally fluent*. It's that simple. Although many people have the impression that the ability to spin ideas into meaningful webs of persuasion must be an in-born skill, probably determined by IQ, the simple fact is that *conceptual fluency is largely a matter of verbal fluency*. A person who has a limited vocabulary has a limited ability to speak—and think—conceptually. Conversely, a person who has a large and diversified vocabulary, and who's willing to use it appropriately in various conversational situations, has a high level of conceptual skill.

Unfortunately, in the contemporary media-based culture of amusement that prevails in most Western societies, conceptual thinking and elegant expression don't seem to be highly valued. Indeed, the celebrities offered to us as icons of success typically behave as if the ability to string a series of ideas together into a coherent thought is not something the "real people" do.

The typical pop star, actor or actress, musician, or sports figure, when interviewed in TV news clips or "fan-mag" shows, models an astonishingly poor command of the language. It's as if sounding "smart" is a terminal career handicap. Maybe the premise is that our celebrities should be at least as dumb as we are—or at least as dumb as the media producers think we are. We don't hire them to speak intelligently; we hire them to sing, play music, tell jokes, act, or do things with a ball.

Without attractive role models who demonstrate the value and power of conceptual expression, and lacking an effective learning experience in school, children are likely to grow up imitating the primitive language patterns they hear from the media celebrities and cultural icons they're exposed to. Teen-agers are notoriously primitive and inarticulate in their use of language, which we can acknowledge and overlook when they're young. The big question, however, which hangs over our heads, is: By what means will they be able to develop the depth of vocabulary and the sophistication of conceptual language without being taught or having it modeled for them? Are we developing an entire generation of people who can't think or explain themselves coherently?

Each of us has three sets of words, or sub-vocabularies, in our total vocabulary:

- *The Recognition Vocabulary.* This is the total inventory of words we've encountered, and whose definitions and usage patterns we understand or can figure out if necessary.
- *The Usage Vocabulary.* This is the portion of our total vocabulary that we actually use—at least occasionally—in expressing ourselves. Most of us use a rather small percentage of our total vocabulary, either because of the situations we encounter or because of choices we've made about how to speak to others. We typically use a somewhat broader range of words in writing than in speaking.
- *The Routine Vocabulary.* This is the small number of words and figures of speech that we use in everyday living. For many people, this smallest sub-vocabulary amounts to only a few hundred words.

A person who has an extremely limited usage vocabulary, for whatever reason, is not likely to be skillful at influencing others with his or her ideas. It's difficult to sell people on your world view if you can't articulate it in a compelling way.

Unfortunately, many people who have a relatively large, or basically adequate, recognition vocabulary limit their usage vocabulary to a small portion of the words they know. For some people, using sophisticated words in conversation doesn't seem right for them—it may seem pretentious, or phony, or just unnatural. A limited sense of self-esteem and self-worth can prevent some people from expressing themselves in a sophisticated way. For some, the social pressure to conform, which they sense from a peer group, can prevent them from deploying their full vocabulary: "We don't talk that way around here."

Whatever the reasons, too many people handicap themselves by restricting their usage vocabulary to the routine inventory, or at most the vocabulary of necessity. This self-censorship acts like a built-in brake on their intelligence. It's often not a matter of growing one's vocabulary that presents a challenge, but actually deciding to use one's existing vocabulary more fluently.

A conceptual word, phrase, or figure of speech is a handle for a big idea. It gives you a shorthand method for calling attention to the concept without having to explain it every time in a long flow of words.

*Case in point*: the simple term *tradeoff*. A tradeoff is a choice that involves two or more options, or courses of action, in a situation in which you may be able to have a part of each option, but not all of both. If you're planning a two-week vacation, for example, you could choose to spend all of the time in one country, or move around among several countries, but not both. You have to *trade off* the value of seeing a lot of any one country with the value of seeing a lot of countries; you can't do both within the *constraints*—the limitations on the time you have available. So a tradeoff is about choices, options, and constraints. This handy expression enables you to capture a lot of thinking in a two-syllable phrase. When you understand and can use the phrase, you understand and can use the concept it encapsulates.

*Case in point*: the word *paradigm*. This is a fancy kind of a word, but one that's becoming more familiar in general conversation. A paradigm is a mental frame of reference that controls the way people think about something. For example, if a person subscribes to a particular religion, the teachings of that religion form a paradigm that shapes the way he or she thinks about a whole range of issues like moral values, marriage, family, and one's role in a community. Again, when you understand how to use the word, you understand and can use the concept.

*Case in point*: the word *context*. A context is a set of conditions that gives a particular situation a certain "meaning." All human interaction takes place within some context or other. The attitudes the participants bring and the behavior they exhibit both shape and are shaped by the context. For example, a religious ceremony is a very specific kind of a context, and most people accept certain rules and policies for behaving there. People generally behave differently, and any person's behavior will be interpreted differently in the context of an airport or a department store than in a place of worship. As with all conceptual-fluency terms, when you understand how to use the word, you understand and can use the concept.

We can teach our children—and ourselves—to develop and use a rich vocabulary for conceptual expression. It takes only the willingness and the diligence to learn and use these tools for thought.

## Notes

1. "Citizenship in a Republic" (also known as "The Man in the Arena" speech.). Speech by Theodore Roosevelt at the Sorbonne, Paris, France, April 23, 1910.

2. Fox, Robin. *Kinship and Marriage.* London: Cambridge University Press, 1996.

3. British author and lecturer Tony Buzan has asserted trademark rights to the terms "mindmapping" and "mindmaps." [See Buzan's book, *Use Both Sides of Your Brain: New Mind-Mapping Techniques.* London: Plume Publishers, 1991.] A more recent work, which refers to the method as "Idea Mapping," is by Jamie Nast. *Idea Mapping: How to Access Your Hidden Brain Power, Learn Faster, Remember More, and Achieve Success in Business.* New York: John Wiley & Sons, 2006.

4. Figure and text adapted from "A Mindmap from IDEO's David Kelley," *Business Week,* September 25, 2006. Website version: www.businessweek.com/magazine/content/06_39/b4002408. htm. Used with permission.

5. One software product designed specifically for building mindmaps is *MindManager,* published by MindJet. The Internet address is www.mindjet.com. Microsoft's Visio product is also well-suited for creating mindmaps.

# 10

## MEGA-SKILL 3
### *"Intulogical" Thinking*

"Logic will get you from A to B.
Imagination can take you anywhere."
—Albert Einstein

HERE ARE TWO FAIRLY EASY THINKING CHALLENGES, or puzzles, which illustrate two contrasting mental processes. Please solve each puzzle and then read the discussion that follows.

Before you begin, here are a couple of tips that may help you solve them more quickly:

1. Try to think metaboxically—think about *the problem* as well as about the ingredients of the problem. Sit back and look at it. Ask yourself, "What kind of thinking will it take to solve this?" "What do I have to figure out?" "What do I know?"

2. Try talking to yourself—aloud—about the problem. When you *vocalize* your thinking process, you call on other mental processes that capture your intermediate results into short-term memory. If you just sit and hope for the answer to occur to you, you may sit for a long time. *Engage the problem actively* by putting your thinking into words.

3. And, of course, *draw a picture or diagram* to set up a "mental scaffold" for your thinking.

## The First Problem

Three men agree to pay two boys for the use of their boat so they can get to the other side of a river. The boat is rather small and won't carry the entire party across in one trip, so the men agree to pay the boys one dollar for every crossing, with the understanding that the boys will end up back on the same side of the river they started from.

The maximum carrying capacity of the boat is 150 pounds. Each of the three men weighs 150 pounds and each of the two boys weighs 75 pounds. Each of the men and each of the boys is capable of rowing the boat single-handedly across the river.

Clearly, they will have to make a series of crossings to get all three men across and both boys back to the starting point. Note, however, that the boat can carry one man alone, two boys together (or one boy alone), but it cannot carry more than one man, nor can it carry a man and a boy.

Figure out how much it will cost (how many crossings it will take) to get all three men to the other side and both boys back to the starting point, considering the limitation of the boat's carrying capacity. *Hint: draw a picture of the situation to help you think about it.*

After you've figured it out (or if you haven't), read the solution in Appendix A, "Solutions to Puzzle Problems."

## The Second Problem

Three ordinary drinking glasses are sitting in a row. Counting from the left, the first three glasses are empty and the next three are full of water. By handling and moving *only one glass,* how can you change this arrangement so that no full glass is next to another full glass and no empty glass is next to another empty glass? *Hint: draw a picture of the glasses to help you think about it.*

After you've figured it out (or if you haven't), read the solution in Appendix A, "Solutions to Puzzle Problems."

## Two Different Thinking Mechanisms

Note that Problem 1 and Problem 2 called for two very different—but intimately related—mechanisms. Problem 1 required you to think *sequentially,* which is basically what "logical" thinking mostly is. You had to arrange the available information, and the elements of a solution, into a series of steps. Drawing a diagram for this process can help to organize the steps as you go along.

Problem 2, by contrast, required you to think *holistically*—or "intuitively" as we often characterize it. The answer comes to you in a flash—one mental incident rather than a series of steps. We sometimes call this process *insight*—an immediate realization of something important that seems to bubble up from the unconscious levels of our thinking.

## THE LOGICAL-INTUITIVE POLARITY: THE L-I AXIS

For some strange reason, many people in Western cultures seem to regard logic and intuition as two antagonistic patterns of thought. We have the usual clichés: "Men are logical and women are intuitive." These half-recognized prejudices can cloud our understanding of both patterns. Logic is often characterized, subtly if not overtly, as somehow "better" than intuition. Intuition is often characterized as feminine, weak, and inconsequential.

We seem to have a kind of hemispheric chauvinism going on. Advocates of an objectively perceived, highly ordered, rule-based world project the attitude: "My sensible, disciplined left hemisphere is better than your scatterbrained right hemisphere." Stubborn defenders of all that's subjective, subtle, spiritualistic, artistic, and magical respond: "My creative right hemisphere is better than your narrow-minded left hemisphere."

It's as if each of the advocates for one of the two alternative cognitive patterns, or styles, has disowned the other pattern. The unvoiced assumption seems to be that, if you're good at one pattern, you can't—or shouldn't—be good at the other one, so you have to build the strongest possible case that your way of knowing is the best one.

Practical intelligence goes beyond the either-or mentality of "logic versus intuition" and embraces the idea of logic *and* intuition. Why not think of both patterns as valuable ways of knowing and valuable sources of success in life? In fact, I propose to marry the two concepts so closely together that they get a new name:

*Intulogical Thinking: A thinking process that
integrates both logical and intuitive patterns
of ideation into a synergistic combination.*

Learning to think intulogically means *valuing* both ways of knowing, deliberately calling on both patterns in a balanced way, and perhaps re-owning whichever one you might have disowned, if either.

Some kinds of thinking challenges not only invite intulogical thinking, but they actually require it. One such challenge is the process of design. Any effective design is an interplay of logic and intuition, objective and subjective thinking, rational thinking and insight.

Consider, for example, the design or redesign of a kitchen in your home. You know some things for sure: you have a certain amount of floor space to work with; there are certain functions that have to be performed there; there are necessary elements such as storage, water supply, stove, refrigeration, and lighting that must be provided; and you may have a budget that must be respected. You can work with the physical dimensions, the number of cabinet doors and drawers, and the sequence of events in getting the project done. These are objective variables, subject to logical consideration.

But the real excitement—or stress, depending on how much you enjoy this kind of an adventure—can come in dealing with subjective variables: the overall style-statement, such as traditional, country, European, cool and sophisticated versus warm and cozy; the color schemes; relationships between elements such as floor color and cabinet color; what to do with the windows; the eye flow pattern as a person looks at the space; the "feel" of the space—what does it "say" to you? These are intuitive variables, to be understood on a different level.

Effective design is usually an unfolding process—it develops in stages, with decisions becoming clearer as previous decisions are made. It's a constant back-and-forth process of objective and subjective thinking; of analysis and insight; of logic and intuition.

## THINKING STYLES: YOURS AND OTHERS'

In the early days of word-processing technology, IBM's software designers were creating special electronic typewriters with display screens to be operated by clerical workers. These new office machines were, understandably, somewhat strange and off-putting for the front-line people who had to learn to use them. Part of the challenge facing the designers was creating an instruction manual or handbook that would help the operators learn to use the systems and become productive as quickly as possible.

After a number of versions and revisions, the designers were frustrated to learn that most of the operators—almost all of whom were young, female, and relatively inexperienced—never opened the manuals. Those who did would typically browse through the pages, pick up a few procedures, and continue trying to learn by trial and error. Or they'd ask their supervisors or other employees for help.

The software experts were at a loss to understand why the workers wouldn't read the manuals, when everything they needed to know to operate the system was thoroughly explained there. In interviews, the operators repeatedly confirmed that they didn't use the manuals and didn't find them helpful. They had few suggestions to offer for improving them except: "Make it simpler."

The developers resorted to a different method of investigation to try to find a solution. They simply sat quietly behind a row of operators in training, observed the way they went about learning the various procedures, and took notes. Occasionally they would ask questions of some of the operators, particularly the very new ones.

In one episode, a researcher was trying to explain a procedure to one of the operators in training. He opened the manual to the appropriate section, which thoroughly explained the basic concepts associated with the procedure, and asked, "Did you read this?" "No," she replied. "Wouldn't it be a good idea to start here?" he asked. "No, that's just information," she replied.

"Just information." A thought-stopping statement. The information that he considered critical to understanding the basic concepts, she apparently looked upon as extraneous.

As the developers studied the operators—and the manuals—further, they came to a difficult realization: the operators *didn't want to know* the "basic concepts"—they only wanted to know "how to do the procedures." They perceived the "information"—the foundation concepts behind the procedures—as extraneous and not relevant to their needs. Maybe it was important to somebody, but not to them.

Most of the designers responded with consternation: "But how," they asked, "can they possibly understand how to do the procedures when they don't understand the basic concepts? How can they 'create a new document' when they don't know what a 'document' is?"

Gradually the realization began to set in: the developers, all of whom were highly educated, theoretically oriented and technically minded, and accustomed to reading detailed technical material, had designed the manuals for themselves. They began to understand that technical experts like them tend to be *deductive learners*—they learn by starting from the "big picture" and proceed to master the specifics. They not only like the "information," the background explanations, but they *crave* it. It suits their favorite information processing style.

Non-technical people, particularly those with relatively limited formal education, are more likely to be *inductive learners*. They proceed from specific cases to a general understanding. This is exactly the opposite mental pathway from that taken by deductively oriented technical people.

Neither pattern of learning, inductive or deductive, is better than the other. Each can be effective or ineffective depending on how well a particular person has learned to use it. However, when a person who favors one learning pattern tries to explain something to someone who favors another pattern, the experience can be difficult and frustrating.

Many so-called "personality conflicts" are actually the result of significant differences in these mental preferences or *thinking styles*. Most of us go through life "talking to ourselves," that is, we tend to project our own preferred mental patterns onto others, and we tend to explain ideas in the way we prefer, not necessarily the way the other person prefers.

Your thinking style is your characteristic way of processing information. It's the way you acquire your knowledge, organize your thoughts, form your views and opinions, apply your values, solve problems, make decisions, plan, and express yourself to others. Just as you have a certain style of social interaction, a style of talking, and a style of dressing, you have a style of thinking.

For many years I've been studying these thinking styles and collecting data on the recurring patterns that seem to dominate human mental process and human interaction. This work has culminated in the *Mindex Thinking Styles Profile,* a self-assessment questionnaire that portrays a person's pattern of preferences for mental activity.

Research into human brain processes has clearly shown the existence of two distinctly different modes of thought. These two modes are associated with the physical division of the brain into the left and right hemispheres, as explained briefly in Chapter 3. For the majority of people, the "left brain" extracts those features of the sensory data stream that are linear, sequential, numerical, symbolic, elemental, and "logical." The "right brain," on the other hand, is oriented to the holistic, spatial, structural, emotional, and "intuitive" processes. These two thinking modes are so highly contrasted that you can recognize them in action by listening to the way a person talks.

Left-brain thought processes show up as statements oriented to logical reasoning, elements, sequences, facts and figures, and conceptual structures. Right-brain thought processes show up as statements about people, feelings, experiences, patterns, relations, and philosophical concepts.

We've recognized these contrasting patterns, at least vaguely, for centuries in the distinction between "logical" thinking and "intuition." We're beginning to understand that these two thinking modes are as fundamental to the mind's operation as breathing is to the body. They are the substance of thought, so to speak.

It's also clear that most people tend to favor one of these two thinking modes over the other as they grow up and develop into adults. This tendency to rely on one predominant mode for the majority of one's thinking processes points to the concept of cognitive style as a framework for understanding how someone thinks, learns, communicates, buys, sells, and decides. This mode preference is one of two important dimensions of thinking style, the dimension of *structure*.

The other dimension of thinking style deals with *what* a person thinks—the *content* of his or her thought. Here the contrast is between *concrete* thinking and *abstract* thinking. People who prefer concrete thinking tend to look for direct, tangible results. They like to deal with what is "real," the here and now, and things they can experience directly. The abstract thinker, on the other hand, likes things that exist in the imagination and enjoys dealing with conceptual or theoretical subjects.

Conceiving of thinking processes in terms of these two sets of polarities—left-brain/right-brain and concrete/abstract—gives rise to four possible combinations, or thinking styles. The four styles are: Left-Brain Concrete, Right-Brain Concrete, Left-Brain Abstract, and Right-Brain Abstract.

To make these four thinking styles easy to understand and remember, I've given them metaphorical names, in terms of colors. In the Mindex model, we can call the left-brained mode of thought "blue" thinking, if only because we tend to think of analytical people as having relatively "cool" personalities, represented by a cool color like blue. We can call the right-brained thinker a "red" thinker, because we think of intuitively inclined people as having "warmer" personalities, as suggested by red.

Similarly, we can give simple metaphorical names to the other dimension—the concrete and abstract levels. We can call them "earth" and "sky," respectively. "Earth" thinking is concrete, immediate, and results-oriented. "Sky" thinking is imaginary, visionary, and conceptual.

Using these metaphorical names for the four key styles, we have:

A.   Red Earth (right-brained concrete);
B.   Blue Earth (left-brained concrete);
C.   Red Sky (right-brained abstract); and
D.   Blue Sky (left-brained abstract).

Figure 10.1 shows these four styles in the form of a two-by-two grid diagram.

Everybody uses all four of these thinking modes, not just one. The brain can shift rapidly from one mode to another, and frequently combines them, according to the demands of the task at hand. However, most people tend to have a "home base" style, one primary mode they employ in most of their dealings with their environments. Some people are highly mobile and able to shift easily from one mode to another. Others are less mobile and have more difficulty with mode-switching. People

## Figure 10.1.　The Mindex Model

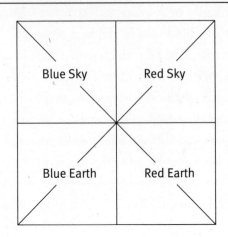

who cannot budge from their primary thinking styles may be handicapped in some situations, not only in communicating, but also in doing the kinds of thinking and problem solving that need to be done. You can think of these four modes as similar to four software "windows" running simultaneously on your computer screen, each processing data in a different way.

The following discussion describes each of the four basic thinking styles from the point of view of a person who favors that style very strongly. People with "combination" styles may not exhibit these tendencies so strongly as those who tend to rely heavily on a single style. The descriptions are intended to clarify the most noticeable patterns of each style and should not be construed to suggest that every person will fit neatly into only one of the four styles.

- Probably the most common style is the Red Earth person. Red Earth is apt to be "intuitive," people-oriented, and inclined toward direct experience. He or she tends to make decisions based on personal impressions, rather than individual facts or figures. Red Earth usually likes to see the outcomes of his or her efforts in concrete, tangible, recognizable form. This person has little interest in technical detail, theories, or elaborate logical processes. To the Red Earth person, feelings are "data." His or her feelings in a situation, and the apparent feelings of others, are just as important as any other "facts." You tend to find a high proportion of Red Earth people in "people" professions like education, sales, social work, and counseling.

- The Blue Earth is a person who values structure and order, logic, and bottom-line results. Blue Earth enjoys organizing things, solving problems logically, and doing work that involves facts, figures, and attention to detail. Fields that tend to attract Blue Earth people are accounting, some kinds of computer programming, and some kinds of engineering.

- The Red Sky is a person who likes the big picture, and is more concerned with the "what" than the "how." Red Sky tends to enjoy entrepreneurial ventures, networking with other people to accomplish big goals, and toying with global concepts and possibilities. Red Sky people tend to be drawn toward fields or activities that reward entrepreneurial thinking, but do not demand a great deal of theoretical knowledge or "detail" work.

- The Blue Sky is the theoretician. This person values abstract ideas, logical reasoning, and relational thinking. Blue Sky also enjoys looking at the big picture, but inclines more toward organizing problems conceptually, creating theories, and working out systematic solutions. You tend to find a high proportion of Blue Sky people in fields like architecture, systems engineering, and strategic planning. The Blue Sky thinker is the one who likes to draw diagrams and models, like the figure given above.

Again, very few people use only one of these styles to the exclusion of the others. But when a person does have a strongly dominant style, it tends to play an important part in his or her thinking processes and interactions with others.

Note that this is an egalitarian model, and especially an apprecia-
tive model. There is no "best" style. If another person with whom you
are dealing does not think the same way you do, neither of you needs
to be "fixed." The other person is not wrong, just different. By understanding these differences and learning to adapt to them, the two of
you can reach a state of "resonance," a highly satisfying condition of
intellectual and psychological rapport.[1]

## SEQUENTIAL THINKING: RE-OWNING YOUR LOGICAL ABILITIES

Fans of Arthur Conan Doyle's fictional detective Sherlock Holmes
know that Sherlock had a brother, Mycroft Holmes. Sherlock conceded
that Mycroft's powers of deduction surpassed even his own.

One reason why the Holmes stories have become so durable in literary history, and still attract a large readership more than a century
after they were created, may be the sense of potency and mastery we
get while reading about these inspiring feats of logic. We can enjoy a
vicarious feeling of being brilliant by identifying with the Holmes character. In one of the few episodes that put Sherlock and Mycroft
together, we get a double dip of this intellectual treat. Here's an excerpt
from a scene in "The Adventure of the Greek Interpreter," narrated by
the ever-admiring Dr. John Watson:

"The two sat down together at the bow-window of the club.

"'To anyone who wishes to study mankind this is the spot,'
said Mycroft. 'Look at the magnificent types! Look at those two men
who are coming toward us, for example.'

"'The billiard-marker and the other?'

"'Precisely. What do you make of the other?'

"The two men had stopped opposite the window. Some chalk
marks over the waistcoat pocket were the only signs of billiards
which I could see in one of them. The other was a very small dark fellow, with his hat pushed back and several packages under his arm.

"'An old soldier, I perceive,' said Sherlock.

"'And very recently discharged,' remarked the brother.

"'Served in India, I see.'

"'And a non-commissioned officer.'

"'Royal Artillery, I fancy,' said Sherlock.

"'And a widower.'

"'But with a child.'

"'Children, my dear boy, children.'

"'Come," said I [Watson speaks], laughing, 'this is a little too much.'

"'Surely, answered Holmes, 'it is not hard to say that a man with that bearing, expression of authority, and sun-baked skin is a soldier, is more than a private, and is not long from India.'

"'That he has not left the service long is shown by his still wearing his "ammunition boots," as they are called,' observed Mycroft.

"'He has not the cavalry stride, yet he wore his hat on one side, as is shown by the lighter skin on that side of his brow. His weight is against his being a sapper. He is in the artillery.'

"'Then, of course, his complete mourning shows that he has lost someone very dear. The fact that he is doing his own shopping looks as though it were his wife. He has been buying things for children, you perceive. There is a rattle, which shows that one of them is very young. The wife probably died in child-bed. The fact that he has a picture-book under his arm shows that there is another child to be thought of.'

"I began to understand what my friend meant when he said that his brother possessed even keener faculties than he did himself. He glanced across at me, and smiled."

As Holmes scholar Edgar W. Smith puts it, "This is the Sherlock Holmes we love—the Holmes implicit and eternal in ourselves."

Actually, the Holmes brothers demonstrate for us *two* very valuable skills related to logical thinking: *keen observation* and *accurate deduction*.

When sizing up a crime scene, they *saw more* than other observers chose to see. They had trained their mental filters to remain open to a full range of information, and not to reflexively exclude more than they admitted. Indeed, they might contend—were they here to talk with us—that observation was the more important element of their remarkable skills.

What if we could all observe and perceive with the searching curiosity that the Holmes brothers displayed? Could it be that our powers of observation are also very keen, but that we simply don't use them and keep them sharp?

How many of us look with tired eyes and see only the few key elements of a scene or situation that seem most relevant to us? How often do we brush aside everything but what we're currently concerned with? Could we understand situations, people, problems, or opportunities much better by searching them more thoroughly and observing more about them?

Here's a small exercise in perception, which can help to condition your biocomputer for logical thinking.

## Exercise in Observation

The next time you eat something, focus only on the thing you're eating and the sensory experience of eating it. Notice how strong the tendency is to shift your attention to other things in your environment. After you've taken a bite of that cookie, or a sip of that coffee, do your eyes automatically wander to look at other things in your environment? Do you taste, chew, and swallow on "autopilot"? Bring your attention fully back to the experience of tasting, savoring, chewing, and swallowing the food. Between bites, look intently at the remaining part. Feel the food in your mouth; feel the texture as you're holding it in your hand. What do you notice about the color? How does it smell? Is it cold, warm, hot? Does it make a sound as you bite into it? If it came packaged in a wrapper, how was the wrapper made? How many different "facts" can you notice about this simple item of food?

Here's a second exercise, this one aimed at connecting the things you observe into a logical pattern.

## Exercise in Logical Deduction

The next time you walk into a supermarket, take two or three extra minutes just to wander around, before you begin your shopping. Try to detect as many of the logical patterns, rules, and relationships as you can that tell you how the store works. See how widely you can extend your consciousness to examine the store as a logical system. Someone designed it the way it is. Why? How do people get into and out of the store? How do the design and layout help to—or fail to—prevent theft? Are all of the fresh perishable items like fruits and vegetables in the same general area? If so, why? Would it make sense to rearrange them? How does the overall visual design—color, use of light, visual variety, and traffic flow enhance or detract from the buying experience? Now imagine that you're an undercover spy and that your mission is to memorize the layout of the store, without drawing a diagram, in order to tell your accomplices exactly where everything is so they can infiltrate the place. Does that intention change the way you observe? Imagine that you're a police officer answering a live burglary call. What would you want to know about the layout of the store that would help you deal with the mission? What do you notice about the place that you might not have noticed before?

## Logical Calisthenics

Sometimes just giving your "logic muscles" some exercise can make a general improvement in your sequential-logical thinking processes. Some people just allow themselves to become mentally sedentary. You might be surprised how much "carryover" effect you can experience from working some simple logic exercises.

Consider, for example, an elementary type of a logic puzzle like the "word ladder." The idea is to start with one word and by changing one letter at a time, transform it into another word, with the requirement that every change of a letter creates another valid word. Punctuations are allowed. Here's an example:

> Change "came" to "went"
> came => cane
> cane => can't
> can't => want
> want => went

Here are some others to practice on. Try talking them through, and if you need to, get your pen and write them out in steps. As you work through each of them, it's important to relax and let go of any anxiety you might be associating with the task, calmly moving through the steps one by one. Pay more attention to the *mental experience* of working through the steps, not necessarily focusing on achieving the final result.

> *1. Change hate to love.*
> *2. Change fall to rise.*
> *3. Change take to give.*
> *4. Change lose to find.*
> *5. Change won't to will.*

Appendix A gives a sequence for each of the problems; there may be others.

With regular practice and determination, maybe each of us can become as skillful a detective as Sherlock Holmes—or even Mycroft.

## TRUSTING YOUR HUNCHES: RE-OWNING YOUR INTUITIVE ABILITIES

Intuition, in contrast to logic, is simply a pattern of ideation that takes place outside of consciousness. We can become conscious of the *results* of intuitive thinking—the "output," so to speak, but we cannot directly perceive the process itself.

The output of any intuitive episode is a "hunch," or a conclusion of some kind, that your mindmodules at the nonconscious level offer up for consideration at the conscious levels. An intuitive conclusion can certainly "make sense": that is, it can be expressed in logical form, so we could say that, in a way, intuition is a quasi-logical process, the steps of which are not known to consciousness.

In fact, we do this routinely. We conjure up a conclusion or a realization at the intuitive level, it is transformed into words—the language of consciousness—and then we can own it consciously. Once we've captured it in verbal form, it seems "normal." Indeed, this process is happening repeatedly, on a rapid-fire basis, in every normal biocomputer, all during our waking hours. It probably goes on even during sleep, except that the conscious expression of the intuitive material is typically impaired when we're not awake.

This easy interplay between intuitive levels and conscious levels is truly what we mean by intulogical thinking. However, not all of the intuitive material that's being produced outside the level of consciousness can ever make it to our conscious mental "view-screen." There's just too much of it. What we call the conscious mind is a very "narrow band" processing system, which means that it actually has a very limited capacity for processing information at any one instant.

We apparently have mindmodules that act as gatekeepers that are continually making decisions about what material will be translated to consciousness. These gatekeeper modules filter out far more information than they pass on. Try a little experiment to illustrate this gate-keeping function.

As you sit reading these words, try to pay attention to the sensations coming from your body. Do you become conscious of the way you're sitting; the feeling of your clothes in contact with various parts of your body; the sensations coming from your digestive system; your breathing; the sounds in your environment? As you tune in to these various signals, do you notice that your consciousness of the words on this page tends to fade? These various signals have been going on all the time, beyond your consciousness. As you tune in some signals, others fade out, because your conscious processor simply doesn't have enough bandwidth to be aware of them all.

Now try another little experiment that can really make a believer out of you, with regard to this narrow-band, gate-keeping effect. Lift your right foot a few inches from the floor and begin moving it in a circular, clockwise direction. Keep it going, and after about five seconds, begin simultaneously moving your right hand in a circular, *counterclockwise* direction. For most of us, even this simple little procedure overloads our main processor. It's like the well-known challenge of patting your head and rubbing your stomach: your brain can only manage one of them consciously, and it has to delegate the other one to an "autopilot" mindmodule.

The *intulogical conversation*—this interplay of intuitive activity and conscious awareness—seems more fluent in some people than in others. It's not uncommon for a person to prefer one level over the other instead of integrating the two. Just as some intuitively oriented people may distrust and disown their logical and systematic thinking processes, some analytically inclined people may distrust and disown their intuitive processes. Clearly we need both, and the more of each we have, the better.

## THE "ZEN MIND": FLOW AND MINDFULNESS

The distinguished Zen master and philosopher D.T. Suzuki attempted to explain what he considered a key aspect of the difference between conventional Westernized thinking—a highly analytical pattern—and the Zen thinking process, which is highly intuitive. He compared two poems, one by the seventeenth century Japanese poet Bashó and one by the English poet Alfred Lord Tennyson, who lived about two centuries later.

The Bashó poem, a classical seventeen-syllable *haiku* (seventeen syllables in the Japanese version), refers to a small wild flower the poet accidentally discovers in an obscure spot:

When I look carefully
I see the *nazuna*
blooming by the hedge!

Bashó's poem does nothing more than sense the flower's existence; he does not attempt to analyze it, classify it, or objectify it. In the Zen sense, the observer and the flower are one, and not separate entities. The poem is about the *experience* of the flower, not some separate entity called a flower.

In Tennyson's poem, according to Suzuki, the poet characterizes the flower as an object, not as part of the same nature as himself:

Flower in the crannied wall,
I pluck you out of the crannies;
Hold you here, root and all, in my hand,
Little flower—but if I could understand
What you are, root and all, and all in all,
I should know what God and man is.

Note, Suzuki says, that the poet Tennyson plucks the flower, confiscating it, trying to make it his own, and kills it in the process. He perceives the flower as a thing, an element of his environment he is entitled to own, control, manipulate, and analyze. The Tennyson poem treats the flower as a thing to be manipulated. The Bashó poem treats the experience of perceiving the flower as a truth in and of itself.

In their thought-provoking book *Zen Buddhism and Psychoanalysis,* Erich Fromm and D.T. Suzuki, together with Richard De Martino, report the exchange of ideas in a groundbreaking psychological conference held in Cuernavaca, Mexico, in 1967. At that time, conventional psychologists and psychoanalysts would have been shocked at the idea of comparing a serious discipline such as psychoanalysis with a "mystical" Eastern practice such as Zen Buddhism. Today, however, the ideas of East and West are considered much more compatible and complementary than ever before, and more worthy of consideration in a new understanding of human mental process.[2]

Re-owning our intuition includes learning to think in that Zen-like way. In those moments when we temporarily set aside our intentions; our definitions; our labels, categories, and classifications; our need for structure, order, and control; and our cause-and-effect thinking, we can *perceive without concluding*. In those moments, the purpose of our perception is perception itself, not getting ready to do something about what we've perceived. This is the state of mind in which we tune in to our inner understanding, the unexpressed wisdom that's waiting to be experienced.

One way to turn up the sensitivity on your intuitive signals is to practice *experiencing without verbalizing*. It's a very common practice for Westerners to, say, walk into an art gallery and review each picture in turn, commenting about it: "I like that," "I don't like that," "What is it?" "It's too busy," or "I don't know anything about art, but I know what I like." The more we verbalize about what we're perceiving, the less we're perceiving it. A statement like "That's beautiful" is a mental event that places a sense of completion, of finishing, on the perceptual experience. Once we've labeled and categorized the thing we're observing, we can move on to the next thing.

## An Exercise in Perception

As an experience in intuitive perception, stand in front of a piece of art and just experience it without saying anything about it. Try to avoid saying anything about it even silently, in your mind. Avoid *intending* to say anything about it. Try to experience it silently and neutrally, without evaluating it, without approving or disapproving. Allow it to just exist, and allow yourself to just exist with it. Feel a sense that you and it are one, or at least parts of the same one thing. How does it feel to share the space with this unclassified and unclassifiable something? What sensations arise in you? Allow your attention to be drawn to whatever features of it attract you at a particular instant. Close your eyes and visualize it as clearly as you can; then open your eyes and see it in a new way.

We can apply this same Zen-like method of intuitive sensing in any situation. Imagine that you're participating in a meeting or a working session associated with your job. Can you "observe with soft eyes," as Zen teachers say—sensing everyone and everything and every happening, without intention. You may find that you become aware of information you might not have otherwise noticed. The way people speak; their tone of voice; the sense of energy, or lack of it, in the group; the undertones and overtones of the conversation, all provide "data" for your intuitive understanding of what's going on.

The more open you are to this kind of non-purposive experiencing of situations, the more richly you can perceive and interact with the situations you encounter.

On a one-to-one basis, with your romantic partner or significant other, or with friends and acquaintances, it's called "being present" or "being in the moment." Instead of listening with intention, we can learn to listen with empathy and curiosity, learning about the other person, and about ourselves, as we respect the depth and richness of what there is to know.

And even when alone, or perhaps especially when alone, we can quiet our minds and tune in to the intuitive conversation that's always going on within us.

> "The worst form of loneliness is not being
> comfortable with yourself."
>
> —Mark Twain

The noted Hungarian psychologist Mihaly Czikzentmihalyi speaks of a special state of consciousness he and others call, simply, "flow." When we become deeply absorbed in something we're doing; when we lose the sense of the immediate present and suspend our sense of time; and when we're experiencing little or no anxiety, we're in the flow

state. People who operate in a state of chronic stress and agitation seldom experience the flow state. Or perhaps it's the other way around:
people who haven't learned to experience the flow state spend more
of their time and energy in the stress zone, or the "panic zone," as
Czikzentmihalyi calls it. Those who've learned to achieve the flow state
can release their natural abilities and perform at a higher level.

According to Czikzentmihalyi, musicians, artists, athletes, and
other performance practitioners do what they do most skillfully when
they get into the flow state. Many skilled performers refer to it as
"being in the zone." Some refer to it as the alpha zone, because it tends
to be associated with the presence of the alpha brainwave frequency,
which ranges from about eight to sixteen cycles per second. [3]

As we've previously considered, a key aspect of the intuitive thinking
state, the zone, the alpha state—whatever one prefers to call it—is the
*absence of anxious intention*. It may seem strange and paradoxical that star
performers largely suspend their conscious intention. It's as if they "don't
care"—consciously—whether the ball goes into the hole, or into the
basket, or over the net; whether they sing the challenging high note;
whether they "connect" with the audience they're entertaining or speaking to. They've delegated the intention to the well-trained mind-modules
that are working skillfully below the level of consciousness. This mental
state is actually what we mean when we say we're "absent-minded."

## An Exercise in Absent-Mindedness

Here's a simple illustration of the potential of "zone-based thinking."
Have you ever wadded up a sheet of paper, absent-mindedly tossed it at
a wastebasket on the other side of the room, and watched it go right in?
Probably you felt slightly elated, and a bit amused. "Wow! Look at
that." Then you try it again, and you miss.

The difference between the first and second attempts is the intention, or lack of it. On the first toss, your mind was "somewhere else," so
your cerebellum—your autopilot for motor activities—handled the
mission. Without interference from the conscious level—the motor

cortex in your cerebrum—the cerebellum simply activated a well-learned script and did the job without expectation, apprehension, or anxiety. It's incapable of those kinds of reactions; it just *does*.

On the second toss, your cerebral process probably took over, and an intentional tug of war ensued. The muscles involved in the toss were getting signals from two command centers at once, the motor cortex of the cerebrum and the cerebellum itself. Chances are, the mixed signals interfered with the coordination of the muscles.

Try a simple practice exercise. Get a dozen or so sheets of scratch paper, or some other items you plan to throw away. Stand across the room from the wastebasket, focus your attention closely on the basket, and detach your thinking from any sense of outcome. Decide that it doesn't matter whether the items you throw go into the basket or not; you're just going to throw them "mindlessly." Concentrate on the basket and picture the item you're going to throw traveling the arc of its trajectory, right into the basket, even while you "don't care" whether it goes in or not.

Practice with many throws, paying special attention to the sense of detachment, passive expectation, and trust in your instinctive knowledge. Each time you feel you've achieved the zone-state, or come close to it, sense the overall body feeling and make an effort to memorize it. The more often you practice, the more quickly and easily you'll be able to access this intuitive zone.

## Notes

1. Portions of the material in this section are excerpted from *Mindex: Your Thinking Style Profile,* a self-assessment instrument developed by Karl Albrecht International. Used with permission. See www.KarlAlbrecht.com/mindex/mindexprofile.htm.

2. Fromm, Erich, D.T. Suzuki, and Richard DiMartino. *Zen Buddhism and Psychoanalysis.* New York: HarperCollins, 1970.

3. Csikszentmihalyi, Mihaly. *Flow: The Psychology of Optimal Experience.* New York: HarperCollins, 1991.

# 11

## MEGA-SKILL 4
### *"Viscerational" Thinking*

> "Man is not rational—merely capable of it."
> —Jonathan Swift

IN THE SLAPSTICK BROADWAY COMEDY *A Funny Thing Happened on the Way to the Forum,* Zero Mostel played the conniving Roman slave *Pseudolus,* who is devising a plot to win his freedom from his master, a young noble who has fallen in love with a courtesan who, unfortunately, has been sold to another man. If Pseudolus can broker a relationship between the two, he might be set free.

Centering on three adjacent houses, the plot spirals into an ever more frenzied complex of just-in-time episodes that become ever more likely to expose him. In one chaotic scene, Pseudolus' assistant, a slave aptly named *Hysterium,* begins to lose his composure and become— well, hysterical.

Mostel, as Pseudolus, grabs him, shakes him, and shouts, "Calm yourself down! I'll tell you when it's time to panic!"

Just then one of the key characters walks in and discovers their mischief. Mostel, after a one-beat pause, calmly pronounces, "It's time." Then he launches into the panic state.

The interplay between what we call rational thought and what we think of as emotion threads throughout almost all of human life. We are, after all, emotional creatures first and rational creatures second.

## THE RATIONAL-EMOTIVE POLARITY:
## THE R-E AXIS

Our everyday conversation and the figures of speech we commonly use acknowledge our understanding of emotion as the buried source of at least some of our behavior. Some people refer to certain decisions as "visceral" judgments, implying that they originate somewhere within the biocomputer, at levels not visible to consciousness. In contrast, we typically refer to "rational" judgments as resulting from a coherent mental process that unfolds at the conscious level. The general meaning of rational thinking typically implies a movement from evidence to conclusions, a progression, which we can recognize and describe.

Both visceral and rational forms of mental process—we can even refer to both of them as forms of ideation—have importance and value in our interactions with our world. Indeed, it would be very difficult to separate the two. It seems more reasonable to regard every mental process as having a conscious or rational component, which is intertwined with a non-conscious or visceral element. This way of thinking about thinking makes a case for a new definition, based on a fusion of both patterns:

*Viscerational Thinking: A thinking process that integrates both rational and visceral patterns of ideation into a synergistic combination.*

We commonly speak of people who act "irrationally"; we wonder: "How can any rational person believe such a thing?" We try to sell our ideas and suggestions as "rational solutions" to problems.

We seem to grasp the concept of rational and irrational thinking—and behavior—at least in a general sense. However, the concept becomes somewhat elusive as we try to define it more specifically, and we soon have to face the proposition that what's rational to one person may be irrational to another.

Consider, for example, that throughout most of Western culture, committing suicide is generally considered an irrational act. We try to prevent people from doing it; we may even punish them for trying. We subject suicidal people to psychotherapy, hoping that they will "get better." Yet in some cultures the act of suicide has more of a noble, romantic, idealized definition than it typically has in the West.

On June 11, 1963, a Buddhist monk named Thich Quang Duc, who was a highly advanced *bodhisattva,* or spiritual master, burned himself to death at a busy intersection in downtown Saigon. He and several other monks arrived at the location by car. Thich Quang Duc got out of the car, walked to the center of the intersection, assumed the traditional lotus position, and with the help of the other monks drenched himself with gasoline. Then he lighted a match and ignited the gasoline. He burned to death in a matter of minutes. The news photo of his self-immolation became one of the legendary images of the Vietnam era.

Historian David Halberstam, then a young reporter for the *New York Times* assigned to Vietnam, witnessed the event:

"I was to see that sight again, but once was enough. Flames were coming from a human being; his body was slowly withering and shriveling up, his head blackening and charring. In the air was the smell of burning human flesh; human beings burn surprisingly quickly. Behind me I could hear the sobbing of the Vietnamese who were now gathering. I was too shocked to cry, too confused to take

*notes or ask questions, too bewildered to even think. . . . As he*
*burned he never moved a muscle, never uttered a sound, his outward*
*composure in sharp contrast to the wailing people around him."*[1]

After he died, Thich Quang Duc was fully cremated; legend has it that his heart did not burn. It's reportedly in the custody of the Reserve Bank of Vietnam.

The purpose of his self-immolation was to draw attention to the brutal repression of Buddhists by the Catholic regime of Ngo Dinh Diem. He had prepared himself for his act through several weeks of deep meditation. He had explained his motivation in letters to members of his Buddhist community as well as to the government of South Vietnam, emphasizing that he did not view his death as an act of suicide in its conventional meaning.

He was not in absolute despair, had not given up all hope, did not suffer from feelings of worthlessness, and did not wish to end his existence—generally recognized aspects of suicidal ideation. Yet he invested his life in making the statement he felt needed to be made. One might even call his behavior highly rational—from one point of view. In the following months, several other devout Buddhist monks publicly burned themselves to death for the same cause.

Consider also the Japanese suicide pilots of World War II, the *kamikaze,* young men in the ages of seventeen to nineteen who flew one-way missions to attack the U.S. fleet, welded into the cockpits of expendable airplanes. An estimated four thousand of them flew their death missions within about five years, and volunteers outnumbered the available planes by three to one.

Each kamikaze pilot received a manual to study before taking off on his last mission. Some excerpts from the manual reportedly included:

"The Mission of To-Go Units. Transcend life and death. When you
eliminate all thoughts of life and death, you will be able to totally
disregard your earthly life. This will also enable you to concentrate

your attention on eradicating the enemy with unwavering determination, meanwhile reinforcing your excellence in flight skills. . . .

"Be always pure-hearted and cheerful. A loyal fighting man is a pure-hearted and filial son.

"Attain a high level of spiritual training. In order to exert the highest possible capability, you must prepare your inner self. Some people say that spirit must come before skill, but they are wrong. Spirit and skill are one. The two elements must be mastered together. . . .

"At the very moment of impact: do your best. Every deity and the spirits of your dead comrades are watching you intently. Just before the collision it is essential that you do not shut your eyes for a moment so as not to miss the target. Many have crashed into the targets with wide-open eyes. They will tell you what fun they had."

"Remember when diving into the enemy to shout at the top of your lungs: 'Hissatsu!' [Sink without fail!] At that moment, all the cherry blossoms at Yasukuni shrine in Tokyo will smile brightly at you. . . ."[2]

Note the use of the "death mantra," the *attention-focusing statement* to be shouted at the last instant, probably intended to distract the pilot's attention from his final impulse of self-preservation.

In the Middle East, solo suicide bombers became ever more numerous after 2003, as the U.S. occupation of Iraq dragged on and as the agonizing standoff between Israel and the Palestinians continued to ferment.

Here's an interesting technical point: the suicide bomber never experiences the pain that precedes death, unlike the kamikaze pilot, who was probably conscious of the defensive machine gun bullets or the crash that killed him. The explosion happens in such a short interval of time—less than a thousandth of a second—that the bomber's brain no longer exists by the time any perceptual signal could have reached it and could have been consciously experienced. The last thing he or she is aware of is pushing the button, not experiencing the blast. This could be a useful sales point in recruiting bombers.

Customarily, the "people on the street" of Western societies have struggled to frame the behavior of "ideological suiciders" within the boundaries of their Western ideologies, with considerable frustration. Many political commentators and everyday citizens seem to dismiss them with an air of contempt: "These people are just crazy," "They don't value human life," "They're not even human." Attaching derogatory labels to them might help the speaker feel less bewildered and impotent to influence the world he or she doesn't understand, but it does little to explain the behavior of ideological suicide.

It seems we have little choice but to conclude that rational and irrational thinking, like "truth," is local to the individual mind where it occurs. Perhaps our best avenue for understanding the rational-emotive dimension of practical intelligence is to consider them as inseparably intertwined—indeed, as parts of the same process. If we can understand how they work in our own minds, perhaps we can understand and even tolerate their workings in the minds of others.

## FIRST WE DECIDE, THEN WE JUSTIFY: IRRATIONAL THINKING EXPLAINED

What we typically call irrational behavior makes sense if you understand its origins. And we can understand it in ourselves and others if we think of it as normal and set aside our tendency to condemn, criticize, or even to evaluate it. We have to understand it as an expression of several competing impulses that arise from unconscious levels, mixed with the influence of the conscious "reasoning" process. If you like, we can consider both levels of ideation as forms of reasoning; it's just that we can articulate one and can't easily articulate the other.

Again the modular-mind concept gives us a helpful perspective on the interplay between conscious and unconscious ideation and the way they influence our behavior. It may help to understand this interplay of visceral and rational ideation, and the conflicts it sometimes involves, by visualizing both levels as illustrated in Figure 11.1. Let's study a simplified example, in slow motion.

## Figure 11.1.   The Rationalizing Process

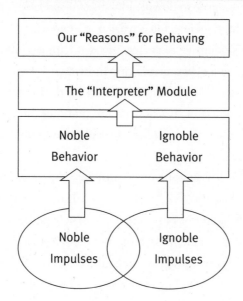

A student is apprehensive about an upcoming exam, which will be important to his grade in a key course. He's fallen behind in the course and has been cramming to catch up. He's worried that he might not be ready for the exam three days from now.

He asks his best friend to help him study so he can catch up. At the conscious level, this seems like the right thing to do. As portrayed in Figure 11.1, this would be a *noble behavior,* consonant with his *noble motive* of wanting to master the material and pass the exam fairly. So far: no conflict.

When he goes over to her house for the study and tutoring session, two other friends are there. One of them has discovered a way to get into the school computer and download the actual exam the teacher has prepared. The computer file containing the exam hasn't been properly safeguarded, the hacker student reports, and can easily be downloaded without detection. He's sure no one will ever find out. "Are you in?" asks his friend.

The students look at one another. One by one, with embarrassed expressions, they agree to download the exam and keep it a secret. There is nervous laughter, joking, and a sense of adventure.

Now our student is experiencing a dilemma, rational-emotively speaking. He's feeling two conflicting motivations; two or more mind-modules are contending for influence over his decision. One is the *noble motive*—the influence of the "honest" mindmodule; and the other is the *ignoble motive*—the influence of the fearful mindmodule that's scared of the consequences of failing the exam.

He's feeling what Stanford professor and psychologist Leon Festinger called *cognitive dissonance,* which is a feeling of anxiety as a result of a contradiction between one's beliefs and one's actions. His conscious, rational mind tells him that studying hard and taking his chances on the exam would have been the *noble behavior.* But his rational mind also observes what he actually does—his *ignoble behavior*—which contradicts his *noble motive.*

If he continues with the ignoble behavior of cheating on the exam, his ignoble motive will have won out over his noble motive. Now he will either have to admit to being downright dishonest, with no excuses, or—the more likely option—he will have to *rationalize* his cheating by making it sound less ignoble and somehow justified.

> "The proper office of a friend is to stick by you when you're in the wrong. Nearly anybody will stick by you when you're in the right."
>
> —Mark Twain

He and his fellow students come up with a variety of reasons why it's "OK" to cheat on the exam. They can minimize the importance of the event: "It's just an exam, it's not the end of the world." They can blame someone else: "If the teacher hadn't been so stupid as to leave the file unprotected on the school's server, nobody could have downloaded it." They can invoke peer support: "Everybody does it these days; if other people could have downloaded the exam, they would have, too." And they can invoke a right of self-interest: "I have to pass this course. If I don't, it could ruin my grade point average. I don't want to be turned down for [a job, or XYZ College] because of that old SOB's course."

Our student can come up with an almost unlimited number of creative reasons why his behavior really was acceptable in terms of his personal code of values. The effect is to resolve his cognitive dissonance by making his behavior seem less ignoble, at least to himself. The effect of the peer pressure is not only to sell him on behaving ignobly, but also to help him rationalize his actions.

Leon Festinger's concept of cognitive dissonance has become a mainstay of psychological thinking about rational and irrational behavior and about the process of rationalizing. It's also a favorite concept of advertising and marketing experts. In simple terms, the theory says that we human beings will usually act to resolve cognitive dissonance, by either restating the belief or idea that's dissonant with the behavior, or we'll explain the behavior in a way that makes it seem less dissonant.

One of the most stereotypical examples of rationalizing as a way to relieve the anxiety of cognitive dissonance is in the ways smokers learn to explain why they haven't stopped. They disapprove of the covert impulse that causes them to smoke—the bodily craving caused by nicotine dependency—so they have to find explanations that make the behavior of continuing to smoke not so bad: "Well, we're all going to die sometime," or "I don't believe all that stuff about smoking causing cancer," or the classic "I can quit any time I want to."

To make the story short and simple:

> *We tend to rationalize our behavior*
> *when we disapprove of the real motive*
> *that's causing it.*

Most of us are somewhat apprehensive at the possibility that our so-called "rational" behavior might actually be influenced by darker, more covert impulses below the level of consciousness. Some years ago when the notion of "subliminal messages" in advertising became the topic of popular conversation, many people suspected that they were being "programmed" to buy various products by hidden messages buried in the TV shows they were watching. The technique turned out to have very little impact, and advertisers made a fanfare of disavowing it—once they saw that it didn't work very well.

Comedian Johnny Carson picked up on the topic in one his monologues at the time:

> "You know, I've never put much stock in this subliminal advertising thing. But the other day I had a funny experience. I was watching TV at home, and I suddenly got up, and I went out and bought a tractor."

The truth is that we human beings are very easily manipulated. We don't like to admit it, but we're unconsciously manipulated every day. Some people make a living by capitalizing on the irrational behavior patterns they can induce in others. In his revealing book *Influence: The Psychology of Persuasion,* Robert Cialdini explains the visceral logic behind con-games and other forms of social manipulation.

One subconscious motive Cialdini identifies is what he calls *reciprocity*—the tendency in all of us to feel obligated and to want to repay some perceived act of generosity. *Hare Krishna* disciples, soliciting donations in airports, have used this method to raise astonishing amounts of money from strangers. In the usual maneuver, a pleasant-looking young woman steps in front of a traveler, most often a man, and hands him a flower. "This is a gift for you," she says. If he tries to hand it back, she refuses to take it: "No, please keep it. It's for you." Then she engages him in a conversation about spiritual practices, offers him some literature, and finally asks for a donation.

By hooking into a subconscious, visceral response program—"She gave me something of value, so I have to give her something"—HK solicitors achieved a remarkable hit rate, the percentage of people so accosted who gave money.[3]

As another example of less-than-rational behavior, consider a seemingly simple game that's sometimes played in bars and pubs, called a "dollar bill auction." The con artist invites two marks—er, patrons— to join into a game, "just for the fun of it." The game moves quickly, and tends to work especially well after a few drinks. The con artist makes the following offer:

1. He puts a dollar bill on the bar and offers to sell it to the highest bidder.
2. The players can bid any amount they like, but when the bidding stops, they both have to pay him the amount they last bid. That is, the one who doesn't win the bidding still has to pay the amount he bid before he stopped bidding. The one who wins gets the dollar bill and presumably makes a profit.

The bidding usually begins with one penny, then rises to five cents or so, and then begins to escalate from there. At some point, each of the bidders comes to the hazy realization that he will lose money unless he wins the bidding. They continue to bid against each other, with the bids getting higher and higher, and usually topping the mid-point of fifty cents. At this point, whether the bidders realize it or not, the person who is auctioning the dollar is guaranteed a profit, because he will collect from both of them.

Still perhaps not thinking very clearly, and now feeling some stress, the bidders begin to compete in earnest. It's not uncommon for them to bid the price up to well beyond a dollar—a clearly irrational act that will mean that one of them will have paid more than a dollar to get a dollar bill, and the other will have paid more than a dollar to get nothing.

At this point the auctioneer (who has probably turned his body toward the door and has scoped out a clear exit path) has them in direct competition with each other, whereas before the tipping point they had the vague idea that they were somehow competing against the auctioneer. After all, the auctioneer was supposed to lose money by selling the dollar for less than a dollar.

At some point, one of the bidders realizes that it's become a game of "chicken," and that even if he wins, he loses; he'll just lose a dollar less than the other guy. But it's not uncommon for a battle of wills to set in, with both bidders running up their losses in order to defend their egos against the thought of "failing." But in fact, they've both been had.

Had either of them realized—*thought rationally*—at the outset what was happening, they could have easily colluded against the auctioneer, agreeing that one of them would drop out after bidding a penny and let the other one win with a bid of two cents. Then they could repay themselves and split 97 cents (perhaps flipping a coin for the odd cent). When they realize they've been had, it's usually much too late for revising their strategy.

Why does this little game so often work? Because *it bypasses conscious reasoning and activates non-conscious impulses.* This is the essential definition of rational and irrational thinking, and the relationship between the two patterns.

## WE'RE ALL NEUROTIC, AND THAT'S OK
### Therapist, n. An emotional baggage handler.

Comedian Woody Allen's characters, and his personal life to some extent, epitomize the kind of person referred to in the language of the popular culture as "neurotic." He's perpetually anxious, apprehensive, and overly concerned with what might go wrong. His *character key,* in the language of comedy writing, is anxiety. It defines him to the viewer and it becomes the platform for much of his humor.

Therapists and others in the mental-health trade tend to dislike hearing ordinary civilians use psychological terms like neurotic or neurosis, because it encroaches on their professional privilege and muddies up the specific meanings they have agreed to for diagnostic purposes.

Unfortunately, we civilians seem to like to confiscate parts of the "psych" vocabulary, and the term will probably continue to be used as a popular lay diagnosis for any type of peculiar thinking we don't like.

But actually, we're all high-functioning neurotics—except, of course, those of us who are dysfunctional neurotics. Nobody escapes neurosis. It's a characteristic of the interaction between conscious and non-conscious ideation.

With apologies to my colleagues in the psychological trade, here's a street-level definition:

> *Neurosis: A pattern of impaired thinking, accompanied by anxiety, which is caused by the repression of an unacceptable emotion.*

That could describe just about all of us.

A disturbance in thinking could be severe enough to be classified as a *clinical neurosis,* meaning that the assistance of a mental-health professional is needed to resolve it. *Sub-clinical neurosis* is the normal kind we carry around with us every day. The more mentally healthy we are, the less of it we carry. Whether we need the services of a therapist is simply a matter of degree—how crazy we actually are.

The extreme version of a neurosis, the clinical kind, involves the repression of a strong emotion of some kind. It could be guilt, anger, shame, sexual desire, or any of the regular inventory of emotions. There's basically a conflict taking place at non-conscious levels.

Certain non-conscious mindmodules are trying to get a message to the conscious level: "Hey! We're feeling distressed down here." Other non-conscious modules, referred to in Freudian psychology as *ego defenses,* are working just as hard to prevent the emotion from coming into awareness. The result of the conflict between these two modular factions is anxiety—a general physical arousal that burns energy in a negative way.

The second effect of the repressed conflict is a warping of certain aspects of conscious ideation, in such a way as to help the defending modules keep the matter out of consciousness. Neurotic ideation shows up in a wide range of possible neurotic behaviors, such as compulsive repetition of some movement or activity, non-stop talking, or ritualistic arrangements of personal space or personal articles.

Extreme forms of neurosis can involve physical symptoms, sometimes severe ones. The anxiety itself can cause various visceral symptoms, such as insomnia, loss of appetite, impaired digestion, and general stress effects. In particular cases, the nonconscious modules may transmit their message to consciousness in code: paralysis of some part of the body or disease or dysfunction of an organ, which might be metaphorically related to the emotion being repressed.

*Case in point*: an associate who's a therapist related the case of a woman who had contracted rectal cancer. In working with her, he noted that she regularly described herself and her problems in the language of victimhood. He speculated that her repressed anger showed up in many of her figures of speech. One of her favorite expressions was "That's a real pain in the a**." Possibly her non-conscious modules took her at her word.

But, getting back to the struggles of us normal, healthy neurotics, let's consider the lessons that are there for us. Emotion is *information*. Emotions are cues and clues; they provide evidence of non-conscious ideation that may be important to our needs and purposes at the conscious level. We can learn to recognize, own, respect, understand, and even cherish our emotions. They won't destroy us, and from the bio-informational standpoint, they're there to help us.

Why do we human beings tend to repress emotion? Ironically, *it's an emotion that causes us to repress emotions*: it's fear. One of the most disabling emotions we can experience is fear of emotions. As a matter of fact:

> *The main cause of bad feelings is the*
> *fear of bad feelings.*

Psychologist Albert Ellis, who pioneered the therapeutic method known as rational-emotive behavior therapy (REBT), preached that we can achieve a high level of mental health by:

1. Becoming aware of and understanding our emotional processes;
2. Reframing our rational processes to make them more sane; and then
3. Integrating both rational and emotional dimensions into a unified pattern of reacting to our experiences.

When we overcome the self-alienation that leads us to disown and repress our natural emotions, we become, at the same time, more primitive and more evolved. We learn to integrate our primal, visceral processes of ideation with our conscious, learned patterns of conscious ideation.

That's actually one of the best definitions of sanity I've encountered.

## THE FIVE PRIMAL FEARS WE LIVE BY: THE PSYCHOLOGY OF RISK

Human beings are notoriously incompetent at estimating risk in situations where the risk is *emotionally loaded*—the outcome has a strong emotional interpretation attached to it.

*Case in point*: for several months after the "9/11" attack on New York City, millions of Americans refused to board airplanes. "I'll never fly again," many of them said. As horrific as the attack had been, and the lives it cost, it did not increase the odds of dying on a hijacked airliner, for any individual, by more than an infinitesimal degree. No matter—millions of Americans had decided that flying was unacceptably dangerous. Considering that more than six thousand flights operate over the United States every single day, and even assuming that there would be a hijacking every day, any one person's odds of dying in a terrorist hijacking remained about equal to the odds of being run over by a bus. But because of the highly charged fear fantasies associated with the 9/11 event, many people adopted a kind of binary fear assessment: if you fly, you die. Amusingly—or ironically—many people who liked to gamble would drive their cars to places like Las Vegas, Reno, and Atlantic City, hoping to beat the odds at the casino while congratulating themselves for cheating death at the hands of imaginary terrorists.

As is our custom, let's adopt a simple definition of fear:

> *Fear: A state of anxious arousal*
> *associated with an expectation.*

We have lots of descriptive phrases and figures of speech for fear, which seem to indicate that there are many kinds of fear. However, aside from the many variations in the situations that invoke fear in us, we actually have a relatively few absolute basic, or primal fears. Based on my unapproved theory of human fear, here's the short-list inventory of what scares us:

1. *Fear of extinction.* Psychologists and anthropologists call it "existential anxiety"—the fear of ceasing to be. The most fundamental of all facts of human existence is that we cannot conquer and control our environments; the best we can do is cope with them to some successful degree. Always at the back of our minds, lurking just below the level of consciousness, is the troubling knowledge that we could be eradicated in an instant. Normal, reasonably well-adjusted adults have learned to both acknowledge and conceal this truth simultaneously. We make jokes about death, dying, and getting old, while we secretly hope it never actually happens to us. Some philosophers attribute great artistic achievements and heroic lives to the primal energy generated by existential anxiety. Certainly religious ideologies, rituals, and ceremonies serve to mask existential anxiety.

2. *Fear of mutilation.* At a fairly primal level, *we are our bodies,* at least so far as our non-conscious ideation is concerned. A physical

injury, mutilation, or loss of a body part has fearful, threatening implications for most of us. It would stand to reason: we have to get through life with the bodies we were issued when we arrived, fully intact. The thought of losing a key part of our anatomy, or having it permanently damaged, elicits a primal form of anxiety and stress. This probably relates to fear of heights and fear of animals like bugs, snakes, and other creatures some people consider "icky." Perhaps this anxiety is what we project onto others who may be disabled or seriously disfigured, or who may have lost body parts. It's probably also part of the apprehension associated with sexual activity with a new partner or concern about eating strange foods.

3. *Fear of loss of autonomy.* We human beings are a self-moving form of life. To be immobilized—seriously impaired physically, crippled, or imprisoned, is to experience a primal form of anxiety, the loss of the capacity to be free. This form of anxiety seems to be at the root of *claustrophobia*—the irrational fear of small spaces. This is probably also one reason why spending a long time in prison is a soul-destroying experience for many: one loses one's fundamental sense of autonomy, one's defining right to move about *ad lib.*

4. *Fear of abandonment.* We human beings are social creatures. We are "wired" for connectedness, even at the same time we are ambivalent about maintaining it. From our early childhood, most of us experience a mixture of the desire for autonomy and the desire for connectedness. The child pulls away from his or her mother, yet comes running back when she gets too far away. To be abandoned is a terrible trauma for a child, and to be completely isolated from all other human beings is a form of suffering that destroys the soul. The so-called "silent treatment" is effective because it can erode the very basis for a person's sense of worth as a human being. People who have an exaggerated fear of abandonment can be jealous, possessive, or hyper-dependent and submissive, and often susceptible to manipulation and control.

5. *Fear of ego-death.* Once we've managed to come to terms with the first four primal fears, we have to deal with the fear that our carefully crafted self-concept might collapse. This primal fear of self-disintegration presents many faces: fear of failure; fear of embarrassment; fear of ridicule by others; fear of shame; fear of guilt; fear of rejection; fear of dependency; and fear of intimacy. Much of what we believe we can and cannot do, what we are or aren't capable of, and what we are or aren't entitled to in life is shaped by our ego-identity and by our need to protect and preserve it.

Primal fears 1 through 3 are fairly automatic, instinctive, self-preserving, and mostly kept comfortably repressed. They activate mostly in threatening circumstances. While some people can become obsessed with them in various forms, or pathologically over-react to threats that can trigger them, most of us live with them at the borderline of consciousness.

Primal fear number 4, fear of abandonment, is somewhat more of a learned pattern than an instinctive one. It becomes pathological when a person behaves in dysfunctional ways in hopes of avoiding it. For instance, a person who experiences feelings of fearful dependence, jealousy, and possessiveness may actually drive away the person he or she is hoping to "own," because the irrational fear of abandonment contaminates the person's rational knowledge of how to be an affirmative, nourishing person whom people will want to know. It can be unlearned by a combination of clear, rational thinking, and experimenting with affirmative behavior toward others.

Primal fear number 5, fear of ego-death, tends to be more socially programmed and less instinctive than the others. It can be nearly as strong and intense as the others, depending on the circumstances that trigger it. And it may activate from below the level of conscious thinking, giving it the sense of an instinctive or self-preservation reaction. But it's the one we have the most chance of changing.

It probably wouldn't be advisable, even if it were easy to do, to eliminate the first three primal fears altogether from our reaction patterns. *Fear is information*: it's a signal or a set of signals that help us know what's going on below the level of consciousness.

If fears are a form of information, and information can be re-patterned, then we can re-pattern our fears, even the primal ones, at least to some extent.

*Case in point*: I once conducted an experiment in which I attempted to use a mind-control technique—a kind of meditative brainstate—to overcome a fear associated with heights and falling. While spending the day with some friends and kids at an amusement park in southern California, I had occasion to go on the "Splash Mountain" ride, which involved climbing into a boat made to look like a hollowed-out log and being terrified as it climbed up steep inclines and then whooshed down the other side. As we were ascending the long climb to the final terrifying drop, I deliberately slipped into the alpha state, using a kind of attentive meditation procedure. As we rocketed to the bottom of the chute, I was aware of the screams of the people around me and the spray of water, but I felt very little of the anxiety usually associated with that kind of experience. I'm sure that my heart rate and respiration barely changed at all, and I remained remarkably calm through the entire descent. But then, of course, the ride wasn't fun any more; the purpose, after all, is to horrify yourself—that's why you do it.

Comedy writer and teacher John Vorhaus talks about overcoming the fear of ego-death in order to become skillful at entertaining people. "You have to *know*, deep down," he says, "that an audience can't kill you— at least not under ordinary circumstances. When you let go of the anxious attachment to their approval—their laughter—you actually become more free to make them laugh. You have to be revved up just enough to be on your game, but not fearful about the results. *You can look foolish and be foolish without feeling foolish.* Once you let go of the fear of ego-death, it's a matter of having great material and getting lots of practice. I guess you could call that confidence."

Public speaking is a similar prospect in which the fear of ego-death paralyzes many people. The first time I ever spoke to a relatively large audience, about five hundred managers in the company I was employed with many years ago, I was extremely apprehensive. I only ate a few bites of the delicious steak and lobster dinner, and I sat through the dessert course thinking, "Why did I ever agree to do this?" and "Why don't they just shoot me now and put me out of my misery?" Once I got up to speak, being well prepared, I got past the fear and into the experience of sharing ideas with them. They reacted very well to my presentation and I've been grateful ever since for the opportunity to face and overcome that particular dimension of the fear of ego-death. Most accomplished speakers will tell you that experience and practice soon overcome the fear.

## SIGNAL REACTIONS: DISCONNECTING YOUR HOT BUTTONS

An old vaudeville routine involves two strangers who get into a casual conversation. One of them innocently mentions the name of an acquaintance—"Martha." Suddenly, the other one reacts maniacally, snapping into a dissociated, glassy-eyed, incoherent state. "Martha!" he shouts. "Niagara Falls!" "Slowly, I turned . . . step-by-step . . ." and he seizes the innocent stranger by the throat and begins to strangle him. The victim's protests bring him back to reality and he apologizes profusely for losing his composure. Minutes later, the innocent participant happens to use some other word that sets him off again. There is a repeat of this maniacal, automated reaction and another episode of strangling.

The running gag is the "trigger" reaction. Another stranger happens along, gets into the conversation, and innocently uses the trigger word, at which time the unstable individual goes into the same recitation and tries to strangle him, too.

It's a comic send-up of a very typical human psychological event: the trigger reaction, also called the "hot-button" response. Some psychologists call it a *signal reaction,* particularly because it's set off by a particular cue—a certain word or expression someone uses; a certain behavior; a facial expression or gesture; almost anything can act as an emotional trigger for someone. Another figure of speech that describes it is the "electrode" response, which suggests that we react so automatically and so immediately that it's as if someone had touched us with a high-voltage electrode.

The signal response mechanism can be, at one and the same time, a valuable feature of your biocomputer's software and a self-destructive one. The same mechanism that ensures our survival as creatures can also derail our rational thinking processes.

Here's how it works. Your brain has an early warning sensor, called the *amygdala,* that alerts your whole body about anything it senses that might pose a threat to your physical well-being. Your amygdala is a small blob of brain tissue located in the limbic region, which is a collection of special-purpose structures located under your cerebral cortex, just above the roof of your mouth.

One of its jobs is to tap into the incoming flow of sensory signals that gather at a nearby gateway structure known as the *thalamus.* All of the signals coming into the brain—through the spinal cord—pass through the thalamus for a quick review before they fan out to the many specialized regions such as vision, audio processing, body sensations, and linguistic recognition.

The amygdala seems to tap into this flow of sensory data, monitoring it for patterns that might imply a threat to our survival. When it detects something to get alarmed about, it shoots a figurative email message to the hypothalamus (the unit that's "below" the thalamus) and tells it to prepare the body for an emergency. The hypothalamus and its partners in the limbic system launch a whole cascade of coordinated arousal signals that kick off the well-known fight-or-flight reaction.

A personal experience brought home to me forcefully how powerfully this simultaneous, multi-level thinking process works. I was walking along the margin of a high, grass-covered cliff overlooking the Pacific Ocean, having just enjoyed lunch at a golf resort nearby. It was a beautiful, cloudless California day and I was immersed in pleasant thoughts. As I strolled along in a state of reverie, I suddenly became aware of something very unusual. For a split-second I couldn't figure out what I was alerting to, but my automatic creature reaction was very strong regardless.

I suddenly felt a whole-body wave of fear as I became conscious of a huge shadow passing over me. Possibly some primitive program encoded deep into my reptilian brain interpreted the flash of the shadow as that of some giant predatory bird and decided to save me from becoming its prey. The instantaneous "fight-or-flight" reaction had kicked in *before I consciously understood what was happening.* A split-second later, as I looked up and scanned around, I realized that a low-flying sailplane had passed silently overhead.

The cliffs area was a popular location for people to enjoy hang gliding and sailplane flying, particularly because of the strong upward air currents rising from the cliffs. The combination of signals—the lack of sound, the sweeping shadow interrupting a cloudless sky—elicited a life-preserving, although unneeded reaction from one or more of my primitive mindmodules.

The good news is that this early warning sensor has probably saved your life many times. The bad news is that the wrong things can set it off. Just as a home burglar alarm can go off as a result of any of a number of extraneous influences having nothing to do with a burglary, so your amygdala can go off inappropriately. When that happens, it's as if the thalamus, the information gateway to your cortex, gets hijacked by the overreactive amygdala. This is what we refer to as the signal reaction.

We modern human beings have trained our amygdalas to react to various experiences and provocations that are not life-threatening. I call these emotional triggers "grabbers"—they grab your amygdala and set off your alarm bells. A grabber is a specific signal of some sort, to which you react with strong negative feelings—anger, guilt, shame, fear, or feelings of inadequacy, for example. The actual signal could be a word, a statement or question, a phrase, the tone of voice someone uses, a facial expression, or other nonverbal cue—anything to which you have developed a negative association.

You can learn to disarm these grabbers by identifying them, studying your reactions to them, and progressively weakening their influences on you.

Here's an exercise that can help you identify your favorite grabbers, and begin working to disarm them.

## Exercise: Signal Reactions

Review the following list of cues and check any that may be grabbers, or triggers, for you. Then add any others you know about that don't appear on the list.[4]

### What Are Your Grabbers?

1. Being laughed at, being made fun of.
2. Being called dumb, stupid, ignorant, foolish.
3. Specific words or expressions such as, "If you were smart, you'd. . . ."
4. Being portrayed as naive or socially inept.
5. Jokes or teasing about your face, body, weight, or physical appearance.
6. Jokes or teasing about various abilities (sports, dancing, singing, etc.).
7. Jokes or teasing about your speech or accent.
8. Jokes or teasing about your clothes or grooming.
9. Jokes or teasing about your aesthetic taste, for example, home decoration, furnishing, etc.
10. Jokes or teasing about your sexual experience or prowess.
11. Jokes or snide references to your ethnic heritage.
12. Gender put-downs, sexist humor.
13. Being criticized; having your work criticized.
14. Being made to seem incompetent.

15. Having your competence or qualifications questioned.

16. Being talked to in a parental tone of voice.

17. Being patronized or condescended to.

18. "You should . . ."

19. Unwanted sexual advances.

20. Tasteless jokes or vulgar humor.

21. Loud, boisterous people.

22. Inconsiderate behavior by others.

23. Being ridiculed for lack of knowledge or skills in some area.

24. Having someone impose on you for favors, etc.; presuming the right to take advantage of you.

25. Being ignored or kept waiting.

The main feature of the signal reaction, and the brain state that it launches, is a loss of coherent, rational thought. Typically it's an angry response, possibly reaching the level of blind rage, although it can also involve other emotions such as irrational fear, self-punishing guilt or shame, or embarrassment.

One useful method you can train yourself to use is the "one heart-beat pause," which allows you to delay or diminish your signal reaction until your rational processes have time to get involved, and you can react less automatically.

To use the "one beat" method, you have to become aware that one of your grabbers has occurred. A person you know has made the same unkind comment about your weight, your hair, your intelligence, or any other feature of your existence that he or she likes to use to "get your goat." Even if you begin to become angry, make a special effort to notice the grabber itself. Then, mentally count one heartbeat, with your mind in a kind of stand-by mode, before you react. One heartbeat, typically about a second or so, is a lot of time, neurologically speaking. It's plenty of time for the higher centers of your biocomputer to decide that this time he or she can't get your goat. The goat is no longer available.

This method is not perfect, of course, and it's not a magic solution. But with diligent practice, you may be surprised how well you can free yourself from signal reactions, or at least reduce their frequency and intensity.

## EMOTIONS AND HEALTH: IF IT'S ON YOUR MIND, IT'S ON YOUR BODY

Neuroscientists have actually solved the so-called "mind-body" mystery, at least theoretically. We now know which mechanisms in the biocomputer actually transform our thoughts into physiological consequences—wellness or illness. What we don't know yet, in any reliable way, is exactly how to create the specific patterns of ideation that do the job. Discovering or isolating those cognitive processes might eventually be one of the biggest single breakthroughs in the history of science. I dearly hope it happens within my lifetime.

According to pioneering hypnotherapist Ernest L. Rossi, the "wiring diagram" of *biocognition* is fairly clear, as illustrated in Figure 11.2.

According to Rossi:

> "The basic idea of the psychobiology of mind-body healing is that information is the central concept and connecting link between all the sciences, humanities, and clinical arts. Psychology, biology, and physics now have information as their new common denominator."

According to the most reliable research, your *hypothalamus,* described above, acts as a translator between your abstract mental processes and your more primitive, visceral processes. It has a number of critical functions, but a key one is serving as a go-between for the conscious and unconscious levels.

Nerve pathways coming down from various regions of the cortex converge at the hypothalamus, which is hooked up to three main sub-systems, each of which qualifies as a sophisticated computer in its own right. These three key sub-systems are:

## Figure 11.2.    How Thoughts Affect Physiology

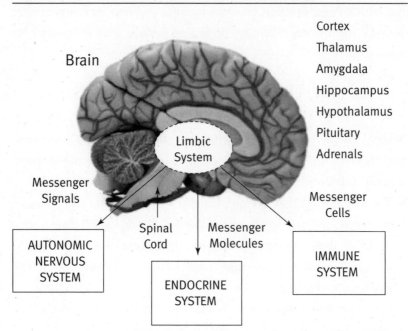

1. Your *autonomic nervous system,* also known as the involuntary nervous system, which has two main branches. The sympathetic branch, or division, is a collection of nerve pathways that act to arouse, stimulate, and increase the tempo of all processes in your body. The other branch is the parasympathetic division, which works as a counter-balance to the sympathetic branch. The parasympathetic nervous system or sub-system becomes more active in order to calm down your bodily processes, preparing you for relaxation, sleep, digestion, sexual activity, and a host of "non-mission-critical" functions. When you're excited or stressed, your sympathetic nervous system is highly active. When you're calm and relaxed, your parasympathetic nervous system is more active.

2. Your *endocrine system,* which is a collection of organs that secrete hormones and a whole array of "messenger molecules"— substances that flow through your bloodstream and body tissues to regulate various far-flung processes.

3. Your ***immune system,*** which is a collection of organs, tissues, cells, and cell products, such as antibodies and messenger chemicals, that identifies and neutralizes potentially harmful organisms or substances that find their way into your body.

These three key systems have a powerful collective influence on just about all aspects of your body's operation, and they directly affect your health and well-being every second of your life. The fact that they are closely integrated with the hypothalamus, and that the hypothalamus converses with the cortical levels of the brain, is a very strong indication of the intimate relationship between our conscious ideation and the most basic functions of our cells. Science has caught up with common knowledge: ideas can make people sick or well; they can kill or heal. Every thought we think has physiological consequences. To repeat the defining mantra of practical intelligence: *thinking is a bodily function.*

For centuries, healers, shamans, witch doctors, gurus, preachers, teachers, therapists, hypnotists, and motivational speakers have sought to discover the hidden codes of conscious ideation that can produce remarkable mind-body effects. The results to date have been frustratingly meager, but the possibilities remain tantalizingly close.

One of the most inviting avenues of investigation into the so-called mind-body effect is the concept of *states of resourcefulness.* A state of resourcefulness, or "SOR," is a brain state, a mind zone, a mood— whatever one would like to call it—that's the right bioinformational set-up for good things to happen in the body.

In Chapter 5 we explored the attitude of gratitude, the attitude of abundance, and the attitude of practical altruism, as possible states of resourcefulness that may promote healing, well-being, and overall health. Much more research needs to be done, and much of it is underway. When and how it will bear fruit is difficult to predict, but the potential gains to the human species are so great as to merit as much talent, time, and energy as we can devote to it.

# CAN YOU MOTIVATE YOURSELF?
# THE "POPEYE POINT"

Singer and actress Tina Turner reportedly endured years of physical and emotional abuse at the hands of her husband and co-star Ike Turner. Displaying the classic coping pattern of denial, rationalization, and self-blame, she had been unable to assert her own individuality and break free from the toxic situation she suffered in.

But one evening, after a particularly vicious beating just before a scheduled appearance, something changed in her. She abruptly walked out, with less than a dollar and a gas station credit card in hand. She went into hiding and, with the help of friends, separated herself from the soul-destroying influence that had been dominating her life. With no money of her own, she spent several months in hiding, existing on food stamps and loans from friends.

Once free, she built a completely new career and, as her ex-husband's career spiraled down the drain, she re-invented herself as a new figure in rhythm and blues. Her autobiography *I, Tina,* became the hit film *What's Love Got to Do with It?* in 1993, and in some ways brought the issue of abuse of women to the front pages.

One can wonder, in the case of Tina Turner and so many women who've escaped from abusive situations: What changed? Why, at that particular time, in that particular place, at that particular moment, did she choose to do something she hadn't been able to do prior to then? What interior mental event enabled her to cross over a bridge she hadn't been able to cross?

People who understand little about the abused-woman syndrome may wonder: "What's wrong with her? Why does she tolerate that? Why doesn't she just get up and leave?" It all sounds rather simple and easy from the safe point of view of the observer who's not the one entrapped in the situation. Certainly, one can say that the entrapped person has choices and has chosen to stay and suffer. That, however, is to say almost nothing. The fact is that almost all of us find ourselves stuck at some point in our lives in situations we wouldn't necessarily choose, but which we find difficult to leave.

How many of us have stayed stuck in toxic relationships, soul-destroying jobs, personal dilemmas, and dead-end situations for far too long, when we—presumably—could have acted assertively to break out of them? Aren't we all, at some point in our lives, in the Tina Turner situation? When we finally do make the move to change our circumstances, what is it that's happened within us? How are we now different? And how did we become different?

I call this decisive internal moment—the decision that says "I'm not going to take this any more"—the "Popeye Point." The metaphor comes from the trademark scene in many of the classic Popeye cartoons, first conceived by Elzie C. Segar in 1929. Our hero Popeye, ever the exemplar of the honorable man, has taken so much abuse at the hands of the bad guys that he's finally had enough. He has to fight back. He makes his quintessentially Popeye announcement: "That's all I can stands, I can't stands no more!" Out comes the can of spinach, which he downs in one gulp. Then, with new-found energy and determination, he mops the floor with his abusers.

I think that's what happens when we finally act against our circumstances and change things for ourselves. We come to the Popeye Point. Something happens in us and we're different.

The most interesting feature of the Popeye-Point phenomenon is that we can explain our reasons for breaking out of the situation very clearly and compellingly—*after we've done it,* but not before. One second before the Popeye Point, we're struggling, feeling confused, and maybe even feeling overwhelmed or defeated. One second after this magical event takes place in our biocomputer, we're in a different reality.

Listen to a person who's decided to break out of a toxic situation and you'll hear considerable energy, conviction, and a sense of confidence in how they describe their new way of thinking about themselves and their lives. "I don't have to put up with that kind of thing." "That situation was not right for me." "I have the right to live my own life the way I see fit."

I suggest that the Popeye Point is not a cognitive event; it's a *pre-cognitive event*. That is, we don't come to it by conscious logic, but by a non-conscious *visceral decision*. Once we make that key visceral decision, we then proceed to explain rationally to ourselves why it was exactly the right decision to make.

We don't change our ways until and unless we come to the Popeye Point. A close friend of mine bemoans the fact that his wife continues to gain weight. "I wish she'd join a weight-loss program, or start going to the gym with me." My response is, "She hasn't come to the Popeye Point yet." He can't make her want to reduce her weight, get back into shape, and take care of her health. Only she can do that.

We can see evidence of the Popeye Point—or the absence of it—in experiences all around us. I recall that when I was very young, my father quit smoking—abruptly. He'd been feeling unwell and already knew that one of his lungs was seriously impaired as a result of dust inhalation. Having been a two-pack-per-day smoker, he came home from the doctor's office and, so far as I know, never touched a cigarette again for the rest of his life. I've often wondered what the doctor must have said to him, or how he said it, because it surely cleaned him up. That day was his personal Popeye Point.

Understanding the Popeye Point as a phenomenon still doesn't answer the basic question that it presents: *How does it happen?* What internal event, what reconstruction of information patterns causes a person to suddenly abandon a dysfunctional behavior and adopt a new, life-serving one?

Heroic attempts at "self-discipline" don't offer much promise. Millions of people go on diets every day and millions fall off. Millions of people "quit" smoking every day and millions go back to it. The success rate for smoking-cessation programs of all types—cold turkey, hypnosis, medicated patches, prescription drugs, support groups, friendly bartenders, falling in love with someone who doesn't want to date a smoker—averages a very consistent 25 percent.

Lots of people screw up their courage and go on aggressive diets, with a death-or-glory mentality that's simply unsustainable. Within a month or two, they've typically lapsed back into their old familiar eating patterns.

Many people ask, "How can I change a habit?" "How can I stop spending so much money on my credit card?" or "How can I be more punctual and stop being late all the time?" The simple answer is: *You have to want to.* And until you come to the Popeye Point for any particular behavior that isn't serving you well, you can forget about changing it.

One might say, "I really want to do more reading." But the simple fact is that if one is not reading more, then the statement is untrue. Here is what's true:

> *If you're wondering what it is you "really" want to do, consider that what you're doing right now is what you really want to do.*

*By definition*: what you're doing right now is what you want to do, because it's what you've chosen to do. If there's something you're doing that's not serving you well, or something you're not doing that would serve you well, then you might "like to" do it, but you don't yet "want to" do it. Your challenge is to turn "like to" into "want to." When you go from "like to" to "want to," then you've passed the Popeye Point.

Maybe the habit you're talking about changing really isn't something you want to change, or even would like to change—maybe it's something you tell yourself you *should* change. You might say, "I should be more organized; I need to keep better records, or arrange my home or room or office more systematically." But deep down, you may not really believe that's what you need. If you're comfortable in a state of creative chaos, why disown that comfort zone and punish yourself for not behaving the way someone else behaves? If you're a dedicated slob, own it and cherish being a slob. It may not be a change you really need, want, or would like to make.

But let's suppose there is a change that you feel would be very beneficial to you, one you can imagine yourself making, if you can mobilize your creative energies to make it happen.

I believe the Popeye Point can be caused to happen, or at least invited to happen, by a *conversation between selves,* between the conscious level of your thinking and the non-conscious levels that are really in control.

If you're thinking about making some changes in your life, get your pen and some index cards and start compiling a "like to" list. After you get a pretty good inventory of candidates, choose one—only one—and begin to think about it. Give it a name. Start identifying the benefits you might experience by making the change. Break it down into small steps: How would you get started? What's a reasonable time line?

The purpose of this self-conversation is to *set things up for the Popeye Point.* You'll probably find that, the more often you bring to mind the idea of the change you're considering, the more reasonable and possible it may seem. The more reasons you find for making the change, the more motivation you give to the non-conscious mindmodules that are incubating the problem. As you dialog it with yourself, and possibly discuss it with others, you may find your sense of motivation growing stronger.

The idea is not to try to motivate yourself directly with heroic ventures based on will power, but to help yourself discover, at multiple levels, the real value of the change. Then you may very well find yourself wanting to make the change and actually moving in the new direction. As you begin making the change, your ongoing self-conversation will be providing you with the reinforcement that makes it easier to keep going.

## Notes

1. This excerpt from Halberstam's writing is widely quoted in a variety of sources. I've been unable to locate the reference to the original 1963 article.
2. Excerpt from website www.hpr1.com/archives/jul2403/gadfly.htm. The sequence of paragraphs has been modified slightly for this illustration.
3. Cialdini, Robert. *Influence: The Psychology of Persuasion* (rev. ed.). New York: William Morrow, 1993.
4. Parts of this discussion are adapted from materials used in the "Brain Power" seminar, developed by Karl Albrecht International. Used with permission.

# 12

## *HOW TO BECOME AN EXPERT PROBLEM SOLVER*

"No problem can be solved from
the same consciousness that created it.
We must learn to see the world anew."
—Albert Einstein

ACCORDING TO A NEWS REPORT, two burglars broke into the basement of a building in Vang, Norway, below a hardware store. Apparently they found it too difficult to get through the door at the top of the stairs leading to the store, so they had to settle for whatever they could find in the basement.

One of the things they found was an old safe, which looked very promising. Having some skill at safecracking, they rigged up a small charge of plastic explosive, pressed it into the crevice around the safe's door, and hid behind a wall while they detonated it, presumably expecting the door to come off so they could get away with some cash to show for their efforts.

Unfortunately, the safe didn't contain any cash: it contained explosives. The basement of the building—and the burglars—were demolished. Investigators surmised the details of the episode from what was left of the crime scene.

One might wonder about the problem-solving process used by these two benighted delinquents—what assumptions they were making; what options they considered; indeed, what they defined as "the problem" they were intending to solve.

In keeping with our habit of specifying simple definitions for the key terms and ideas we're trying to think about, here's a very basic definition:

> *Problem: A state of affairs you have to change in*
> *order to get what you want.*

You're dissatisfied with some part of reality; you're not getting what you want; what you want to happen is not happening; you think you see an opportunity to make things better, but you don't know yet how to go about it. So you go into some kind of a special thinking mode—a mental process you hope will enable you to figure out how to change the state of affairs so you can get what you want. That's problem solving.

## FORGET THOSE "FIVE STEPS"
## THEY TAUGHT YOU

If your educational experience has been fairly typical, somewhere along the way they taught you about the "problem-solving process." They probably told you "there are five steps in problem solving"—or six, or seven, according to the favorite method espoused by the teacher or the school. The method probably involved steps like "define the problem," "gather information," "identify options for solving it," "select the best option," and maybe "take action" based on the solution you chose. They might have also included an extra step, such as evaluating results to see whether the solution actually worked.

Here's a trick question: *When did you last use that five-step problem-solving process?* Is that really the way your mind works? Do you sit down and say, "Now I'm going to solve Problem X. Let's see, the first step is to define problem X"?

It's very likely that Problem X is interwoven with various other things you have to think about and decide on; it's less likely that you get to attack it in a step-wise process. You may have been thinking about various aspects of it well before you officially declared it a problem. You may have partly solved it intuitively even before you began to deal with it consciously. Problem solving tends to be a much messier process than we'd like to believe. However, understanding that intrinsic messiness, and using it to our advantage, can make us much more skillful problem solvers than if we tried to follow a formal step-wise method every time.

Not many years ago, as I was pondering the problem-solving process for the umpteenth time, I had a sudden realization—sort of a "blinding flash of the obvious." I'd been teaching and touting the standard problem-solving process for decades (I used a six-step model), and *I realized it's not actually the way I problem solve.* Nor is it the way most skillful problem solvers whom I've observed problem solve.

*Effective problem solving is not a series of steps;*
*it's an adaptive process that unfolds based on the*
*nature of the problem that's being solved.*

I began thinking more carefully about the flow of mental processes that come into play in various kinds of decision-making and problem-solving situations. I finally found myself pushed to the conclusion that the "five-step process" we all had to learn was basically a convenient intellectual fiction—something we tell ourselves in order to support our belief in a logical, rational world. When you give up on the idea that all thinking has to be logical and rational, not only do you have more fun, but you become a much better problem solver.

## USING HEURISTIC (A.K.A. NATURAL) PROBLEM SOLVING

A more accurate description of the flow of mental processes involved in a typical problem-solving experience might look something like the following:

- You sense that something's wrong—you become aware of the symptoms; or someone tells you something's wrong; or several people agree to declare something "a problem." You bring the problem to a conscious level—yours or that of a group of people who are concerned about it.
- You get more information—you ask a few questions; explore the symptoms further; what, if anything, has been done so far to try to solve it?
- You reflect on some possible solutions—what actions might possibly solve it? Which options seem most promising? Are there options no one has yet thought of?
- You get more information—how did this problem get to be a problem? What caused it or allowed it to happen? Who's affected by the problem? Who has a stake in seeing it solved? Are there people who don't want to see it solved?
- You search more vigorously for options; you, and others if it's a team problem-solving effort, put on your explorer hats and stretch the boundaries of what might be possible. You try to get a fresh perspective; look for more connections and possibilities.
- You gather more information—what are the limits or constraints you have to consider? What kinds of options are ruled out once

you understand the nature of the problem in more detail? Has anyone else solved this kind of a problem, or some variation of it? If so, what can we learn from their experience?

- You restate the problem—based on a clearer understanding of the situation, the possibilities, and the constraints, now you have a more concise understanding of the outcome that's desired. What would a solution have to look like if you had one?
- "Et cetera, et cetera, et cetera," as the King of Siam liked to say. Eventually, you work your way to a solution.

At first glance, this hypothetical flow of mental process might sound confused and disorganized—and in a way, it is. Where are the "five steps" your teacher said you had to use? At what step did you "define the problem"? At what step did you "gather information"? At what step did you "define options"? It's all in there, but not in a neat, step-wise order.

The sample process just described doesn't follow the standard five-step recipe we all learned, but it's actually more like the natural process by which we move from problems to solutions. It's what information scientists call a *heuristic thinking process*: what you do at each point in the process will depend on everything you've learned so far.

Heuristic thinking, in addition to being a very natural thinking process, is a fairly clever way to think. We think of it as "seat-of-the-pants" or "trial-by-error" learning. We can define it as:

*Heuristic thinking: arriving at a result by intelligent guesswork rather than by following a pre-established formula.*

For the technically minded, heuristic thinking can be contrasted with *algorithmic thinking,* which follows a fixed, step-wise process. An algorithm is a stepwise formula, with pre-defined branching procedures.

Suppose we think of solving any problem as a *learning process*; you "learn" your way to a solution by increasing your understanding at every stage of the journey. Let's call it a "learning journey." Rather than slavishly trying to follow a pre-determined set of steps or an algorithm, we use our natural wisdom—our common sense—together with our capacity to learn, discover, and conclude, to navigate from symptoms to solutions. We shift our focus from reliance on the "five steps" to trusting our own natural intelligence.

## YOUR FIVE KEY MINDZONES

Heuristic thinking and problem solving don't have to be completely random or instinctive. By applying some of the basic findings of brain research and cognitive psychology, we can indeed give form to the heuristic thinking process. We can augment its natural, exploratory, discovery-based patterns with a conscious process of managing our mental strategies as the problem unfolds before us.

One useful way to think about the problem-solving process is by considering the various kinds of mental processes we can engage in along the way to the solution. Let's call these patterns or processes *mindzones*. A mindzone is a mental "territory"—a place you go in your mind for a particular kind of thinking. There are five useful mindzones that can come into play when you're in your problem-solving mode, illustrated in Figure 12.1.

- *The Neutral Zone.* This is the central playing field for the thinking process, sort of the "town square" where ideas meet, and the place to which the participants in a group discussion keep returning to evaluate their progress toward the solution. In the neutral zone we build a "model" of the problem and get all of the key elements into one place so we can think of them in a complete context. Here we also connect the dots; we trace the relationships among various elements of the problem and describe the solution as it unfolds.

## Figure 12.1. High Speed Problem Solving Model

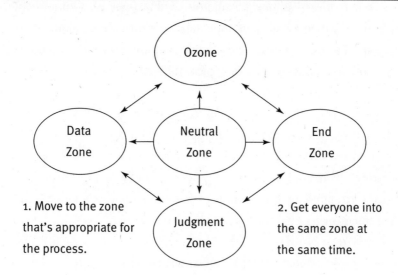

1. Move to the zone that's appropriate for the process.

2. Get everyone into the same zone at the same time.

- **The End Zone.** This is the goal line—the place we'll be when we have the solution basically scoped out and we're ready to define all the details: what will be done, by whom, by when, at what investment in cost and time, and the criteria we'll be using to evaluate the solution to be sure that it actually solved the problem.
- **The Data Zone.** This is the land of evidence: facts and figures; basic "truths"; logical conclusions we can pretty much depend on; assumptions we agree to make (and test for accuracy); speculations we agree to consider (and test for validity); hypotheses, properly identified (and tested); opinions, properly characterized as opinions; expert judgments; reports we will consider as valid.
- **The Ozone.** This is the "option zone," the "outer space" of thinking, idea generating, brainstorming, and harvesting possible options that might become ingredients for a solution. Here, no judging or evaluating is allowed; the only acceptable activity is divergent thinking.

- *The Judgment Zone.* This is the place for critical evaluation, where ideas, options, possibilities, and prospective solutions are subject to impartial and impersonal scrutiny. Here judgment is specifically permitted and officially required; the only acceptable activity in this zone is convergent thinking.

One reason why so many people are not more skilled in problem solving is that they tend to muddle up their thinking processes by mixing mindzones willy-nilly. Instead of becoming conscious of the process of moving from zone to zone, many people simply wander through the process, responding impulsively to whatever thoughts run through their minds or to whatever options happen to arise.

> "Get your facts straight first. Then you can distort
> them as much as you please."
>
> —Mark Twain

To paraphrase the Biblical verse, there's a time for judging and a time to refrain from judging; a time to gather evidence and a time to put the evidence to use; a time to consider far-out ideas and a time to come back down to earth and see which ones have promise. Expert problem solvers can typically navigate through these five mindzones with ease and fluency. So can you.

## THE HIGH SPEED PROBLEM SOLVING PROCESS

As I pondered further the fundamental mental processes involved in problem solving, I began to consider the ways in which the five key mindzones we've just recognized can come into play and how they can work together in some synergistic way to get us to good solutions. I evolved a heuristic problem solving process, based on skillful navigation between the five mindzones, which I christened "high speed problem solving" or "HSPS." It works particularly well with a group of people who are trying to combine their best ideas, knowledge, and life experiences to solve some complex problem. The more complex the problem, the better this heuristic process seems to work.[1]

The key elements, rules, or policies of HSPS are:

- Get the right people in the room. Assemble a collection of brains—or biocomputers—that has the needed knowledge, expertise, and open-mindedness to tackle the problem.
- Start by putting aside, as much as possible, all preconceived ideas of what the solution should be. Go at the problem with a clean sheet of paper.
- Keep everyone in the group in the same mindzone at the same time. When various people are jumping around through various zones at the same time, they tend to waste mental energy and make idea-synergy much more difficult. This "one-zone" rule may spell the need for a skilled group leader or a trained process facilitator.
- Go to the mindzone that's most appropriate, in the best judgment of the participants, for the stage of development you've reached on the way to the solution.
- Move fluently among the five mindzones, staying conscious of how the collective understanding of the problem is evolving.
- Avoid groupthink: it's not *who* is right that counts, but *what* is right.
- Trust the intuitive nature of the process; all participants can allow themselves to draw upon their individual, natural intelligence as they decide which mindzone to visit next and what they need to accomplish in that mindzone before they leave it and visit another one. Very often, if we simply set aside our habitual patterns of advocacy and adversarial persuasion and look at the problem through "innocent eyes," as Zen practitioners like to say, we may find that the information speaks to us. It may tell us its story, and we may see the elements of the solution looking back at us.

Let's illustrate the power of heuristic problem solving by tracing a hypothetical journey through the mindzones. Here is one of a vast number of sequential possibilities, the particular value of which will depend strongly on the particulars of the problem being solved:

1. Let's begin in the *neutral zone*. We could get started, for example, by itemizing the symptoms of the problem. Maybe we don't have an agreed-upon "definition" of the problem at the outset, but we probably know what unsatisfactory state of affairs it's causing. In the neutral zone we begin to build a preliminary "model" of the problem. What are the undesirable consequences we or others are having to cope with?

2. If it's a fairly complex problem, or one that affects a number of people in different ways, we might decide to go to the *ozone* for a round of divergent thinking. We could identify as many undesirable symptoms or side-effects as we can. Then, perhaps, we bring the laundry list of symptoms back to the *neutral zone* and capture them for later use.

3. Back at the *neutral zone,* we might be ready to ask for some preliminary "statement of the problem." I often like to phrase this inquiry something like: "Please state the apparent problem with which you propose to deal." When we characterize it as "the apparent problem," we give ourselves the right to rephrase and revise the problem statement as many times as we choose, until we arrive at a way of conceptualizing it that we find compelling and actionable.

4. Next, we might go to the *end zone* and begin trying to describe what the solution might look like when we find it. What symptoms will go away? What new state of affairs will we enjoy? Who will be doing or saying what, and in what way, that benefits us? By going to the *end zone* early in the process, even before we know what solution we want to implement, we can pretend to look backward from the solution—even if we only know its

general characteristics, if not its actual form—to the current state of affairs. This can help us begin to trace out a line of action that can eventually bring us to a solution.

5. Next, we might visit the *data zone*: have we assembled all of the important or relevant facts, figures, key ideas, concepts, and "truths" we'll need to consider? The evidence from which we proceed will illuminate the process of learning, discovery, and development that makes for effective problem solving. If we neglect the evidence-gathering process, we'll be less able to identify and evaluate viable options for a solution.

6. Now, we may need to come back to the *neutral zone,* the figurative "town square" to which we keep returning as we paint an ever-clearer picture of the problem, share our understanding of it, and begin to see more possibilities for solving it.

7. At this point, if we've evolved a fairly clear understanding and consensus about the nature of the problem, we might want to go to the *ozone* and begin itemizing some of the promising options for solving it. Here we simply generate options—divergent thinking—without evaluating or judging any of them yet. We take them back to the *neutral zone* and add them to our developing picture of the problem.

8. As the set of promising options becomes more and more clear and our understanding of the problem continues to develop and mature, we might want to go to the *judgment zone* to sort the solution options down to a manageable number. In the *judgment zone* we can further narrow down the scope of the problem, and perhaps come back to the *neutral zone* with a more focused attack. Note that returning to the *neutral zone* tends to serve as a kind of "sanity check" on the process. Are we progressing reasonably effectively and efficiently toward a solution?

9. As the process unfolds, we tend to sense a movement toward consensus, a convergent pattern. We may go to the *judgment zone* for a final evaluation process, as we narrow down the possible

solutions to the preferred option and we specify what it would
look like in real life.

10. Presuming we have the basic ingredients of the solution, we can
then visit the *end zone* to specify the "who, what, where, when, and
how" of the course of action. The *end zone* thinking process can be
as detailed as we like, depending on how precisely we need to spell
out the solution. This is where we commit to the solution, spell it
out in the necessary detail, and invite the various participants to
take responsibility for their share of the implementation.

This process may seem rather loose, vague, and disorganized for
some people, particularly those with a high preference for structure,
order, and discipline. People with a low tolerance for ambiguity and
complexity may wish that it could somehow be reduced to an easier
formula. The bad news is that the problem solving process is typically
confused, evolutionary, and exploratory. But that's also what makes it
fun for some people.

The good news is that, if you study and apply this five-part mindzone model of HSPS, it begins to seem more and more natural as you
become more familiar with it. It may even begin to portray a kind of
intellectual elegance that may appeal to your aesthetic sense of moving
from chaos to intelligent order.

Considering the general state of problem solving that seems to
prevail in our world today—confused, haphazard, emotionalized, and
adversarial—a method that invites humility, suspended judgment, and a
continuous learning process can fill an important need.

## Notes

1. Parts of this discussion are adapted from materials used in the "Brain Power"
seminar, developed by Karl Albrecht International. Used with permission.

# 13

# SUCCESS PROGRAMMING
## Causing the Outcomes You Want

"The greatest discovery of my generation is
that human beings, by changing the inner
attitudes of their minds, can change the outer
aspects of their lives. . . . It is too bad that
more people will not accept this tremendous
discovery and begin living it."
—William James
(Pioneer of modern psychology)

IN HIS BEST-SELLING BOOK *PSYCHO-CYBERNETICS,* physician and
plastic surgeon Dr. Maxwell Maltz laid the groundwork for a large part of
the field of self-help psychology. As a successful plastic surgeon, Maltz had
seen many times the psychologically disabling influence on his patients of
significant disfigurations. Many people with deformations—unattractive

physical images—also carried around very negative self-assessments and a low sense of self-worth—negative mental images of themselves. These negative self-images restricted their ambitions and motivations and limited their beliefs about what was possible in life for them.

What surprised him, however, was the number of patients who became significantly more attractive as a result of the surgery, but who never changed their negative self-concepts. They continued to think of themselves as unattractive, unlovable, and unworthy. Their new appearances might reduce their negative self-evaluations somewhat, but not to a level one might expect. He concluded that their negative self-perceptions were not caused by their disfigurement, but by deeper-lying mental disfigurements.

Maltz began to study this self-concept issue very carefully, and he eventually developed a theory and a set of strategies for affirmative thinking, which he called *psycho-cybernetics,* based on the analogy between the human mind and the computers that were being developed at the time. His book, of the same title, hit the best-seller charts, sold over thirty million copies, and remains to this day one of the most respected sources for the psychology of self-esteem.

Maltz, and other motivational experts such as Andrew Carnegie, Norman Vincent Peale, and Napoleon Hill, preached, as we have discussed in previous chapters, that we human beings think and behave based on our mental models, which often override the influence of our current perceptions of reality. Once a person builds and internalizes a model of any aspect of experience, including a model of the self, he or she typically doesn't revise or update it without having a strong reason. Many of Maltz's patients had their physical appearances updated, but never updated their mental models of themselves.[1]

It's pretty clear that if we want something more or different from life than we're getting, we have to change the mental software. We have to "reprogram" the biocomputer with updated models of ourselves, our situations, our possibilities, our beliefs, and our intentions.

Almost the entire journey of exploration we've pursued in this discussion up to this point has been intended to update our mental software. What we now need to do is provide our biocomputers with new and better data. We have to update the *models* that define what we want for our lives. This is what *success programming* is designed to do.

## USING WHAT WE'VE LEARNED

Let's recap and review the basic methods and skills we've been studying in this exploration of practical intelligence and dedicate ourselves to putting them to use, diligently, every day of our lives. The key dimensions of PI we've explored are:

- *Four Key Mental Habits*: Mental Flexibility, Affirmative Thinking, Sane Use of Language, and Valuing Ideas. These key habits, applied every day, can release and channel our natural intelligence, the built-in capacities of our biocomputers.
- *Four Key Mega-Skills*: Bivergent Thinking (including Metaboxical Thinking), Helicopter Thinking, Intulogical Thinking, and Viscerational Thinking, applied every day, can vastly enlarge our mental "bandwidth," the range of mental processes and mental competence we can engage in. They are our toolbox for thinking. These four polarities, or dualities, can serve you well when you integrate them into a synergistic combination.

Some key principles that bear remembering and applying every day:

- Thinking is a bodily function.
- You have many minds, or mindmodules.
- If you want to have lots of good ideas, you must write your ideas down—constantly.
- You organize much of your experience in the form of mental models, which shape your perceptions and reactions.

- You have a number of brainstates available, which support the rich variety of mental experience.
- You slip into and out of a "normal" trance state many times in a typical day.
- Emotions are a valuable kind of information, and they deserve to be integrated into your overall mental process, not to be suppressed or avoided, but to be understood and accommodated.
- Problem solving is a free-flowing, adaptive learning process, not a set of standard steps.

Some readers might nominate various other concepts and principles as more important to them personally. The list above is simply intended to re-activate much of what's been learned to this point by refreshing the associations between ideas.

Appendix B, "Fifty Tips for Better Thinking," provides a somewhat more comprehensive review of the key points and can serve as a study guide.

## MINDMOVIES: WHO'S PRODUCING YOUR LIFE'S STORY?

Have you ever thought of your life as a movie? Your life story might not be particularly exciting to a Hollywood producer, but it's important to you. It's the record of where you came from, where you've been, and how you got to be where—and who—you are.

You know what the movie has been, up until this moment, or at least you remember large parts of it. But what comes next? What will the rest of your life movie be about? Have you considered that the "rest of the movie" is pretty much up to you? It will result from the choices you make from here on.

Actually, considering the way your biocomputer works, the concept of living a movie is a fairly good analogy. The difference is that, instead of the usual two channels of drama—video and audio—that normal movies have, your mental movies have three. Your biocomputer is constantly recording information on a *visual* channel, an *auditory* channel, and a *kinesthetic* channel. The visual and auditory channels are probably familiar to you, but the kinesthetic channel deserves further explanation.

In addition to what we see and hear, our bicomputers are always processing what we *feel* as well. In this discussion, we refer to the feeling channel—the kinesthetic information—as including bodily sensations, visceral signals, emotional state, and even sensations such as smell and taste. When you bring up a "memory movie," a scene or progression of scenes you've experienced in the past, it comes up with a feeling or a combination of feelings attached to it.

Simply imagine that you're going through your daily life experiences as if you had a movie camera or a video camera on your shoulders. Everything you see, hear, and feel comes in. Most of it goes unnoticed, much of it is lost, and some of it is recorded.

As an exercise in becoming aware of your mindmovies, call to mind some very significant event in your personal history. It might be your first date, graduating from school or college, your first day of your first job, or some other event that's vivid in your memory. Close your eyes and imagine that you're watching the memory movie you recorded as the event unfolded. The scenes in the movie will almost certainly appear from the angle and perspective from which you looked upon them. Now, as the images become clearer and more abundant, listen for any sounds you heard during the experience—the voices of others, your own voice, music, or background sounds. Next, recall as intensely as possible the way you felt during the experience.

What you're doing, to continue the movie analogy, is replaying the movies you've already made. What if you could make your movies in advance? What if you could design the movies you want your life to reflect and then create those movies in your imagination? Would rehearsing important experiences before they happen make them more likely to unfold as you want them to?

That's the basic idea behind mindmovies. You decide in advance how you want a particular situation or experience to unfold, you create the script for the "success" movie of the experience, you "shoot" the movie in your imagination, you "replay" the movie a number of times, and it becomes part of your intention for the experience when it occurs.

## ALPHA PROGRAMMING: MAKING THE MOVIES YOU WANT

If you like the analogy of the mental movie, the key question becomes:

*If your life is a movie, are you the one who's*
*producing the movie? Or are you just the*
*camera operator?*

Most human beings live their lives passively. They're like the camera operator: they point their mental video cameras at whatever's happening and their life movies are mostly recordings of what they experience. Of course, all people make decisions from time to time, but how many of our decisions are merely selections from the menu of options presented by other people or by circumstances? How many of our decisions are proactively arrived at and consciously planned? How many of us make the movies we really want in life?

Rather than thinking of your life from here on out as a single big production, it's probably more realistic to think in terms of making many movies—or episodes, if you like—in the long-running series that's your life.

Experts in the theory of *neurolinguistic programming,* or NLP, refer to the mindmovie method as *future pacing.* The idea is to make the prospective future experience as real as possible to your various minds by creating images and sensations that are similar to those you'll experience in the real situation. Self-concept expert Maxwell Maltz contended, many years ago, that the unconscious mind can't differentiate between fantasy and reality if the fantasy is detailed enough.

You can make mindmovies for just about any experience you're anticipating. For example, I have a close friend who's a mid-level executive with a large company made a mindmovie to help him cope with a stressful situation in his job. He believed he was being treated unfairly by his senior management, and his competence was being questioned regarding a matter that he believed represented a failure of company policy. He was due to meet with the senior executives to discuss the situation.

He asked me to help him prepare for the meeting. In particular, he didn't want to go into the meeting feeling defensive and didn't want to allow them to put him in a one-down position in relation to the problems caused by the failed policy. After some discussion, he decided that his best strategy for the meeting was to reframe the issue from "who's wrong" to "what's wrong." He decided to approach them as a member of the management team, not as a "defendant," and to point out that he and they shared a responsibility to create and enforce policies that could prevent the problem from occurring or recurring. He decided to take the initiative from the first word of the discussion and change the context to a problem-solving situation.

Once he'd settled on his strategy for the meeting, we built a mindmovie for the meeting as he wanted it to unfold. I guided him through a relaxation and visualization process, in which he rehearsed the sequence of events from the time he got out of bed on the morning of the meeting; through getting dressed; eating breakfast; driving to work; walking into his office; working until the time for the meeting; walking into the meeting room; greeting the executives; sitting down at the conference table; taking the initiative to frame the conversation; expressing his views clearly, forcefully, and non-defensively; dealing with their concerns; and concluding the meeting by having them agree to his proposed course of action.

After he built his mindmovie, on a Sunday evening, I suggested that he replay it at least two or three times before the meeting the next morning—before going to bed that night and at least once in the morning.

The next evening, he called to report the results. "It was amazing," he said. "The meeting went exactly as I wanted it to. It was just like seeing my movie again, only this time it was the real thing. I got everything I wanted."

His experience made him a fan of using mindmovies for other situations in his life. "What made it successful," he concluded, "was that *I had a movie and they didn't.* They just walked into the meeting cold, without having thought through what they wanted to happen. In a way, I'd already been through the meeting and I knew how it was supposed to turn out. I knew the plot, so to speak, because I wrote the script."

I've used the mindmovie technique many times, to help me deal with difficult or challenging situations, and to avoid allowing others to make me stressed or angry. You can make your mindmovies especially effective by:

- Choosing a very definite, specific outcome or sequence of events that you want.
- Specifying the details of the experience: the physical environment, who will be there, the sights and sounds, the actions of others, and the procedures.
- Designing a complete script: who does what, when, in what sequence; what do you do, and how do others act or react?
- Rehearsing the movie at least three times, with all three channels going: visual, auditory, and kinesthetic.
- Holding a very confident expectation that the experience will match your movie fairly closely, while being prepared to deal with any deviations from the script.
- Reviewing the results afterward and learning from the experience. How can you make your next movie even more effective?

Mindmovies tend to work best as short features, not mega-productions. You'll get better results by taking on one particular opportunity or challenge, focusing on a specific outcome or self-change you want to make, and creating a movie just for that.

If you become a fan of mindmovies, as I have, you'll find that with experience you can make them more and more compelling, and you'll find creative ways to build the stories. Eventually, you'll get to the point where you can build a custom-made mindmovie for a specific experience, within a matter or seconds. Then you can rehearse—or "shoot it," if you prefer that metaphor—also in a matter of seconds. A few screenings, and you'll be ready for the real thing.

## YOUR LIFE WHEEL: TAKING STOCK, SETTING PRIORITIES, AND MAKING CHANGES

Equipped with our inventory of PI resources—the four key mental habits; the four key mega-skills; the attitude of practical altruism; the states of resourcefulness available through the various mind zones, meditation, and alpha programming; and the various methods such as card writing and high-speed problem solving, we can obtain a clearer sense of where we are in life, what we want our lives to be, and what we can do to proactively close the gap between what is and what ought to be.

The Life Wheel is a useful concept, model, and planning tool that can help you review your possibilities, set some priorities, focus your energies, and concentrate on a few key areas that are special and important to you.

Figure 13.1 shows a typical example of the Life Wheel, although your personal version might have different areas of focus or *key result areas,* as they're also known. You can draw the diagram with the categories that mean the most for you.

## Figure 13.1.   The Life Wheel

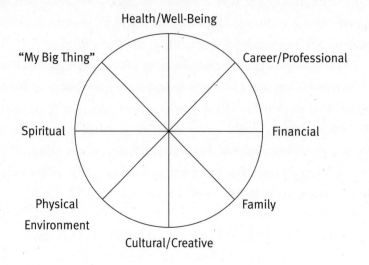

One helpful way to use the Life Wheel is to think carefully about each of the key result areas, one at a time, and then together in a group. Think about what each category suggests to you in terms of the activities, intentions, and rewards associated with it. Then give each category a rating, say on a 10-point scale, to indicate how satisfied—or, perhaps, dissatisfied—you are with it at the moment, relative to the others. Do some categories call your attention right away? Are there several, or perhaps one, that stands out as one you'd like to make some changes in, set some goals and priorities for, and devote special energy to?

Some categories you might want to consider are:

- Health and physical well-being.
- Family.
- Personal relationships.
- Intellectual activity.
- Education.
- Career and professional progress.

- Financial status.
- Cultural experiences.
- Aesthetic, expressive, artistic experiences.
- Spiritual pursuits.
- Physical environment (your personal space and what's in it).
- "My Big Thing" or MBT, which might be a very specialized area of interest for you.

If you include a large number of key result areas in your life wheel, you might be inclined to diffuse your energies. As the Japanese expression goes, "If you chase ten rabbits, you may not catch one." About six or eight categories might be sufficient.

Once you've ranked your key result areas in terms of priority for action, consider setting just one achievable goal in each of the top three categories. You don't have to disown or ignore the other categories, but it helps to concentrate your energies where you most want to see results.

Write down your plan if you like, or just write the key result areas and the goals on an index card and carry it around with you.

Review the goals and categories from time to time, and revise them in whatever way feels right for you.

## Notes

1.  Maltz, Maxwell. *Psycho-Cybernetics: A New Way to Get More Living Out of Life* (reprint ed.). New York: Pocket Books, 1989.

# A

## Answers to Thinking Exercises

*IMPORTANT:* Please read only the solution to the problem you're working on. If you read ahead and look at the other solutions before you work the problems, you'll take the fun out of the process and deprive yourself of a learning opportunity.

### Chapter 6. Solution to the "Inference" Problem

Statement 1 is True. The evidence—the text of the story—specifies this.

Statement 2 is Unverifiable (we must check "?"). The text of the story provides no information with which to determine whether or not any or all of the employees denied taking the money.

Statement 3 is Unverifiable. We know from the story that Joe A was on vacation when the incident occurred; that doesn't prove anything about whether he took the money.

Statement 4 is Unverifiable. Jane B has refused to make any statements and has insisted on talking to a lawyer. It would be a value

347

judgment—not a provable fact—to say that she has "refused to cooperate."

Statement 5 is Unverifiable. We know that Jim C has volunteered to take a lie detector test, but we don't know whether Joe A—or any of the other employees—did or did not.

Statement 6 is Unverifiable. We know that all three of them knew the combination to the safe, but not whether they were the only ones. If you like to split hairs, we could even question whether they "knew how to open the safe"—we only know that they each knew the combination.

Statement 7 is Unverifiable. We know that a sum of $1,500 is "unaccounted for." We don't actually know whether it was in the office safe, and the story does not establish whether the money was *stolen,* either from the safe or elsewhere. The notion that the incident was a robbery would be an inference.

Statement 8 is Unverifiable. We can't verify, from the evidence given in the story, whether the safe was robbed.

Statement 9 is Unverifiable. Same reason as Number 8: we can't verify, from the evidence given in the story, whether the safe was robbed. It could possibly have been robbed, and, if so, the thief could possibly have been identified; but we can't prove or disprove the statement from the evidence given.

Statement 10 is Unverifiable. By now, we can see that the whole proposition of a robbery is inferential, and the involvement of the three employees in a supposed robbery is entirely circumstantial.

Note that *the only verifiably true statement* is Number 1, which is explicitly confirmed by the text of the story. All of the other statements are inferences—they *might* be true, and it's easy to see how a person listening to the story might be tempted to *assume or infer* that they're true. But they're all inferences, which is the key point to be learned in this exercise.

Note also that a statement we can't verify as true does not automatically become false. Consider statement 5, for example. The story identifies Jim C as the one who has volunteered to take a lie detector test, whereas the statement to be evaluated identifies Joe A as the one who volunteered. However, this does not prove the statement false; Joe A might also have volunteered, but the story gives us no evidence about this one way or the other.

## Chapter 7. Solution to the "Bookworm" Problem
See Figure A.7.1 below.

First, recognize that the bookworm travels to the *right* to get to the last volume, because of the normal way the books are stacked on the shelf (volume one on the left, then volume two to the right of volume one, and volume three to the right of volume two). This means that he doesn't have to travel through the page block of volume one— only through its front cover, to get to the back cover of volume two.

**Figure A.7.1. The "Bookworm" Problem**

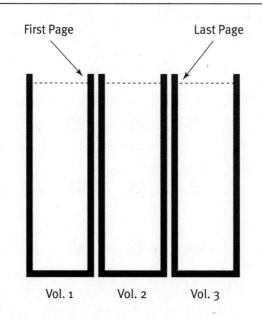

Then he has to go all the way through volume two—back and front covers plus the page block in between—to arrive at the back cover of volume three.

And because the last page of volume three is just inside the back cover, he doesn't have to travel through volume three's page block to get there—just through the back cover.

In all, he only has to travel through one complete book—volume two—plus the front cover of volume one and the back cover of volume three. That adds up to four one-eighth inch covers (equal to one-half inch), plus one book block equal to one inch. His total journey is one and one-half inches.

## Chapter 7. Solution to the Famous Nine-Dot Problem

See Figure A.7.2 below. The solution will be explained in words, without a final diagram, in order to remove the temptation to look at it before you've had a chance to try to solve it. Here are the nine dots, numbered for reference.

Starting at dot 9, draw a diagonal line that passes through dot 5 and goes to dot 1.

## Figure A.7.2.    "Nine Dot" Problem

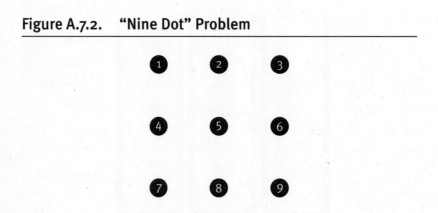

Then without lifting the pen from the paper, draw the next straight line going toward the right, passing from dot 1 through dot 2 and dot 3. *Extend the line beyond dot 3,* far enough that its end point lines up with an imaginary line running from dot 6 diagonally through dot 8.

Again without lifting the pen from the paper, draw a diagonal line running through dot 6 and dot 8, *extending the line* to a point below dot 7 that lines up with dots 1, 4, and 7.

Now extend the fourth line segment upward through dot 7 and dot 4, to dot 1.

## Chapter 7. Solution to the Anagram "teralbay"

Rearranging the letters of teralbay, you can come up with betrayal.

## Chapter 10. Solution to the "Boat" Problem

Note that, because no one can accompany any of the men in the boat (it would exceed the safe weight limit), it would be futile to start by having any of them row the boat to the opposite side. There would be no one to take it back.

That means that both boys will have to row the boat over on the first trip, one has to row it back, and the other will stay to bring it back after one of the men takes it over.

Next, one of the men takes the boat over and the boy on the opposite side brings it back.

Note that these four crossings form a repeatable cycle. Two boys go over, one boy comes back, one man goes over, the other boy comes back; and both boys end up one the side where they started (which is part of the deal).

By running this cycle three times, they get all three men to the other side and both boys back at the starting point. That makes three cycles of four crossings each, for a total of twelve crossings. So the men pay the boys twelve dollars for the use of their boat.

## Chapter 10. Solution to the "Water Glass" Problem

See Figure A.10.1 below. Note that the instructions refer to handling and moving only one glass, but say nothing about the water in the glasses. You simply pick up glass 5, the second full one as viewed from let to right, and pour its contents into glass 2, the second empty one in the line. Then you put glass 5 back in its original position.

*Mental check:* did you unconsciously assume that each glass and its contents had to be an inseparable unit?

### Figure A.10.1.    The Water Glass Problem

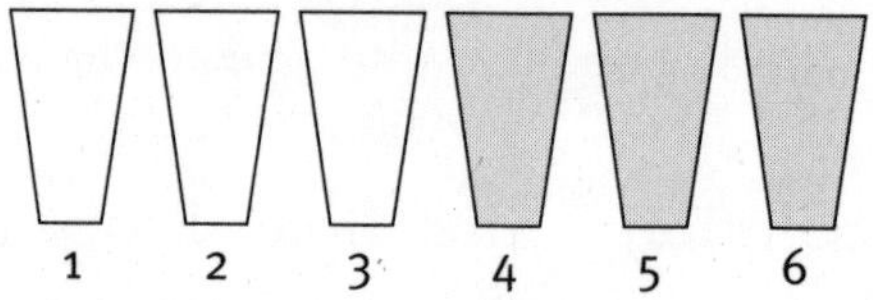

## Chapter 10. Word Ladders

Here are the sequences of words to change from the starting word to the target word:

1. Change hate to love: hate, have, hive, live, love
2. Change fall to rise: fall, fill, file, rile, rise
3. Change take to give: take, sake, save, gave, give
4. Change lose to find: lose, lone, line, fine, find
5. Change won't to will: won't, want, wand, wind, wild, will

# B

## *FIFTY TIPS FOR BETTER THINKING*

THESE TIPS ARE ADAPTED from materials used in the "Brain Power" seminar, developed by Karl Albrecht International. Used with permission.

1. Respect all levels of your mind (e.g., subjective experience and knowledge as well as verbal thought); remember that thinking is a bodily function.
2. Respect all ways of knowing, in yourself as well as in others.
3. Practice humility: intellectually, socially, and emotionally.
4. Promote a high respect for evidence, in yourself and others; many problems contain their own solutions when you understand them well.
5. Write your ideas down. Keep pens and index cards within reach wherever you are.

6. Pay attention to differences in thinking styles; remember that each person has his or her own unique way of constructing reality.

7. Explain things in the other person's thinking pattern, not always your own.

8. Combine your hunches with your logic; they make great partners.

9. Keep your opinions in draft form; this can make you more alert for new perspectives.

10. Suspend judgment when hearing something new.

11. Check to see whether the brain you're talking to is "on line."

12. Listen for the subtext: facts, feelings, values, and opinions.

13. Delay your signal reactions; don't let your amygdala get hijacked.

14. Practice an attitude of gratitude, generosity, and practical altruism.

15. Own your value judgments, assumptions, and inferences.

16. Practice non-allness thinking and talking (minimize use of "all," "every," "always," "everybody," etc.).

17. Practice gray-scale thinking ("to what extent. . .").

18. Practice self-reference ("It seems to me. . . ." or "So far as I know. . . .").

19. Remember that arguing is one of the least effective ways of changing someone's mind.

20. Remember that *context* communicates as strongly as *content*. In a meeting or other group situation, notice the process as well as the content.

21. Use the language of leadership and big ideas, and people will be more inclined to treat you as a leader.

22. Re-own the parts of yourself you may have rejected earlier in life.

23. Declare your intellectual civil rights: "I don't know," "I made a mistake," and "I changed my mind."

24. Remember that your sense of humor is your stress barometer; when it seems like there's nothing to laugh about, you're probably overstressed.

25. Find at least five minutes every day for quiet reflection; find a private place, close your ideas, go into the alpha zone, and just be.
26. Get to know your mindmodules; watch them in action and learn when and how they vie for influence over your behavior.
27. Constantly remind yourself that self-worth is not something you have to prove, or a conclusion you arrive at; it's an assumption you start from.
28. Remember that there is often more than one "right answer."
29. Beware of slogans; they often invite reaction without reflection.
30. Remember that "truth" is local to the individual brain-mind system in which it arises, and to the language system used to construct it.
31. Don't fear or avoid logical thinking; facts are your friends.
32. Practice positive "sensorship"; you can choose to concentrate your attention on positive inputs.
33. Spend more time reading than you spend watching television.
34. Constantly monitor your self-talk; prefer positive language.
35. Shun toxic people and those who push negative thinking; remember that you can fire anybody from your life.
36. Don't play victim or martyr; accept responsibility and authority for the consequences in your life.
37. Monitor your mood; keep yourself "up"; when you're in a bad mood, don't kick the dog, the cat, or anybody else.
38. To change the way you're feeling, change what you're doing.
39. Always be learning; try to discover something new every day.
40. Don't give advice; suggest options.
41. Notice the cultural holograms, the unspoken background patterns and rules that shape everyday behavior.
42. Avoid clichés like the plague; keep your language fresh and original.
43. Don't kill ideas when you first hear them; use the "P.I.N." formula (Positive first, then Interesting, then Negative aspects).

44. Make good use of metaphors and word pictures; they add color and power to your language.

45. Don't mistake a haphazard "brain-dump" for a conversation; explain your ideas clearly; use a discursive strategy to escort others to your truth.

46. Use the power of bivergent thinking; know when to diverge and when to converge, and do it by conscious choice.

47. Don't be bullied into groupthink; as Aldous Huxley said, "It's not who is right that counts, but what is right."

48. Use idea maps and card-writing to take inventory of the elements of a situation; use whole-brain thinking to combine the bits and pieces with the big picture.

49. Steer an even course between cynicism and gullibility; don't accept everything on face value, and don't look for diabolical motives in everything.

50. Always be ready to smile in the next second, and let it show on your face.

# C

# A VOCABULARY FOR
# PRACTICAL INTELLIGENCE

THIS GLOSSARY IS ADAPTED FROM MATERIALS used in the
"Brain Power" seminar, developed by Karl Albrecht International.
Used with permission.

**Affinity Diagramming** A method of organizing and associating items of
information by writing them on cards or slips,
putting them on a wall, and moving them around
to form *affinity groups,* or coherent groupings of
information.

**Affirmative Thinking** A pattern of selective attention and ideation that
supports a high level of mental health.

**All-ness Orientation** The psychological (and verbal) tendency to think
in terms of absolutes: "all people," "every time,"
"always," "never," and so forth. The all-ness orientation shows up in language as "all-speak."

| | |
|---|---|
| **Alpha State** | A mental state characterized by slow brain-wave activity and the absence of intention, in which a person is alert and attentive, but in which outside distractions are mostly excluded. |
| **Alpha Programming** | A process for changing attitudes, overcoming mental obstacles, and setting life goals that takes advantage of the benefits of the *alpha state*. Alpha programming can help you reduce stress, concentrate, remember, perform tasks more effectively, and build motivation for future action. |
| **Attribution** | The mental act of assigning motives, intentions, or attitudes to another person's behavior; it can often lead to misunderstandings and reciprocal conflict. |
| **Biocomputer** | The total information system of the human brain, nervous system, and all levels of mental activity. Also called the brain-mind system. Emerging theories such as *psychoneuroimmunology, neurosemantics,* and *cognitive therapy* begin with a concept of the human biocomputer as an information system. |
| **Bivergent Thinking (Divergent and Convergent)** | A thinking process that integrates both divergent and convergent patterns of ideation into a synergistic combination. It's the process of deploying both thought patterns fluently and interchangeably to consider the various elements of information in a problem situation and to sort through them to arrive at an effective decision, solution, or plan of action. Bivergent thinking is the basis for virtually all recognized models of problem solving. One of four key polarities, or mega-skills, of practical intelligence. |

| | |
|---|---|
| **Blue Earth Mode** | One of the four Mindex thinking patterns, characterized by left-brain thinking at a concrete (experiential) level. People who favor a Blue Earth pattern tend to prefer facts and figures, concrete results, procedures, and analytical or logical thought processes. |
| **Blue Sky Mode** | One of the four Mindex thinking patterns, characterized by left-brain thinking at an abstract (conceptual) level. People who favor a Blue Sky pattern tend to prefer systematic thinking, planning, organizing, and highly structured thought processes. |
| **Brainstates** | Distinctive patterns of activity in the brain-mind system, such as ordinary wakefulness, reverie, dreaming, meditation, concentration, excitement, and others, each of which has its unique set of bioinformational and conscious characteristics. |
| **Brainstorming** | A disciplined method for generating a large number of ideas, options, possibilities, designs, or solutions; pioneered by advertising executive Alex Osborn, the process has a specific set of rules and procedures, based on separating the process of idea production from the process of evaluation. |
| **Complex** | A consistent combination, or cluster, of ideas, which may be both verbal and preverbal, often associated with an emotional state, that form the basis for one's reactions to certain experiences. Example: the well-known inferiority complex, which every human learns early in life, deals with the experience of being subordinate, intimidated, or incompetent. Complexes are not necessarily pathological, although some are. They're a normal aspect of the way the biocomputer assembles its "data." |

**Conscious Mind**

The collection of mental functions that centers on awareness, and which receives the results of mental processes going on at non-conscious levels.

**Convergent Thinking**

A thinking process that reduces a large set of ideas or options to a select few. It's the trajectory of thought that progresses from the general to the specific, narrowing down the field of discussion, rejecting various options, and converging toward a conclusion, decision, or specific topic of focus. It excludes rather than includes; narrows rather than expands; and decides rather than explores.

**Cognitive Dissonance**

A mental sense of unease, experienced as a pressure to resolve a basic conflict between two closely held ideas; first studied by Professor Leon Festinger of Stanford University. Example: (1) "I know that smoking is very bad for my health" and (2) "I smoke cigarettes." Unconscious methods for resolving cognitive dissonance can include denial, rationalizing, selective perception, and "demoting" one of the conflicting ideas to less important status.

**Data Zone**

In the high speed problem solving model, it's the mind zone we use to gather, assemble, and interrelate the elements of evidence we need to find worthwhile options for the solution.

**Divergent Thinking**

A thinking process that branches out from one idea to other, related ideas. It's the trajectory of thought that progresses from the level of details and specific topics to the level of concepts, possibilities, options, and relationships. It includes rather than excludes; expands rather than narrows; and explores rather than decides.

| | |
|---|---|
| **Dichotomizing (Dualistic Thinking)** | The tendency to think of situations or issues in terms of only two opposing choices, without being able to appreciate a range of alternatives; also called black-and-white thinking or bipolar thinking; the antidote is gray-scale thinking. |
| **Ego-Neutrality** | An attitude that involves separating your sense of self from a situation, interaction, or conflict and reacting to the situation on its merits, rather than taking offense, defending, or counter-attacking. |
| **Emotional Intelligence** | The capacity to integrate one's emotional processes into one's overall mental functioning and to incorporate emotional experience into the total process of perceiving, reacting, interacting, and dealing with others. |
| **End Zone** | In the high speed problem solving model, it's the place we seek to arrive at, after having carefully worked through the elements of the problem. It's the mind zone in which we specify the "who, what, when, and how" of the accepted solution. |
| **Four-Channel Listening** | Paying attention to the *subtext* of a conversation or a message or to persuasive messages in the media; it involves separating the elements of the message into four components: Facts, Feelings, Values, and Opinions. |
| **Future Pacing** | A process of mental rehearsal in preparation for some challenging experience; it involves creating a mindmovie (that is, a visual, kinesthetic, and auditory fantasy) and making the imaginary experience conform to your plan. This creates the sense of having already been through the experience when it occurs and reinforces your confidence in the outcome. |

**General Semantics**    The field of study founded by Alfred Korzybski, which deals with the psychology of language and its effect on human thought, interaction, and emotional adjustment.

**Grabber**    Any signal (a word, statement, gesture, tone of voice, implication) to which a person reacts with dysfunctional intensity, such as anger, shame, fear, frustration, or guilt. Also known as a "trigger" or a "hot button." See *signal reaction*.

**Gray-Scale Thinking**    The capacity to think in terms of a range of possibilities rather than become imprisoned by dualistic thinking, which sets up an issue or proposition in terms of only two opposing choices.

**Groupthink**    The process, first clarified by Professor Irving Janis of Yale University, in which a group of people have a high need for consensus, regardless of the merits of differing points of view, and in which the "in-group" applies social pressure to coerce the dissidents to join in the false consensus.

**Helicopter Thinking**    A thinking process that integrates both abstract and concrete patterns of ideation into a synergistic combination. It's the capacity to think and express ideas on a wide range of levels, from the concrete level of direct experiences, actions, and examples to the most abstract level of concepts, philosophical discussions, and possibilities. One of four key polarities or mega-skills of practical intelligence.

**High Speed Problem Solving Model (HSPS)**    A heuristic, ·creative, non-sequential, problem solving process that includes five key mind-zones, each of which supports a particular kind of thinking, depending on the stage of development of the thinking process. The two rules of HSPS are to consciously choose the mindzone that's most suited for the current stage of the problem solving process and to get everyone who's working on the problem into the same mindzone at the same time.

**Hologram**    A consistent pattern of ideas, beliefs, values, and imperatives, often unconsciously formulated, that circulates throughout a culture and that forms the basis for the cultural "rules" and behavior patterns. This is an analogy to the photographic hologram, in which each small piece contains a replica of the overall picture. Cultural holograms are also sometimes called *memes*.

**Idea Mapping**    Also called mindmapping or radial thinking. A system diagramming method, also used for divergent thinking and brainstorming, that involves writing a key idea in the middle of a paper and then associating other, related ideas to it by means of radiating lines and branches to other ideas.

**Incubation**    The process by which mental activities below the level of consciousness work on problems and challenges while the conscious mind is attending to other things. The incubation process can often come up with clever ideas, options, and solutions that conscious reflection does not produce. Incubated ideas often break through into consciousness in the "light bulb" experience or the "Aha!" event.

**Inference-Observation Confusion**    The inability to distinguish between various levels of certainty, particularly the difference between a direct observation (or an accepted factual report), and various inferences that might possibly be drawn from it. This is a fuzzy-thinking habit that leads people to jump to conclusions (or confusions).

**Intulogical Thinking** A pattern of thinking that integrates both logical and intuitive processes into a synergistic combination. One of four key polarities or mega-skills of practical intelligence.

**Judgment Zone** In the high speed problem solving model, it's the mindzone we visit—occasionally, and by agreement—to consciously evaluate options, potential solutions, and propositions that may be considered in building the solution.

**Kinesthetic Channel** One of the three sensory channels that form our mindmovies; it includes direct sensory experience, taste, smell, emotional arousal, and *proprioception,* or the ability to sense the position and activity of various parts of the body.

**Lateral Thinking** A form of mental agility, made popular by Edward de Bono, in which one becomes aware of the limits of a convergent pattern of thought ("vertical" thinking or "monorail" thinking) and deliberately abandons it in order to approach possible solutions from a radically different angle. Lateral thinking is one type of "metaboxical" thinking.

**Life Wheel** A life-planning diagram, used for personal assessment and priority-setting, which involves a pie chart showing a number of significant dimensions of one's personal life; categories can include health, financial status, career, social activities, cultural experiences, education, and others.

**Mental Flexibility** The willingness to let yourself be changed by your experiences. It includes commonly recognized habits like open-mindedness, tolerance for ambiguity and complexity, absence of dogmatism, respect for evidence, and willingness to consider various points of view.

**Mental Scripts**  Routine patterns of actions, or "menus," that prescribe many of our unconscious, preverbal, and conscious actions; these range from micro-scripts such as reciting one's telephone number to more complex social scripts that dictate how to behave in certain contexts.

**Metaboxical Thinking**  The process of detecting and freeing one's self from self-imposed boundaries, constraints, and limitations—unconscious "mental boxes"—that can limit one's imagination in solving problems. The origin of the cliché "Let's think outside the box."

**Metaphor**  A figure of speech that substitutes a concrete experience for an abstract concept. Example: the expression "We're barking up the wrong tree" may convey one's meaning more efficiently than "We seem to be pursuing a course of action that will not lead us to our objective."

**Mindmap, Mindmapping**  See Idea Mapping

**Mindmodules**  Hypothetical brain structures, which may be micro-regions or associated collections of brain processes, that carry out various mental functions; the multi-mind theory contends that the brain-mind system is composed of many elementary mindmodules, many of which are vying for influence on behavior at any one time.

**Mindmovies**  The natural structure of human memory, in which the brain accumulates a composite of visual imagery, auditory input, and kinesthetic (sensory, olfactory, gustatory, and proprioceptive) information; a mindmovie has three "tracks" or channels, corresponding to these three channels of sensory processing.

**Mindex Model**
The four-dimensional model of thinking styles, developed by Dr. Karl Albrecht, and presented in his instrument, *Mindex: Your Thinking Style Profile.*

**Mindset**
A fixed arrangement of ideas, beliefs, values, and conclusions that shapes the way a person perceives, reacts, and behaves.

**Mindzone**
Any of a number of mental states, characterized by a particular pattern of attention and ideation, e.g. reverie, critical thinking, or creative idea production.

**Multiple Intelligences**
The concept that human intelligence is not best represented in terms of a single factor (the "g-factor," as early researchers called it), but rather as a collection of competencies. Developed extensively by Professor Howard Gardner of Harvard University.

**Multiplexing**
A conversational habit of mixing two or more streams of discussion or hopping back and forth between multiple topics; this causes stress for people with certain kinds of thinking styles, but may be perfectly comfortable for others.

**Neurolinguistic Programming (NLP)**
The systematic study of the structure of subjective inner experience, including the ways in which human beings record, represent, process, recall, and communicate at the level below consciousness.

**Neutral Zone**
A mindzone characterized by ego-neutrality, a willingness to suspend judgment and consider various points of view, and an avoidance of preconceived

|                     | beliefs or conclusions. In the high speed problem solving process, it's the center point of the thinking process, the "town square" to which we keep returning to assemble our understanding of the problem and develop a model for the solution. |
| --- | --- |
| **Ozone** | In the high speed problem solving model, it's the "option zone," the fuse we go to for divergent thinking, generating options, brainstorming, conceptual or philosophical thinking, and big ideas. |
| **Pattern Paradox** | The ironic conflict between the human brain's need for patterns and structures in its basic operation and the imprisoning influence that various patterns can have on our capacity to think creatively and originally. |
| **P.I.N. Formula** | An acronym for "Positive First," then "Interesting," and then "Negative," as a policy for reacting to new ideas. |
| **Popeye Point** | A mental event of clarity and conviction, characterized by a sudden sense of determination and purpose, leading to decisive action. Analogous to experience of the cartoon character Popeye, in which continued abuse by others triggers his sense of injustice. |
| **Practical Altruism** | The attitude of generosity and good will toward others that is based on the proposition that one gives in order to get. It includes the concept of the "karmic loop," which is the time span over which one feels he or she will be rewarded for affirming and supporting others. People who are attached to the idea of a short karmic loop (consciously or unconsciously) insist that they be compensated immediately for generosity. People |

|  | with longer karmic loops believe that compensation eventually results, but don't concern themselves with the "when." |
|---|---|
| **Projecting (Projection)** | The mental act of incorporating one's own preoccupations into one's perceptions of people or experiences in such a way as to color one's interpretation of them and one's responses to them. |
| **Radial Thinking** | Also called *idea mapping* or mindmapping. |
| **Red Earth Mode** | One of the four Mindex thinking patterns, characterized by right-brain thinking at a concrete (experiential) level. People who favor a Red Earth pattern tend to learn by experience, prefer concrete results, and refer ideas and information to their own experience or to a human context. |
| **Red Sky Mode** | One of the four Mindex thinking patterns, characterized by right-brain thinking at a conceptual (philosophical) level. People who favor a Red Sky pattern tend to prefer conceptual, big-picture thinking, and they like to consider issues and problems in a global context. |
| **Resistance to Enculturation** | Abraham Maslow's term for the capacity of an individual to substitute his or her own judgments and interpretations for the ready-made propositions (cultural holograms) projected by the surrounding culture. Ernest Hemingway called it, simply, "crap detecting." |
| **Route 350** | A metaphor for the process by which a listener's mind may wander, because the mind can process speech at about 500 words per minute, while most people can talk at about 150 words per minute; this leaves about 350 words per minute of unused brain capacity, which will go toward |

|   |   |
|---|---|
| | other sources of stimulation. Keeping a person's attention on your message involves keeping him or her "off Route 350." |
| **Self-Concept** | A unique complex of ideas, evaluations, conclusions, and emotional responses connected with each person's sense of him- or herself as an actor in society. |
| **Self-Talk** | A running mental commentary in which a person verbalizes self-approval or disapproval, or an emotional response to immediate experience. Maladjusted self-talk can lead to maladjusted thinking and behaving. |
| **Self-Esteem** | A comprehensive self-estimate, which incorporates a person's sense of his or her own lovability, capability, and worthiness. |
| **Semantic Flexibility** | The habit of using words, figures of speech, and language patterns that support adaptability, openness to new information, and willingness to consider various points of view. |
| **Signal Reaction** | A sudden, irrational, emotional reaction to a specific cue such as a statement, action, or nonverbal gesture made by another. |
| **Social Intelligence** | The ability to get along well with others and to get them to cooperate with you. |
| **Socratic Method (Questioning)** | A questioning process for developing ideas, which leads the thoughts of others in a specific direction or that discloses deep-lying attitudes, beliefs, values, or needs that may be important in dealing successfully with them. |
| **State of Resourcefulness** | Any of a number of brain states that involve a sense of self-efficacy that can enable a person to function effectively in challenging situations. |

| | |
|---|---|
| **Strength-Weakness Irony** | The principle that any personal quality that serves as a strength can, when taken to extremes, become a weakness or a handicap. |
| **Target Fixation** | Also known as "tunnel thinking." The tendency to become so focused on a particular problem, challenge, or desired outcome that one ignores other significant aspects of the situation that can defeat one's purpose. |
| **Thinking Style** | A unique pattern of processing ideas and deriving meaning from one's experience. See *Mindex model*. |
| **Tipping Point** | Also called the "evidentiary threshold"; the point at which enough evidence accumulates to cause a person or a group of people to change their mindset, opinion, or value judgment. Example: in a stock market boom, early evidence of a possible downturn tends to be rejected or explained away, but as additional evidence contradicts the accepted doctrine or dogma, it reaches a crossover point at which people abandon their conviction or lose faith in it. |
| **Tolerance for Ambiguity** | A psychological competence, first emphasized by psychologist Abraham Maslow, that involves the ability to function effectively in the absence of simple answers, clear structures, and clear rules for behavior. |
| **Toxic and Nourishing Behaviors** | The basic patterns of your behavior toward others that lead them to move with and toward you (nourishing behavior) or away and against you (toxic behavior). Nourishing behavior promotes empathy and a sense of connectedness; toxic behavior destroys it. |

**Unconscious Mind**  A collection of mental processes that operate outside of consciousness. Includes intuition, hunches, and creative incubation, as well as repressed emotions and conflicts.

**Verbal Pathologies**  Various learned habits of speech that encode forms of mental and psychological rigidity, such as all-ness thinking, dogmatic thinking, or dualistic thinking.

**Viscerational Thinking**  A pattern of thinking that integrates both rational and visceral—or emotional—processes into a synergistic combination. One of four key polarities or mega-skills of practical intelligence.

# D

## *A CODE OF INTELLIGENT DISCOURSE*

THIS CODE OF DISCOURSE IS ADAPTED from materials used in the "Brain Power" seminar, developed by Karl Albrecht International. Used with permission.

I recognize and affirm that the sane use of language is an important aspect of applying my intelligence in every interaction with other people. I promise myself that I will diligently strive to follow these key principles of intelligent discourse:

1. *Self-reference.* I will regularly use "to-me" language, to remind myself and others of the self-locality of my views, value judgments, beliefs, assumptions, and conclusions, and to explicitly affirm the rights of others to hold their own views.

2. *Non-aggression.* I will refrain from personal attacks on those who disagree with me, such as name-calling, labeling, sarcasm, ridicule, and imputing disreputable motives to them.

3. *Non-directiveness.* I will carefully limit the use of "should" language and coercive "verbal bludgeons," which others may perceive as bullying, unwanted advice, or pressure to behave as I dictate.

4. *Non-attribution.* I will refrain from attaching dishonorable motives to the behavior of others or attributing disreputable ideologies to those who disagree with me.

5. *Non-allness.* I will regularly use "limiters and qualifiers" in my statements, to remind myself and others that generalizations are inevitably limited in their applicability.

6. *Non-dogmatism.* I will regularly use expressions that remind myself and others of the relativity and self-locality of "truth" and affirm that each person is entitled to his or her own "perspective."

7. *Non-polarization.* I will carefully limit the use of "either-or" expressions, which tend to dichotomize the discussion of a topic and suggest that it must be thought of only in terms of two polarized extremes.

# E

## LEARN TO MEDITATE IN "ONE" LESSON:
### The Harvard Mantra

MEDITATION IS A SPECIAL KIND OF MENTAL EXPERIENCE that can help you gain easy access to the "alpha zone," and to the states of resourcefulness that can make your mindmovies more effective. The most basic form of meditation, sometimes called "mantra meditation," is a procedure that's easy to learn, pleasant to experience, and beneficial to mental and physical health. There are lots of good reasons to do it on a regular basis, and almost no reasons not to. So if you don't yet know how, it's probably time to learn.

Skilled meditators and practitioners of esoteric mental disciplines use various advanced techniques, but ordinary civilians like us can easily pick up the basic "mantra" method. Here's how.

*Note: this will be an eyes-closed exercise, so be sure to read the whole procedure before you begin.* Allocate about twenty minutes for this lesson, which is best done in a quiet place where you won't be disturbed or distracted by people or events. Disable the telephone if possible and turn off other potential distracters. Note the time and tell yourself that your eyes-closed session will last for twenty minutes—you may be surprised at how accurate your internal clock is.

Sit comfortably in a comfortable chair, with your feet flat on the floor and preferably with your hands in your lap or resting easily on the arms of the chair.

Take three deep, refreshing breaths, and as you exhale the third time allow your eyes to close. [With practice, you'll be able to use the closing of your eyes as a signal that triggers a memory-wave of complete relaxation throughout your body.]

Allow a minute or so for your body to relax progressively. During that time, turn your attention to your breathing. [Breathing serves as a bridge between your conscious and unconscious mental processes. It's the only "automatic" body function you can consciously control to some extent.]

Taking care not to interfere with your breathing in any way—*don't try to control it*—begin counting your breaths as they come and go. Observe attentively and respectfully as the breath comes in; then there's a pause at the turning point; then the breath goes out; there's another pause; and the cycle repeats endlessly. Passively observe each inhale and each exhale, and wait patiently for the turning points. Count ten breaths as they come and go. You'll become less and less aware of your body signals as you become more detached and ultra-relaxed. You'll become less and less aware of your physical environment.

Now that you're becoming more relaxed, begin to withdraw your attention from your body and shift it to an imaginary point a few inches in front of your eyes. Visualize as vividly as you can a clear crystalline ball floating there in front of your face.

Now, allow a *mantra* word to begin repeating in your "mind's voice." A simple and familiar word, like "one" (the "Harvard Mantra" is recommended by Harvard psychologist, Dr. Herbert Benson), works very well as a mantra. [You can choose almost any word you like that's simple and effortless to pronounce.] Listen for your mantra word and hear it repeating incessantly, slowly, rhythmically. You know that you're the one saying it, and at the same time it may seem to be coming from somewhere else.

The combination of the focus on the crystal ball and the repeating sound of the auditory mantra will bring your attention to a clear focus. The noise level in your mind will fade, and you may sense yourself as much closer to the real origins of your thinking process.

The method of meditation in this case is basically just to continue hearing the mantra word over and over for the full time of your meditation period, which is typically twenty minutes or so. That's all there is to it.

From time to time, you'll almost certainly discover that the mantra word has been displaced by other thoughts, usually words, phrases, fragments of sentences, and fragments of ideas that drift up out of the pool of your memory. As soon as you become aware that the mantra word is no longer playing in your mind, you simply drop the thought that's momentarily playing and return to the mantra word. The first few times you meditate, you may find that the mantra gets displaced very frequently. With practice, you'll find that you can stay tuned to the mantra for longer stretches of time and return to it easily whenever it fades out.

You may also discover that you occasionally "tune out" completely—you'll become aware that you've "gone somewhere else" and that you've just returned to awareness. No one seems to know where the mind goes during this tuning-out state, but most experts agree that it's a normal and potentially healthy state—and may even be more restful and restorative than ordinary sleep.

That's about it. You just allow your mind to hold the mantra for the duration of the session. At some point, you'll probably find yourself taking in a full breath and feeling that you're ready to open your eyes. Just make sure you allow a minute or two to rejoin the world you left, and that you're fully aware of all parts of your body and alert to do whatever you need to do.

# INDEX